The Irish Parliament, 1613–89

Series editors
DAVID EDWARDS & MICHEÁL Ó SIOCHRÚ

The study of early modern Irish history has experienced something of a renaissance in the last decade. However, studies tend to group around traditional topics in political or military history and significant gaps remain. The idea behind this series is to identify key themes and set the agenda for future research.

Each volume in this series comes from leading scholars from Ireland, Britain, North America and elsewhere, addressing a particular subject. We aim to bring the best of Irish historical research to a wider audience, by engaging with international themes of empire, colonisation, religious change and social transformation.

Already published

The plantation of Ulster: Ideology and practice
Micheál Ó Siochrú and Éamonn Ó Ciardha (eds)

Ireland, 1641: Contexts and reactions
Micheál Ó Siochrú and Jane Ohlmeyer (eds)

The Scots in early Stuart Ireland: Union and separation in two kingdoms
David Edwards and Simon Egan (eds)

Debating Tudor policy in sixteenth-century Ireland: 'Reform' treatises and political discourse
David Heffernan

Studies presented to the International Commission for the History of Representative and Parliamentary Institutions XCVIII
Études présentées à la Commission Internationale pour l'Histoire des Assemblées d'États

The Irish Parliament, 1613–89

The evolution of a colonial institution

COLEMAN A. DENNEHY

Manchester University Press

Copyright © Coleman A. Dennehy 2019

The right of Coleman A. Dennehy to be identified as the author of this work has been asserted by him in accordance with the Copyright, Designs and Patents Act 1988.

Published by Manchester University Press
Oxford Road, Manchester M13 9PL
www.manchesteruniversitypress.co.uk

British Library Cataloguing-in-Publication Data is available

ISBN 978 1 5261 3335 9 hardback
ISBN 978 1 5261 6472 8 paperback

First published by Manchester University Press in hardback 2019

This edition published 2022

The publisher has no responsibility for the persistence or accuracy of URLs for any external or third-party internet websites referred to in this book, and does not guarantee that any content on such websites is, or will remain, accurate or appropriate.

Typeset by Servis Filmsetting Ltd, Stockport, Cheshire

Dedicated to my mother, Elizabeth Dennehy
&
in memory of my father, Coleman Dennehy

Sir James Barry, 1st Baron Santry.
MP for Lismore in 1634–35, he was created 2nd baron of the Exchequer and thus attended the Lords as a judge in the 1640s. He was chairman of the Dublin convention in 1660 and, being created Baron Santry and appointed lord chief justice of the King's Bench in that year, he attended the House of Lords as a judge and sat as a member in his own right. He desired the speaker's chair while the lord chancellor was a lords justice, but was left disappointed.
Image reproduced by kind permission of The Honorable Society of King's Inns.

Contents

List of tables	*page* viii
Series editors' preface	x
Acknowledgements	xi
Abbreviations	xiii
1 Introduction	1
2 Petitions and the administration of justice	18
3 Making law: bills and acts	58
4 Officers and servants of parliament	110
5 Privilege, precedent, and self-regulation	168
6 Conclusion	207
Bibliography	212
Index	231

List of tables

2.1	Overall number of petitions	p. 43
2.2	Overall frequency of category	43
2.3	Number of petitions by members petitioning their own house	43
2.4	Success rate of petitions	44
2.5	Number of petitions rejected outright	44
2.6	Number of petitions by one or more females	44
2.7	Frequency of categories of female petitioners	45
2.8	Frequency of category when peers petition their own house	45
2.9	Frequency of category when MPs petition their own house	46
2.10	Frequency of 'absence'	46
2.11	Frequency of 'appellate'	47
2.12	Frequency of 'debt'	47
2.13	Frequency of 'election'	47
2.14	Frequency of 'enlargement'	48
2.15	Frequency of 'fees'	48
2.16	Frequency of 'fines'	48
2.17	Frequency of 'government'	49
2.18	Frequency of 'legal practice'	49
2.19	Frequency of 'legislation'	49
2.20	Frequency of 'miscellaneous'	50
2.21	Frequency of 'privilege'	50
2.22	Frequency of 'property'	50
2.23	Frequency of 'Church of Ireland'	51
2.24	Frequency of 'trade'	51
2.25	Frequency of 'unknown'	51
3.1	Bill starting point	72
3.2	Committal of bills	81

3.3	Re-committal of bills	81
3.4	Committal of bills to a grand committee	82
3.5	Bills per days sitting	82
3.6	Bill committed in both houses/one or the other	86
3.7	Acts per parliament in the House of Commons	94
3.8	Acts per parliament in the House of Lords	94
3.9	Acts as a percentage of bills read in the House of Commons	95
3.10	Acts as a percentage of bills before the House of Lords	95

Series editors' preface

The study of early modern Ireland has experienced a renaissance since the 1990s, with the publication of a number of major monographs examining developments in the country during the sixteenth and seventeenth centuries from a variety of different perspectives. Nonetheless, these works still tend to group around traditional topics in political, military or religious history and significant gaps remain. The idea behind this new series is to identify key themes for exploration and thereby set the agenda for future research. Manchester University Press, a leading academic press with a strong record of publishing Irish-related material, is the ideal home for this venture.

The fifth volume in the series is the second monograph to appear. Written by a leading young scholar with a growing reputation, the book focuses on the Irish Parliament, a key institution central to the tumultuous events of the seventeenth century. Despite its importance, knowledge of how parliament functioned has not been explored in detail, with students of Stuart Ireland lacking an equivalent to Richardson and Sayles' seminal guide for the medieval period. This book finally fills that gap. Despite government efforts at harmonisation, it reveals that the early modern Irish Parliament developed along significantly different lines to its counterparts at Westminster and Edinburgh. While the book addresses the idea of Irish constitutional exceptionalism in detail, it also succeeds in placing the Irish Parliament firmly within the wider historiographical context of Stuart constitutional history. We expect it to establish itself as a foundational study for all students of the early modern period.

David Edwards
Micheál Ó Siochrú

Acknowledgements

This book originates from research for which John McCafferty's expert guidance and encouragement was crucial. My initial foray into early modern parliamentary history was under the tutelage of James McGuire, and more recently I have had the benefit of Ivar McGrath's mentorship. Along with these three from University College, Dublin, David Smith at Selwyn College, Cambridge helped this project along and I am most grateful for all of their support. Although this book was not purely the focus of it, my postdoctoral grant (Irish Research Council Marie Skłodowska-Curie Elevate Fellowship) gave crucial support, time, and space to think further about the issues surrounding parliamentary, and particularly legal, procedure. Thanks also to Dennis Finn and Tony Brady at Malahide Community School for an earlier grounding in the historical sciences.

I would like to acknowledge the advice of Micheál Ó Siochrú and David Edwards who kindly accepted my book into their series, Caro McPherson for her copy edit, and also Emma Brennan, Meredith Carroll, Lianne Slavin, and Alun Richards at Manchester University Press who guided me through the process in a most expert and patient fashion.

More generally, in Ireland I have had colleagues and students from whom I have learned much: Neil Johnston, Eoin Kinsella, Frances Nolan, Emma Lyons, John Bergin, Suzanne Forbes, John Cronin, Ida Milne, Lynsey Black, Ian O'Donnell, Marian Lyons, Raymond Gillespie, Colm Lennon, Sarah Feehan, Shane Lordan, Elaine Pereira Farrell, Liam O'Rourke, Jennifer Wells, John McGrath, Patrick Walsh, Noreen Giffney, David Hayton, Jane Ohlmeyer, Tadhg Ó hAnnracháin, and of course Bríd McGrath.

My membership and council activity of two particular organisations has greatly informed my academic outlook and my knowledge of parliaments and the law. At the International Commission for the History of Representative and Parliamentary Institutions, good friends have been John Young, Paul Seaward, Henry Cohn, Alastair Mann, Joseba Agirreazkuenaga, Mario di Napoli, Maria Sofia Corciulo, John Rogister, Eva Jedruch, the recently deceased Valerie Cromwell (Lady Kingman) and, a little less recently, Alex Cowan. At the Irish Legal History Society Robert Marshall, Sir Donnell Deeney, David Capper, Niamh Howlin, Paul Egan, John Gordon, Felix Larkin, John Larkin, Sir Anthony Hart, Colum Kenny, Tom Mohr, Patrick Geoghegan, and Yvonne Mullen.

London, and University College London in particular, was my home for two years. Jason Peacey was a wonderful mentor and colleague, as were Patrick Glen, Kathleen Walker-Meikle, Julian Hoppit, Margot Finn, Stephen Conway, and my legal history partner-in-crime, Danica Summerlin; at the History of Parliament Trust, Patrick Little, Robin Eagles, Paul Hunneyball, Hannes Kleineke, Charles Littleton, Emma Peplow, and Ruth Paley; at the Seventeenth-Century British History Seminar of the Institute of Historical Research, Ed Legon, Tim Reinke-Williams, Justin Champion, Laura Stewart, John Miller, Richard Bell, and Elliot Vernon; at the Institute of Advanced Legal Studies Legal History Seminar, Ian Williams, Michael Lobban, Catherine MacMillan, and Paul Brand.

At *Das Max-Planck-Institut für europäische Rechtsgeschichte* in Frankfurt (where much of the writing of this book took place) and at *Das Institut für Rechts- und Verfassungsgeschichte* at the law faculty of the University of Vienna, I must thank, in particular, Donal Coffey and Stefan Vogenauer at the former and Gerald Kohl at the latter.

There are too many librarians and archivists to mention, but I cannot let this opportunity pass without particular mention of Avril Patterson at UCD library, Eugene Roche and Evelyn Flanagan at Special Collections UCD, Jason McElligott at Marsh's, Renate Ní Uigín at the King's Inns and the staff at the Parliamentary Archives.

My fellow siblings and in-laws Andrew, David and Adrienne, Adam, Marian, and Serena, along with the younger generation for whom I will never be forgiven if I fail to mention personally: Alfie, Cian, Leon, Ailish, Aoife, Una, and Aidan-Coleman, Ronan McNulty, Lucy Hill, Simon Cassidy, Robert Rowan, Andrew Doyle, Marcus McNulty, Sebe Mtshali, Patrick Moloney, and their families.

Coleman A. Dennehy
Frankfurt-am-Main, 2017

Abbreviations

AH   *Analecta Hibernica*
APL   Armagh Public Library
BL   The British Library, London
Bodl.   The Bodleian Library, University of Oxford
CSPI   *Calendar of state papers, Ireland*
CJ   *The journals of the House of Commons of the Kingdom of Ireland*
DIB   *Dictionary of Irish biography*
EHR   *English historical review*
IHS   *Irish historical studies*
JRSAI   *Journal of the Royal Society of Antiquaries of Ireland*
LJ Eng.   *The journals of the House of Lords*
LJ   *The journals of the House of Lords of the Kingdom of Ireland*
NAI   National Archives of Ireland, Dublin
NHI   Moody, T.W., Martin, F.X., and Byrne, F.J., eds, A *new history of Ireland, vol. 3: early modern Ireland, 1534–1691* (Oxford, 1976)
NLI   National Library of Ireland, Dublin
ODNB   *Oxford dictionary of national biography*
PRIA   *Proceedings of the Royal Irish Academy*

1

Introduction

HISTORIOGRAPHICAL TRENDS IN IRISH PARLIAMENTARY HISTORY

There is a near absence of historiographical debate on the Irish Parliament as *parliament* in the seventeenth century. The English assembly has had a different experience. Victorian historians, often personified by the now much maligned Stubbs, subscribed to what has now become known as a 'whig interpretation of history'.[1] As such, a vibrant and confident Victorian society sought to place its parliament, erroneously considered at the time as 'the mother of all parliaments', at the centre of England's perfectly balanced constitution.[2] Parliament, so the argument ran, and in particular the Commons, had since its inception at some vague point in the mists of time striven to emphasise and safeguard the just liberties of the English people against their monarchs. As far as the seventeenth century went, the Stuarts were frequently portrayed as the bogeymen. Criticism of Stubbs and his colleagues appears now to be somewhat unfair – they were the first generation of professional or near-professional historians and, when compared with practitioners in other countries, they do not come across as particularly poor. Simply put, they took the first steps in the modern professional era and so naturally errors were made and perspectives were skewed. Above all, they looked at the parliament then in existence and attempted to work their way back.

What has been described as an 'orthodox' school of thought came to the fore in the first half of the twentieth century to take the study of English parliaments to its next logical step.[3] Lewis Namier and John Neale, working on the eighteenth and the sixteenth centuries respectively, moved away from the idea of a progressive and just body of MPs fighting 'the good fight' against authoritarian and absolutist-minded monarchs.[4] Instead, they portrayed parliament as being involved in near-constant confrontation with central authority. Wallace Notestein, in particular, wrote an influential article on the winning of the initiative by the House of Commons in the early seventeenth century, which he argued led king and parliament on a 'high-road to civil war'.[5] This work was characterised by concentration on moments of high drama and of political conflict. These historians also overemphasised the role of members of the lower house, especially their religious attitudes and apparent alliances.[6] A consequence of the prominence of this school of thought led to the establishment of the History of Parliament Trust. Its approach, in turn, led to vehement reaction by the revisionists from the 1960s onwards.

George Sayles, a rare historian of both Irish and English medieval parliaments, made a valid point when he wrote that

> to still pretend that the history of the medieval parliament is being written when the sparse and uninformative details of the obscure lives of obscure men are laboriously collected because they made a fitful appearance among the commons is merely to veil the hard realities ... the place of biography in constitutional history is a subordinate one. If we see in parliament merely a public spectacle of political struggles between crown and commons and of democracy in embryo, we shall certainly never understand the medieval parliament.[7]

Elton shared these sentiments when he wrote of 'Namier's obsession with the persons of individuals – his belief that the history of parliament equals the history of individual members of the commons ... The lords, once again, lie forgotten.'[8]

This criticism is perhaps somewhat excessive. Biographies of people who sat as members of the Commons are, of course, very useful.[9] Nonetheless the dominant form of parliamentary history took the focus off the institution of parliament, and apparently supported the assertion that the history of parliament is the history of the House of Commons. From the late 1960s onwards, a revisionist school emerged in early modern parliamentary history that rejected the idea that there was a sure emergence of a strong opposition in Elizabeth's time. Michael Graves, Conrad Russell, Geoffrey Elton and Sheila Lambert, among others, all played a role in this. In rejecting the 'orthodox' specialisation (some would say obsession) on the House of Commons and party politics, they opened the door to the study of the Lords also, and highlighted the need to study parliament as part of the state apparatus, rather than just as a political event. At the very core of this approach was a widespread consideration of the activity of parliament over a long period rather than just tracking back from the civil war looking for its causes. New approaches flourished. Statistical analysis of 'work rate' began to demonstrate the way in which all elements of parliament (for the most part) cooperated in the process of getting the business of parliament done. Developments in procedure were no longer to be seen as constitutional weapons in a political war, but rather as aids in allowing parliament to dispatch its constantly growing workload. As the early modern state expanded at a fast pace, so too did all of its constituent courts and administrative departments and parliament was caught up in this process. Above all, the speed at which legislation could be processed came to be treated as the barometer of parliaments.[10]

So what about the Irish Parliament in the early modern period? It does not make much sense to take English historiographical developments and baldly apply them to an Irish question. The Irish assembly was a different institution which operated in a different environment and under different conditions. Most famously, the provisions of Poynings' Law made the process of legislation considerably different and introduced a fourth part to the parliamentary trinity: Lords, Commons, king and English council, and lord deputy and Irish council.[11] Although there were religious pressures in the English Parliament, the differences were all the more stark in Ireland, and the ethnic distinctions made the situation a little more volatile. While many ambiguities of the Irish situation were not formally clarified until the 1720 Declaratory Act, Ireland was clearly treated more as a colony than a co-equal kingdom or, at very best, a little brother.[12] However, there were also some important similarities.

In many respects, the Irish Parliament had developed in a similar fashion to the English one simply because so many other facets of royal government were modelled on England. However, because the Irish Government was generally staffed with figures from the Irish lordship up until the growing anglicisation of government from the mid-sixteenth century onwards, there were aspects of parliament that had local particularism in organisation and development.[13] For example, the clerical proctors remained in the Irish Parliament a long time after they had disappeared from its English counterpart. An indication of the growing anglicisation of government affecting parliament can be seen in the abandonment of the law with regards to MPs' residency and property qualifications in the boroughs they represented and the laws regulating where parliament should sit. This was not just for reasons of political expediency, but also because government ministers' knowledge of parliaments rested on their experiences and that of their assistants in the English assembly.[14] As such, then, while we must be cognisant that the Irish Parliament was dependent on local conditions for its development as an institution, it was also explicitly shaped, particularly from the mid-sixteenth century onwards, by the knowledge of the workings of the English Parliament.

Much of the writing on the Irish Parliament has concentrated on confrontation, though not always on that between executive and commons. More often it has highlighted religious and ethnic distinctions. When reading more generally on Ireland in the seventeenth century the same issues are usually mentioned. In 1613, the fall-out from the election of the speaker and a sharpening religious divide in the Commons created by the wholesale creation of Protestant-dominated boroughs is usually highlighted. In 1634, denial of the graces and the creation of a government grouping to play the settler interest against the Catholic interest is prominent, and in 1640–41, partially as a result of policies and practices in the previous parliament, the fall of Wentworth.[15] In 1661, an all-Protestant Commons (frequently mistaken for an all-Protestant parliament) and the land settlement feature, and in 1689 Catholic domination and the land settlement – a swinging pendulum to the previous assembly. In most histories of seventeenth-century Ireland, parliament is used to illustrate the growing distrust and animosity between the competing interests. While it is important to acknowledge that the Irish Parliament could of course be an important forum in playing out the confrontational episodes of Irish history, an institutional study of parliament will give us a different perspective. For example, the 1634–35 parliament can be regarded as being, legislatively at least, a very active parliament. In this parliament, the Lords read 78 bills in 77 days sitting and the Commons read 103 bills in 104 days sitting, a much higher rate than any other. Having said that, one aspect of the English revisionist school is a strong emphasis on the production of legislation, an emphasis which, if unchecked, could distort an understanding of the Irish Parliament. During the seventeenth century, the English Parliament, and the Irish for that matter, took on a massive number of legal cases, which consumed much of parliament's time and attention.[16] According to the sources available to us, the Irish houses considered 1,664 petitions or counter-petitions usually (though not exclusively) initiating or answering either first instance or appellate cases. This aspect of parliament's, and especially that of the upper house's, work has been to a large extent ignored by historians in Ireland. The exception is especially revealing when these petitions were politicised, such as in 1640 and 1641.[17]

The Irish Parliament has not been without institutional histories. Richardson and Sayles's work on the medieval Irish Parliament took the institutional route, as does much of Steven Ellis's work and that of D.B. Quinn.[18] On the eighteenth century, much of the work of David Hayton follows an institutional approach, as does James Kelly's recent work on Poynings' Law.[19] Indeed, the collaborative project on Irish legislation by David Hayton, James Kelly, John Bergin, and Andrew Sneddon, on the Queen's University Belfast website, is a superb example of such an approach, with legislation at its core.[20] A more thorough examination of the various works is made in each relevant chapter.

Perhaps we should pay special heed to the call of David Hayton to study 'the achievements rather than the rhetoric'.[21] Although it may be relatively novel to Irish historiography in general, he was simply reiterating arguments advanced by Elton, Graves, and Smith.[22] Importantly, he recognises that in Irish historiography, parliamentary process and institutional history have become totally subordinate to a dominant political narrative. As such, a more thorough understanding of parliament can be achieved if we study how parliament worked. Political studies of parliament both for its own sake and for the sake of understanding the political world of Stuart Ireland have served the reader well in the past and continue to do so, but they are of less use in a study of parliamentary mechanics in its own right.

This book will attempt to study parliament purely for its own sake. It is essentially an investigation into how parliament processed the business put before it, and how, while conducting this business, the component parts interacted with each other – and indeed how parliament interacted with other aspects of government and administration in the kingdom as a whole and occasionally outside of it. Generally speaking, it could be described as an administrative and legal history of the Irish Parliament. It is not seeking to overturn any previously held beliefs or advance any particular interpretation beyond that of the validity and necessity of institutional history as an essential tool for political historians to understand parliament in order to understand the parliamentary event. It will naturally share some characteristics with the revisionist school in England, but because parliament in Ireland had a different position within the constitution, and because it continues to occupy a different position in the thinking of modern historians, it will be distinct.

The parameters of this work have been set for purely practical reasons. The earliest parliament in this study began in 1613. This date has been chosen not because it was the first Stuart parliament or because it was the first parliament to have representatives from constituencies spread across the entire island (that is merely coincidental), but because it is the first parliament for which we have journals. Had the journals emerged in the Tudor period, this book would have begun in 1585, 1569, or even earlier. Nor is the end-date set by the watersheds in Irish political history in general. The year 1689 has been chosen as a logical end as, from the point of view of many historians of parliament, 1692 represents the beginning of the long eighteenth century. However, the 1689 parliament does throw up some difficulties. The journals for the Jacobite parliament, as explained in greater detail below, did not survive the 1690s and so a thorough examination is not possible in the way that it is for the period 1613–66. However, that is not sufficient reason to exclude it. The Lords' journals are missing for the Jacobean parliament and segments are also lost for parts of the 1640s. References to the 1689 session are therefore less numerous, and statistical analysis is not always possible. Yet peers and MPs who sat in 1689 saw themselves as part of an assembly that was legitimate and so it would make no sense whatsoever to exclude it on the basis that Williamite politicians in both London and Dublin subsequently declared it to be illegal. On the same reasoning, there would be little use in studying the English Parliament between 1649 and 1660.

The chapters are essentially divided on the basis of needing to understand parliament in the work that it undertook and how this workload was dispatched. Therefore, there is a chapter on petitions and the adjudication of law (Chapter 2), a topic on which there had been very little work done, but to which the Irish Parliament devoted an increasing amount of time. There is, naturally, a chapter on legislation (Chapter 3). Irish historians have spent a lot of time on the issue of legislation; sometimes on the content and effects of it, and particularly in the seventeenth century on the thorny issue of Poynings' Law, but curiously few have spent much energy on how it moved through the houses of parliament. This chapter will concentrate mostly on the internal processing of legislation. Chapter 4 follows and is concerned with the staff of the Irish Parliament, for in a study of how parliament conducted itself, these people are at least as important (if not much more so) than the members. And finally, in Chapter 5, we deal with privilege. Like the study of petitions and law, this increasingly demanded the attentions of the Irish Parliament, both private and public. The common thread that runs through all of these chapters is that it deliberately avoids political commentary. It is an acknowledgement of the view that institutional developments in parliament tended to come about organically, generally as a response to the shifting way in which it conducted its business. Above all, this study makes much use of how parliament recorded its own proceedings: the journals of the House of Commons and of the House of Lords.

This book might have been written differently. There may well be a case made for a standalone chapter on committees. As it was written, committees as a regular cog in the parliamentary machine feature throughout this study. Writing a separate chapter on the parliamentary committee, ad hoc, standing, or grand, would in effect produce repetition both of the theory and the practical examples. The same might be said of the history of parliamentary elections, something many historians have written on already.[23] Elections feature in this study only when the House of Commons took an interest in disputed elections after the House had assembled. Elections could, of course, be intensely political, but when viewed through the prism of administrative history, they are best understood as being part of the borough or shrieval administrations, rather than as a particularly parliamentary affair. Paying homage to the standard English authorities such as Elsynge or Selden has been avoided, for the most part. This is due to the fact that most of these sources, with the exception of Hooker's *Orders and usage* and the *Modus tenendi parliamentum*, were unknown at this time in Ireland to the best of our knowledge.[24] They are certainly not cited by members or servants of the House for guidance in their work, and although they could have been circulated in manuscript, they were not published until after the parliaments in this study had sat.

It may seem strange in a study of a colonial institution in Ireland in the seventeenth century that the influence of Scotland is not more emphatic. In fact, Scotland and the Scots make virtually no appearance in this study at all. Although Scottish MPs and peers did feature in parliament on occasion, the longer history of Ireland's parliament suggests that it is very much an English colonial institution, that either by design or by chance it developed in ways primarily based on an English model, and that precedents cited by officers and members make it clear how they felt their institution should develop. Furthermore, the nature of appointments by the government in the seventeenth century to posts relating to parliament (both high and low) effectively cut out the Scots, thereby drastically reducing any possibility of Scottish influence over the development of the Irish Parliament.[25] However, there are historiographical developments in the study of the Scottish Parliament that are worthy of our attention, and might, in another study, make for a fascinating comparison.[26]

THE NATURE OF THE PARLIAMENTARY JOURNALS AND OTHER SOURCES

Most historians use the journals as their prime source for the history of parliament. In the seventeenth century, there were few Irish diarists and even fewer from those who attended parliament. Even when some did keep diaries, they rarely wrote much about the institution or the political developments that may have occurred within parliament. Newspapers in Ireland during the seventeenth century were rare, and in any case, parliament forbade reporting on its debates, votes, and resolutions.[27] State and private papers supplement our knowledge, but they tend, naturally, to focus on political issues and rarely give much information on the procedural aspects of parliamentary activity. As such, the journals are our source for the day-to-day events in parliament. In most cases, in a fashion quite similar to the English parliamentary records, they record many of the activities of the house but not usually in any great detail.[28] For instance, they may record a debate or discussion that will have taken place but rarely leave details of who spoke or exactly what was said.[29] The journals also keep a record of when bills were read, when oral or written messages were sent or received, when protests were made in the lords, and when petitions were read and the resultant decisions made. They generally recorded divisions and subsequent decisions. Speeches were rarely recorded, except those of the speaker when addressing the chief governor. The same may be said for the content of warrants or letters dispatched by the speaker. On certain days, the journal record may be merely a few sentences, yet on others it will be several pages long. It is incorrect to assume the length of the journal entry reflects the amount of work that the house did on a day. Upon the reading of petitions, for example, the journals might record the actual petition in full, the resultant decision, and any follow up issues such as reading a counter-petition, the order for the production of a warrant for an arrest, the admittance of counsel to plead, further investigation, or committal. This could quite easily all be achieved in just a few minutes but the entry may be several paragraphs long. Whereas the entry for the reading of a bill could be just one sentence long, the reading and subsequent discussion of the bill, if it were a second or third reading could take several hours and have far greater political ramifications.

For the most part, the journals of the House of Lords are quite similar in their layout and content to those of the Commons. The Lords' journals regularly contain an attendance list for the day, the compilation of which was obviously a much easier task as its membership was so much smaller. It is not clear whether the seating arrangements were as regimented as on the ceremonial days all of the time or if robes were worn at all times.[30] In the Commons, the only way we can ascertain whether a member was attending was if he happened to be mentioned on a committee list or if he had been recorded for some other reason, which is not very dependable.

The journals have done much to preserve the parliamentary heritage of the seventeenth and eighteenth century, but there are pitfalls in being over-reliant on this source. The main problem is one of accuracy. It is inevitable that there are occasions when the editor or printer made an error. Printers might make an error in more substantial matters, such as a record of numbers in a vote, or perhaps mistakenly recording, for example, the bishop of Cork instead of the earl of Cork. There were after all five episcopal sees that shared names with secular titles.[31] During the restoration parliament there were four members who shared the Boyle surname, two more had Boyle as a first name, and there was a represented town, in Roscommon, called Boyle.[32] The MP for County Carlow was John Temple and the MP for the borough of the same name was also a John Temple, son of the knight of the shire. In many cases there are committee lists or other instances in the Commons' journals where there is only a reference to a Mr Boyle or a Mr Temple.[33] Comparison between the manuscript copy and the printed journals for 1640 show there are several occasions when names were mistaken.[34] Still, many of these errors and confusions are minor and infrequent and do not necessarily change our general interpretation of the decisions the journals sought to record.

Detailed examination of the text shows up a number of errors in the printed journals in our period of study.[35] In acknowledgement of the issue, the Lords, early in the first session of Charles I's first Irish Parliament, ordered a committee to peruse the journal books to 'amend what mistakes or mis-recitals they found' and this order was repeated on several occasions and in later parliaments.[36] There are certainly several minor variations between the printed text of the later eighteenth century and the contemporary manuscript found in the National Library of Ireland.[37] Another obstacle to the effectual report and recording of business in the House of Lords is the fact that even before the printing of the journals, some of the rough journals – which were the original record of the clerk as business took place – had been missing for some time. A note under the date of 16 July 1634 says that 'There doth not appear upon the Fair Journal any entry of 16th July – and, upon Inquiry, the Rough Journal is said to have been missing many years.'[38] There clearly was a sitting of the House of Lords on this day, as the Commons reported in their journal that they visited the House of Lords and, with the lord deputy present, they presented Serjeant Catelin as their proposed speaker.[39] Even when the rough journal did survive, it was not always intact; as was the case in mid-1644, when a report mentions that 'It appears that the proceedings of the 11th July have been torn out of the Rough Journal'.[40] Occasionally a few errors appear, such as in 1642: despite entering the patent promoting the earl of Ormond to the marquis of Ormond in the journal only seven days earlier, the journal refers to him twice as the earl of Ormond.[41] Also suspicious is the attendance list for 29 October 1640 and the next recorded attendance list of 9 November 1640.[42] The numbers recorded as in attendance are identical each day, the Lords containing 26 sitting lords, 41 represented by proxy, along with the lord chancellor, but there is a drastic change in the personnel sitting and those represented by proxy. This can probably be explained by the non-attendance of some peers holding a large number of proxies who were replaced with other government supporters who held an equal number. However, the bishop of Elphin is once described as Henry (Tilson, bishop from 1639 to 1655) and seven days later called Thomas.[43] This is hardly an error that erodes any trust we might have in the journals as a whole, but it does indicate that errors could be made and were recorded, despite the supervisory efforts of the peers themselves.

The Commons seem to have had a less perfect record. For example, in 1613, an order was recorded to have the 'sheriff of Wexford', Cantwell, sent for by warrant for not paying the wages of the knights of the shire; but Cantwell was the sheriff of Waterford.[44] In the following parliament, a bill for several charges imposed upon the lands and persons of *cestunique* use was recorded as having a second reading, but no first.[45] This is an occasional occurrence in the Commons' journals throughout the century, particularly in the first half. In 1661, a letter of the speaker permitting fundraising on behalf of Philip Ferneley, although ordered to be entered into the journals, never made it into printed version.[46] This surely is the fault of the printers as Ferneley was the clerk in the Commons and the letter was financially beneficial to him.[47] In October 1665, the Commons made reference to the example of the calling of new elections to replace Lord Lisle and Lawrence Crawford due to their absence in England without permission. The order for new elections was made on 9 April 1644, but the restoration journals of the Commons refer to the order as having been made on 19 April 1649 (after parliament had been dissolved).[48] In March 1666, the Commons agreed to remit the fine on Matthew Harrison for non-attendance in late January of the same year after the truant member made sufficient argument or excuse in a petition.[49] However, on inspecting the journals for the day the house was called, on the long list of eighty-four members fined between £10 and £50, Matthew Harrison (MP for Callan in Co. Kilkenny) is not to be found. It may be the case that as his fine was remitted for some good reason, his name should have been omitted from the original list (not usual in other examples of fines), but this in itself would, in most cases, have necessitated another entry in the journal. There was also deliberate misrepresentation of actual events through efforts to adjust the journals. The content of the journals was overseen by a committee of the House, which obviously created room for modification of content. There were also times when the House voted to remove material from the record of previous parliaments for political reasons. The restoration parliament removed material from the journals of the 1640s sessions and the 1695 parliament passed legislation to destroy the 1689 journal in its entirety.[50]

When working with the journals, it is absolutely critical to remember that they were composed and preserved as a court record. They were primarily to be used by the officers of the house, speakers, and individual members both as a record of past events and also as a guide as to how parliaments should function. Precedent was, for example, referred to on several occasions, not just by members seeking to have a certain procedure followed, but also by litigants (who were sometimes members) who brought their cases to parliament. They were simply asserting their rights under *stare decisis*, as they could do in any other court of the kingdom.[51] The journals were never produced or preserved for public consumption – indeed, as in England, the parliamentarians jealously guarded their privilege not to have their activities reported upon in the public sphere.[52] For those interested in the history of parliamentary politics, particularly high politics, the very fact that the journals do not generally report speeches makes them seem somewhat dry and of limited use other than as a guide for dating the reading of certain bills or other politically significant happenings. However, to the historian of parliamentary procedure, the journals are an invaluable source. And while one must always be sceptical and careful with sources, an internal record that was never compiled to relay an interpretation of political events or to convince an individual as to the merits of one argument over another (as personal letters, pamphlets, and news-sheets might) must surely be regarded as relatively safe and relatively un-biased. This is not to suggest that procedural issues could never be contentious; and as a result, could the reporting of differences not be contentious also? In general, the reporting of differences of a procedural nature, either between the houses or between individual members, tended to be recorded in the journals in a fairly neutral fashion. Some of the major disputes from procedure and procedural innovations of the 1690s, such as the (mis-) use of heads of bills and the drawing up of money bills are outside of the boundaries of this work, but there were differences between the houses over the issue of headwear and seating arrangements during conferences, and also differences over precedent between individual peers in the Lords.[53] While there might be dangers associated with such episodes with regards to the politicisation of what would normally be a very neutral report in the journals (particularly during interhouse differences), these disputes are useful for historians. The very fact that those involved tended to research and provide arguments in support of their respective points of view means that we are provided with even more detail on the procedural history of parliament, both in the seventeenth century itself, but also on the perceptions that seventeenth-century parliamentarians might have had of both Irish and English parliaments before 1613.

That, of course, is not to say that other sources should be ignored, for although the journals of the Lords and the Commons make up a largest part of the material used in this study, there are other sources which provide useful insight. The statutes of the Irish Parliament in the seventeenth century are of some use.[54] Although none of the private acts are preserved, the texts of almost all public acts were printed up, and as only the titles of bills were usually mentioned in the journals, the actual text of the acts is useful. On occasion parliament legislated to regulate its own procedures. Those of the seventeenth century and also from previous centuries that continued to regulate parliaments with regards to elections, the calling of parliaments, the passing of legislation, the location for convening, and also the regulation of parliamentary privilege are of particular use.[55]

State material can also be very useful. These are papers such as the State papers Ireland, State papers domestic, Carew state papers and the Acts of the Privy Council of England.[56] State papers are mainly the written communications between state officers in Ireland or communications between the Dublin and London executive. Reports on the proceedings in parliament can sometimes be a little skewed despite (or perhaps because of) the fact that many members of both houses were members of the executive also. For a procedural history, they become quite important when they deal with warrants and the like, which may have been used to control the prorogation, calling, and dissolution of parliaments. State papers frequently contain detail as to how bills were drawn up and also information on various officers, their responsibilities, and pay. Following the state papers, there are occasional references to parliament in general collections in Irish and English repositories such as the Carte papers at the Bodleian in Oxford or Wentworth Woodhouse Muniments at the Sheffield City Archives. The nature of holding government papers in the seventeenth century meant that state papers ended up in personal collections. Frequently these papers are of a political nature and relate primarily to the interests of the individual, as not many outside parliament had any real interest in procedure.

NOTES

1 W. Stubbs, *The constitutional history of England* (3 vols, 5th edn, Oxford, 1891–98).
2 First recorded in *The Times* (19 January 1865) reporting a speech by John Bright the previous day in Brighton. It is very difficult to find the origins of an institution that develops across Europe in many different legal, national, or political environments, but the Icelandic Althing (first recognised meeting in 930) holds a strong claim. P.S. Barnwell and M. Mostert (eds), *Political assemblies in the earlier middle ages* (Turnhout, 2003); M. Hébert, *Parlementer: assemblées representatives et échange politique en Europe occidentale à la fin du Moyen Âge* (Paris, 2014); C. Jones (ed.), *A short history of parliament: England, Great Britain, The United Kingdom, Ireland and Scotland* (Woodbridge, 2009); J. Madicott, *The origins of the English Parliament, 924–1327* (Oxford, 2010); A. Marongiu, *Medieval parliaments: a comparative study* (London, 1968); J.F. O'Callaghan, *The cortes of Castile-Leon, 1188–1350* (Philadelphia, 1989).
3 M.A.R. Graves, *Elizabethan parliaments, 1559–1601* (Harlow, 1996), p. 20.
4 For a very interesting summation of the influence and work of Namier, Neale, and others, see J.P. Kenyon, *The history men: the classic work on historians and their history* (London, 1983).
5 W. Notestein, 'The winning of the initiative by the house of commons', *Proceedings of the British Academy*, 11 (1924–25), pp. 1–53.
6 For greater insight, see Elton's attack on his former Ph.D. supervisor's promotion of the existence of a 'puritan choir'. G.R. Elton, *The parliament of England, 1559–1581* (Cambridge, 1986), ch. 14 ('The myth of an opposition').
7 G.O. Sayles, *The king's parliament of England* (London, 1975), p. 18.
8 G.R. Elton, *Political history: principles and practice* (London, 1970), p. 35. Both Sayles and Elton were venting their frustration at the History of Parliament Trust, but since then the trust has recently published a section on the English House of Lords, including volumes on the House as an institution considering its operations, business, and procedures. R. Paley (ed.), *The House of Lords* (5 vols, Cambridge, 2016); R. Paley and P. Seaward (eds), *Honour, interest & power: an illustrated history of the House of Lords, 1660–1715* (Woodbridge, 2010).
9 For Ireland, biography of members of the Commons has been relatively well served. See B. McGrath, 'The membership of the Irish house of commons, 1613–1615', Unpublished M.Litt. thesis, Trinity College, Dublin, 1985; 'A biographical dictionary of the membership of the Irish house of commons, 1640–1641', Unpublished Ph.D. thesis, Trinity College, Dublin, 1997; A. Clarke, *Prelude to restoration in Ireland: the end of the commonwealth, 1659–1660* (Cambridge, 1999). There is still considerable work to be done on the work the membership of the restoration Irish parliament (1661–66) and the Jacobite parliament (1689). Like the History of Parliament Trust in the past, we have largely ignored the peers, although there are some excellent sub-chapters in J.H. Ohlmeyer, *Making Ireland English: the*

Irish aristocracy in the seventeenth century (New Haven, 2012). In her six-plus-one-volume, 3,392-page history of the post-Jacobite Irish Parliament, Johnston-Liik unforgivably ignores the Lords, not considering them 'as a separate entity, partly because of its constitutional status as part of a dependent legislature and its nebulous quality, for honours tended to be spread across the British Isles and not precisely confined to Ireland, and partly because it was so integrated with the Irish house of commons'. E.M. Johnston-Liik, *History of the Irish Parliament, 1692–1800* (6 vols, Belfast, 2002), vol. 1, p. 7; *MPs in Dublin: companion to the history of the Irish Parliament, 1692–1800* (Belfast, 2006).

10 For a useful synopsis, see D.L. Smith, *The Stuart parliaments, 1603–1689* (London, 1999), pp. 1–3; Graves, *Elizabethan parliaments*, pp. 19–24.

11 See J. Kelly, *Poynings' Law and the making of law in Ireland, 1660–1800* (Dublin, 2008).

12 M.S. Flaherty, 'The empire strikes back: *Annesley v. Sherlock* and the triumph of imperial parliamentary supremacy', *Columbia law review*, 87 (1987), pp. 593–692; I. Victory, 'The making of the Declaratory Act' in G. O'Brien (ed.), *Parliament, politics, and people* (Dublin, 1989).

13 B. Bradshaw, *The Irish constitutional revolution of the sixteenth century* (Cambridge, 1979); S.G. Ellis, *Reform and revival: English government in Ireland, 1470–1534* (London, 1986), p. 294. The decision of Lord Deputy Sidney to dispense with residency rules may have been influenced by the MP for Athenry, John Hooker, a specialist in English procedure. See *Parliament in Elizabethan England, John Hooker's order and usage*, ed. by V.F. Snow (Yale, 1977). Indeed, by 1634, the Irish House of Commons had deposited a copy of Hooker with the clerk that 'he shall give copies thereof unto such as desire them, to the end, those, that have not been formerly acquainted with the orders of parliaments, may the better inform themselves, how to demean themselves in the house'. *The journals of the House of Commons of the Kingdom of Ireland* (hereafter *CJ*), 18 July 1634.

14 33 Henry VIII, Sess. II, c. I (An act for the adjournment of the parliament, and the place to hold the same, and what persons shall be chosen knights and burgesses); 18 Edward IV, Sess. IV, cc. VII (An act for the construction of an act of parliament as to qualification of knights, etc., returned to serve in parliament referred to lords spiritual and temporal in parliament and council), VIII (An act that the governors of Ireland not to call parliaments to meet, etc., at any places save Dublin and Drogheda).

15 Indeed, it is very interesting the number of historians who consistently speak of 'the Irish parliament of 1640–41' and give the impression that they at best disregard the entire seven years of parliament sitting, and at worst may not even know that it exists. This, it would seem, is all on the basis that all issues of political interest have concluded by the time the rebellion breaks out in October 1641. For some welcome relief in this matter, see chapters by C.A. Dennehy and by B. McGrath in P. Little (ed.), *Ireland in crisis: war, politics and religion, 1641–1651* (Manchester, 2019).

16 J. Hart, *Justice upon petition: the House of Lords and the reformation of justice, 1621–1675* (London, 1991); C.C.G. Tite, *Impeachment and parliamentary judicature in early Stuart England* (London, 1974).

17 A. Clarke, *The Old English in Ireland, 1625-42* (2nd edn, Dublin, 2000), ch. 8; M. Perceval-Maxwell, *The outbreak of the Irish rebellion of 1641* (Dublin, 1994), ch. 3.
18 Ellis, *Reform and revival*; D.B. Quinn, 'Parliaments and great councils in Ireland, 1461-1586', *Irish historical studies* (hereafter *IHS*), 3 (1942-43), pp. 60-77; H.G. Richardson and G.O. Sayles, *The Irish Parliament in the middle ages* (Philadelphia, 1952).
19 Kelly, *Poynings' Law*; D.W. Hayton, 'Introduction: the long apprenticeship' in D.W. Hayton (ed.), *The Irish Parliament in the eighteenth century: the long apprenticeship* (Edinburgh, 2001), pp. 1-26.
20 http://qub.ac.uk/ild/ (Accessed 31 October 2018).
21 Hayton, 'Introduction: the long apprenticeship', p. 7.
22 Elton, *Political history; the parliament of England, 1559-1581*; Smith, *The Stuart parliaments*; Graves, *Elizabethan parliaments*.
23 B. McGrath, 'Electoral law in Ireland before 1641' in C.A. Dennehy (ed.), *Law and revolution in seventeenth-century Ireland* (Dublin, 2019); 'Sex, lies and rigged returns – the Kerry county parliamentary election of 11 June 1634 and its consequences', *Parliaments, estates and representation*, 37 (2017), pp. 241-55; 'The Irish elections of 1640-1' in C. Brady and J.H. Ohlmeyer (eds), *British interventions in early modern Ireland* (Cambridge, 2005); S. Carroll, 'The Dublin parliamentary elections, 1613' in W. Sheehan and M. Cronin (eds), *Riotous assemblies: rebels, riots and revolts in Ireland* (Cork, 2011).
24 M.V. Clarke, *Medieval representation and consent: a study of early parliaments in England and Ireland, with special reference to the* Modus tenendi parliamentum (London, 1936); *Parliament in Elizabethan England*, Snow; *Modus tenendi parliamenta in Hibernia*, ed. by A. Dopping (Dublin, 1692).
25 D. Edwards, 'Scottish officials and secular government in early Stuart Ireland' in D. Edwards with S. Egan (eds), *The Scots in early Stuart Ireland: union and separation in two kingdoms* (Manchester, 2016).
26 For example, see J.R. Young, 'Charles I and the 1633 parliament' in K. Brown and A.J. Mann (eds), *The history of the Scottish Parliament* (3 vols, Edinburgh, 2005), vol. 2; A.R. MacDonald, 'Uncovering the legislative process in the parliaments of James VI', *Historical research*, 84 (2011), pp. 601-17, whereby earlier assertions by Rait and Terry, that procedure was 'haphazard' and that parliament was 'vicariously and indirectly a legislature', are firmly put to bed. R.S. Rait, *The parliaments of Scotland* (Glasgow, 1924), p. 124; C.S. Terry, *The Scottish Parliament: its constitution and procedure, 1603-1707* (Glasgow, 1905), p. 143. In perhaps a similar vein, and much more recently, Johnston-Liik opined, quoting Lord Chancellor Clare, that 'Ireland before the accession of James I, never had anything like a regular government or parliamentary constitution'. Johnston-Liik, *History of the Irish Parliament*, vol. 2, p. 91.
27 *Mercurius Hibernicus* in 1663 is one of the few examples. It lasted for just 15 numbers and there were a handful of poorly organised news-sheets in the 1680s. R. Gillespie, *Reading Ireland: print, reading and social change in early modern Ireland* (Manchester, 2005), pp. 170-72. The banning of reporting on Irish parliamentary activity extended to England where a news-sheet was being published,

primarily reporting on the emerging land settlement in 1662. There was also an earlier case in May 1641, where William Bladen, the bookseller and a significant figure in Dublin politics, was deprived of his remaining stock of the printed *Queries* and was ordered that 'he sell or utter no more of the said books, being falsely printed'. Interestingly, Bladen became, in 1641, the king's printer, although was not referred to as such in May of the same year. *CJ*, 29 May 1641, 7 July 1662; Mervin to Nicholas, 9 July 1662, the British Library, London (hereafter BL), Egerton MS 2538, f. 85.

28 In addition to the ongoing anglicisation of the Irish Parliament and all state machinery in general, the very similar layout between the Irish and the English journals is almost certainly down to the fact that William Bradley was sent to effectively serve an apprenticeship of sorts at Westminster, just at a critical point when the Irish journals were first being used and the English Parliament 'was rapidly organising its own procedures, records etc'. R. Bagwell, *Ireland under Stuarts and during the interregnum* (3 vols, London, 1916), vol. 1, p. 108; D.J.T. Englefield, *The printed records of the parliament of Ireland, 1613–1800: a survey and bibliographical guide* (London, 1978), p. 1; *Calendar of state papers, Ireland* (hereafter *CSPI*), *1611–14*, p. xxxviii; Chichester to Salisbury, 17 February 1611; 'Memoranda for the Parliament to be held in Ireland', February 1611; English Privy Council to Chichester, 7 March 1613; James I to Chichester, 31 March 1613; English Privy Council to Chichester, 13 April 1613, *Acts of the Privy Council of England*.

29 One exception to this rule is in the House of Commons' journals for the 1613–15 parliament, where there is some detail of debates and hearings. For example, see the committee report on the attempt by Paul Sherlock to corrupt Thomas Jones, archbishop of Dublin and lord chancellor (interestingly the lord chancellor petitioned the House of Commons in this instance rather than his own house, which would have been the norm later in the century, followed by a conference between the houses), *CJ*, 27 April 1615; the report of an inter-house conference on the matter of wages of the knights and burgesses, *CJ*, 10 May 1615; and the debate surrounding the return of recusant lawyers to their practice, *CJ*, 3 May 1615. Perhaps also we might consider the entry for the House of Lords' journals in March 1640, where there is greater than usual depth to the detail of discussions over the relatively banal and unimportant discussion of sending a messenger to the Commons to advise them of the Lords' intention to hold a conference: *The journals of the House of Lords of the Kingdom of Ireland* (hereafter *LJ*), 24 March 1640. It is not clear why more detail is given in certain instances. There is nothing in particular that marks the detailed accounts as being of more significance than others. Perhaps one explanation is that there was a brief change to the personnel at the clerks' desk and, as a result, there was a change to the normal operating procedures with regards to the level of detail expected in the journals. Entries for consecutive days can also show up some differences in spelling; for example, in March 1640 there is a distinction between the spelling of Byse and Bisse and also Rives and Reeves. It is not with any certainty that we might say who is responsible for this distinction between spellings. What might be a more convincing explanation is that there was a sudden change in personnel either at the clerks table or at the printers.

30 It would appear not, as when certain peers were introduced it was occasionally difficult to find two other peers from the same bench who were in attendance with their robes. *LJ*, 2 November 1692 (Rule 41), 12 November 1640, 3 February 1645, 20 May 1661.
31 The earls of Ossory, Cork, Meath, Kildare, and Limerick.
32 Sir Richard Boyle (MP for County Cork), Sir Joshua Boyle (MP for Clonakilty), Murrough Boyle (MP for Kilmallock), Nathaniel Boyle (MP for Clonmines), and Sir Boyle Smith (MP for Tallow) and Boyle Maynard (MP for Youghal).
33 *CJ*, 27 May 1662, 18, 31 July 1666. A similar and probably longer list can be drawn up for instances of the use of 'Mr Temple'. In addition to the two Johns mentioned above, we may add William Temple (MP for County Carlow) and Henry Temple (MP for the borough of Wicklow).
34 For example, within a week, there appears to be a discrepancy between the two versions over the place of either the earl of Ormond or earl of Thomond on a committee, and just a week later there appears to be confusion between Lord Ranelagh and the lord chancellor, the printed record claiming that Ranelagh collected a Commons message from the bar, whereas the lord chancellor would of course have been the much more likely figure for this job. Chart, Historical Manuscripts Commission, *Various collections*, 8 (1913), p. 201; *LJ*, 24, 31 March 1640; National Library of Ireland, Dublin (hereafter NLI) MS 9607, pp. 7, 8, 18.
35 This study allows for only a brief glimpse of such a comparison. For the benefits of a more in-depth comparison on the English journals of the House of Lords, see G.R. Elton, 'The early journals of the House of Lords', *English historical review* (hereafter *EHR*), 84 (1974), pp. 481–512.
36 *LJ*, 1 August 1634, 17 April 1635, 9 November 1640.
37 C.A. Dennehy, 'Surviving sources for Irish parliamentary history in the seventeenth century', *Parliaments, estates and representation*, 3 (2010), 129–43.
38 *LJ*, 16 July 1634.
39 *CJ*, 16 July 1634.
40 *LJ*, 4 June 1644.
41 *LJ*, 17, 24 November 1642.
42 *LJ*, 29 October 1640, 9 November 1640.
43 *LJ*, 29 October 1640, 9 November 1640.
44 *CJ*, 29 April, 1 May 1613.
45 *CJ*, 4 December 1634.
46 *CJ*, 17 July 1661.
47 *CJ*, 7 August 1641. This is in relation to the 1635 Act for the naturalisations of all the Scottish nation, which were ante-nati, born before his late majestie king James, of ever blessed memorie, his happy accesse unto the crown of England and Ireland, &c. (10 Charles, Sess. III, c. IV) which, despite being a public act, had many benefits more akin to private legislation. The Commons voted, in August 1641, to tax locally the subjects of Scottish background in Ulster who benefitted from this naturalisation act; but obviously autumn 1641 was possibly the worst possible time to collect revenue and so Ferneley had to bide his time until a subsequent confirmation could be issued by the restoration parliament.

48 *CJ*, 9 April 1644, 30 October 1665.
49 *CJ*, 22 March 1666.
50 Dennehy, 'Surviving sources for Irish parliamentary history', pp. 135–37.
51 N. Duxbury, *The nature and authority of precedent* (Cambridge, 2008).
52 See n. 26 above, and also J. Peacey (ed.) *The print culture of parliament, 1600–1800* (Edinburgh, 2007); K.W. Schweizer (ed.), *Parliament and the press, 1689–c. 1939* (Edinburgh, 2006).
53 See Chapter 5 on privilege, and also C.A. Dennehy, 'Privilege, organisation and aristocratic identity in the seventeenth-century Irish house of lords' in F. Soddu and A. Nieddu (eds), *Assemblee rappresentative, autonomie territoriali, culture politiche. Atti del 59°Congresso dell'International Commission for the History of Representative and Parliamentary Institutions. Alghero 9–12 luglio 2008* (Sassari, 2011), pp. 117–30.
54 *The statutes at large.*
55 C.A. Dennehy, 'An administrative and legal history of the Irish Parliament, 1613–89', Unpublished Ph.D. thesis, University College Dublin, 2011', appendix I.
56 *Acts of the Privy Council of England* (46 vols, London, 1890–1964); *Calendar of the Carew manuscripts preserved in Lambeth Palace Library* (London, 1867); *Calendar of state papers, domestic series* (81 vols, London, 1856–1972); *Calendar of state papers relating to Ireland during the reign of Charles II* (London, 1905).

2

Petitions and the administration of justice

THEORY AND PRACTICE

A great deal of parliamentary time was spent dealing with petitions, both from its own members and also from individuals or groups of non-members.[1] For instance, in the period between the outbreak of the rebellion in autumn 1641 and the effective dissolution of parliament in summer 1648 just one piece of legislation passed, and the representative nature of parliament was severely reduced by the fact that most of the territory of the island of Ireland was in the hands of rebels of varying religious or political outlooks.[2] During such periods, petitions took up a large share of the attention of both houses.[3] Any study of parliamentary procedure should devote considerable attention to consideration of petitions presented to either house, the ways in which public access to parliament could be achieved, and finally what might result from this access. Members' own petitions and their outcomes also deserve attention.

Petitions in general, according to Brian Weiser in his study of those presented to Charles II's court, 'had a special resonance. The fact that the right to petition the king was, in theory, universal, and that in petitions subjects could explicitly inform the king of their requests, imply that petitioning presented a direct avenue of access to the monarch.'[4] Not only did a physical request allow subjects a form of access to higher levels of government, but it also made it more difficult to be overlooked. Irish subjects could petition both the monarch and the Irish Parliament. Gwilym Dodd, in his study of the medieval English process, puts it well when he states that

> petitions created a crucial interface between the king and his subjects, and that for the most part they enabled individual men and women, and local communities, to initiate and shape this interface on their own terms. Petitions not only made possible, but also gave expression to, a remarkable degree of initiative on the part of medieval people seeking to improve their individual or collective fortunes.[5]

Irish petitions either to Dublin Castle or Whitehall in the restoration period, for instance, were usually asking for one of two things: preferment in employment or restitution of estates lost during the civil wars and Cromwellian regime. Yet petitions to parliament in Ireland were different to those sent to London or the Castle. They were a request to a similar, albeit a more limited, power and they had the same form as those sent across the Irish Sea. The theory and the practice of petitioning was almost identical, but sharp differences lay in the requests made and in the response of parliament.

Until recently it was believed that none of the manuscripts of parliamentary journals had survived the Four Courts fires, and as such there is little chance that loose sheets such as petitions would be extant either.[6] Although the assumption is false for the former, it seems to be true for the latter. There are, to the best of our knowledge at present, no surviving manuscript records of the petitions made to the Irish Parliament of the period and it was rare for a copy of a petition to be recorded in the printed journals of the two houses. What survives is usually, but not always, just a synopsis of the request and the judgement that parliament decided to make in reference to it. The journals are usually just the bare minimum of facts and sometimes not even that. For example, in the journals for 24 May 1641 the following record is made:

> It is ordered, that the petition of Lieutenant Thomas Prescott, esq., is referred to the consideration of the committee of grievances, and, in the mean time, the defendant Richard Heaton, clerk, shall be forthwith summoned to appear before the said committee, and answer in writing unto the said petition.[7]

There is no record of what the committee reported, what the final verdict was, or even what the issue, complaint, or request was. The Lords could be just as vague: on the 12 December 1662 'The petition of the Lord Baltinglass, read. Ordered, that the same be referred to the committee of privileges and grievances'.[8] In this instance we are not given the defendant's name, details of the case, or the outcome. We cannot be even sure if it were a case or there was a defendant.

There are some complete petitions in the printed records – roughly twenty-five. Petitions of the houses to the lord lieutenant or directly to Whitehall, many of which are recorded in the journals, will not be considered here. There are several reasons for this. Primarily, the petition was the presentation of a grievance, or else made in anticipation of justice being dispensed. This avenue of access to parliamentary, and indirectly to royal, power is the main concern of this chapter. As such, when parliament in Ireland petitioned either the monarch or his representative in Dublin Castle they may well have been looking for a similar redress of grievance, but it was a different petitioner, petitioning a different power. In petitions from a house of parliament to the monarch or lord lieutenant, it really is a method of communication between two negotiating teams. There is a substantial difference between that and petitions to parliament by subjects.

In terms of public petitioning to parliament, what follows is a petition to the House of Commons read on 6 December 1661, which serves as an example:[9]

> To the right honourable the House of Commons in Ireland assembled.
> The humble petition of Thomas Robertson and Henry Goldsborow,
> Humbly shewth,
> THAT your petitioners were, upon the complaint of Sir William Dixon, knight, a Member of this honourable House, ordered by the serjeant at arms attending this House to be attached, to answer before this honourable House the prosecution of Richard Dixon, Esq; son of the said Sir William Dixon in an action of trespass in the Manor-Court of Mountmellicke, the said Richard Dixon being, by the laws of this land, which your petitioners were altogether ignorant of, not to be impleaded; and that your petitioners, upon knowledge, that the said Richard Dixon was a son to a worthy Member of this House, and ought not to be impleaded, did desist from further prosecution, and have, since the same, humbly submitted to the said Sir William Dixon, and as we do hereby, to this honourable House, your petitioners being heartily sorry they should, by their ignorance, intrench the honour of any Member of this honourable Assembly; therefore your petitioners humbly pray the discharge of this house from further attendance: and they shall ever pray, & c.
> Thomas Robertson
> Henry Goldsborow

Although any conclusions drawn from just a few examples are tentative, some interesting points arise from this 1661 petition. Its formulaic wording is identical to that of other petitions that arrived in parliament and indeed in the royal or vice-regal court, which began with the address to the petitioned, followed by the name or names of the petitioners. After the introductions, the apparent facts of the case are set down and towards the end of the petition, the request or explanation is stated. The petitions always end with a phrase containing the words 'and they shall pray', followed by the signature of the petitioner.

The fact that they closely resemble petitions made to the Irish executive and to the English Parliament shows that these seventeenth-century Irish examples are part of the same tradition represented in the writing of Dodd and others. So far, Irish medievalists have not conducted substantial research into their survivals. For the most part, the medieval Irish petitions tend to have had a similar layout and procedure as their seventeenth-century successor.[10] Of the fifty petitions preserved from the Hilary parliament of 1393 in Kilkenny, ten are made by those of the upper house, one by a clerk, two by the corporations of Waterford and Galway (these were presented by their representatives in parliament), and the remainder by private individuals.[11] The subject matter of these petitions is just as varied as the seventeenth-century petitions. Some are judicial in nature, such as seeking a writ of error or an effort to expedite judgements in the King's Bench. Others are more practical, such as a petition for payment of fees of royal officials and petitions for the right to mine for minerals.[12]

As petitions became more frequent from the second third of the seventeenth century onwards, parliament reacted by producing a system of procedure better able to cope with the increase in day-to-day business. In March 1641, the Commons ordered that 5 shillings per petition was to be added to the clerks list of fees. Indeed, the clerk did very well out of the litigious nature of the Irish public in the 1640s. Fees determined on 3 March 1641 gave substantial payments to the clerk for processes related to petitioning and access to parliament. For the entry of every order, either in the house, or in committee, 5s; for the reading by the defendant of each answer to a petition, replication, or other pleading, 5s; for the entry of every protection by a member or by his servant, 5s; for the appearance of every delinquent, 2s 6d; for every bond or bail to abide the censure of the house, 5s; for cancelling of each aforementioned bond or bail, 5s; for every warrant from the house or grand committee, 5s; for every discharge of delinquent, 5s; and for each summons made by the house, 2s 6d.[13] It is quite clear that the legal process begun could be expensive for both plaintiff and defendant and highly profitable for the clerk. This order for fees was repeated in the commons on 5 June 1641, that

> no petition shall hereafter be presented to be read before this house, or before any committee, but the clerk is to have his fee first paid him for the reading thereof; except of the petitions of the members of this house, for which he is to have no fee; and that the said clerk is to promote the petitions in order, viz., the publick petitions in the first place.[14]

On 2 September 1662, a committee was formed to peruse the journals of the House of Commons 'for finding out whether petitions presented to parliaments did not use to be drawn in parchment that the like precedents may be observed in this parliament'.[15] Two days later, the committee reported to the House that a perusal of the journals 'showed on 20th July, 1641, all petitions to the house of commons were ordered to be drawn in parchment'.[16] The House re-confirmed this order. This episode seems interesting for several reasons. First is the importance attached to the process of petitioning. Considering that bills were read twice on paper before being engrossed onto parchment, it would seem that both Commons and Lords regarded petitioning their respective houses as a solemn procedure.[17] Indeed, the Commons spent much time in summer 1641 considering the ills brought about generally by paper petitions. The issue was formally moved in a petition to the lord deputy on 7 November 1640 and later emerged in the protestation against the preamble of the first subsidy bill, with judgements on paper petitions being seen by the

Commons as an integral part of 'the introducing of a new, unlawful, arbitrary, and tyrannical government'.[18] By 22 June, the Commons had drawn up a bill concerning such petitions and proceeded to discuss it in detail over the coming months, going to grand committee on 26 and 28 June and 1, 3, and 5 July.[19] The Commons made the aforementioned order concerning paper petitions to their own house on 20 July,[20] and by 7 August ordered a committee to 'prepare a bill concerning paper petitions, and other proceedings not warranted by the laws of the land'.[21] The outbreak of the insurrection in Ulster ten weeks later meant that no such bill was ever passed.

Aside from the importance of this theatre of parliament, we also must consider the idea that many of these amendments to established procedure were brought about at a time when the house was receiving more petitions than it ever had and, as such, was using this newer system to prevent too many claims of lesser importance overwhelm them, and perhaps to limit the number also.

An order such as this (parchment-only order) also sheds light on some of the practical aspects of petitioning either house as a member or as a non-member. Parchment was of course not the only cost in petitioning parliament. As Weiser points out, a petitioner would have to employ the services of a scribe.[22] Once the petition was physically written, it would have to be presented to the clerk of the house for which it was intended. Once again, the House of Commons ordered in 1665 that 'no petition [is] to be read in this House until the clerk shall first receive his fee of 5s. due for each petition'.[23]

Once all of the regular payments had been made to a scribe and to the clerk, the petition was then left to the mercy of the House. Although there is only partial evidence for bribery during the restoration parliament, it is certain that some extraordinary payments were made. A letter, found in the state papers, by Thomas Juxon (MP for St Johnstown in Donegal) early in the restoration parliament reads

> But although you empower us to apply to parliament it is thought fit by a very good friend that you should particularly address to the parliament by a petition that will have a greater sense and influence over them. That it may be done to reach all our concernments and be worded so as to answer the objections that are made here, I have desired the said friend to draw a draft of one to send to you, yet I have some regrets for I have no money. 'That is the oil to the wheels and a prevailing argument. If we were masters of that we could with very good profit lay out £100 or £200 and procure many advocates and you would thank us for so doing'.[24]

Unfortunately the fate of the proposal is unknown.

Once the petition had been drawn up it was lodged with the clerk of either house. There is no mention of a bag at the back of the speaker's chair, as is the case in the English House of Commons, but there may have been one.[25] The clerks held all documents and determined the order of business with the speaker. In the peers' house, the clerk was ordered to receive all petitions, and immediately deliver them to the committee established to examine and lay aside all 'scandalous' petitions before they could be read out.[26] This committee resembles the process of 'trying' a petition in the medieval Irish Parliament, which also used a small, well-qualified committee as a filter.[27]

Accused persons delivered their petitions to the lords at the bar.[28] It was also the clerks who read the petition aloud to the House. In October 1614, the Commons ordered that all petitions to be read had first to be moved by a member.[29] This raises the question of what the consequences were for an individual MP who sponsored a 'scandalous petition', but the journals are silent on this matter. In the Commons in 1635, all petitions regarding the privilege of either the House or the member, had to be submitted first to the Committee of Privileges.[30] On 17 July 1641, the House set up four committees to deal with the sheer volume of petitions coming from each of the four provinces. All the members of the committee were drawn from the relevant province, and were, for the most part, balanced in terms of religious make-up.[31] After this stage, petitions were read before the House where its fate could be immediately decided, or, if sufficiently complex or in need of further examination, it could be committed – usually to the Committee of Grievances.

After the petition was read, there was sometimes a call to have the petition committed. Of the 1,664 petitions on record between 1613 and 1689, 725 were committed during the period under study. This represents roughly 43% of the total. There was no absolute rule as to why some petitions were committed. Generally, if there was something that was contentious or deemed to need further consideration, it was committed. Once committed, there were several options. In the Commons, petitions regarding members usually went to the Committee of Privileges and those of non-members went to Grievances. In the Lords, these two committees were generally combined into one. On occasion there was a standing committee for religion or trade and so petitions related to these would be sent there. The final option was for the petition to be sent to an ad hoc committee (sometimes a committee of the whole) if sufficiently important. If deemed necessary, the committee was given power to call persons and papers regarding the issue at hand.

Once the committee reported, the house would usually vote on it. In cases where there was a plaintiff and defendant, the House sometimes chose to hear both and then to proceed to a judgement. The lord chancellor had the sole right to administer oaths in the Irish Parliament and so, if the Commons wished to examine witnesses, they had to send them to the higher house for swearing in along with a representative to indicate to the Lords what examinations were to be made.[32] Once a formal decision was taken on an issue, the petitioner was entitled to take a copy of the order (paying the clerk his fees). If there was a person petitioned against, such as somebody who may have breached a member's privilege, a warrant would be issued to the effect that the guilty party should be attached by the serjeant at arms and held in custody until the house decided otherwise. This was usually just a matter of a few days. It also appears that by the end of the restoration parliament in 1666, details of petitions were being advertised on what was effectively a noticeboard within the House of Commons. An order for putting Sir Francis Peisley into possession of an estate was suspended, since he had failed to make sufficient answer to the petition of Robert Nugent, 'though the cause had been posted up for a hearing that day'.[33]

There was no set time as to how long a petition might take to proceed through the House, though six days was close to being a norm. In many cases, a petition could, if it were not committed, take the amount of time it took to read the petition aloud and then vote upon it. The fact that this organic institution was constantly developing methods to dispatch its business more quickly and efficiently indicates that both houses were coming under pressure from their workload. In the Commons, the standing committees of privileges and of grievances tended to meet twice a week, and ad hoc committees were generally ordered to sit the same afternoon as their creation.

Obviously, certain factors could slow a petition down. In the earlier half of the century, travel times were slower, so if a witness or defendant was to be summoned to Dublin from, for instance, Donegal or Kerry, it could take several weeks for a case to be processed. Baltimore in County Cork was the furthest parliamentary borough from Dublin, sitting roughly 220 miles away. The average travel time in Ireland at the end of the seventeenth century has been calculated at roughly thirty English miles per day.[34] Thus, it would take at least seven days for a message to get from the parliamentary complex in Dublin to some of the further reaches of the kingdom. As such, the fastest a witness or defendant could be expected to arrive from Kerry or Cork would be fourteen days at the least.

On occasion, petitions were handed over to the judges in the House of Lords for their opinion. Petitioning for justice became popular in Ireland in the mid-seventeenth century partially due to the backlog in the regular courts.[35] In some cases, defendants needed extra time to answer, such as Robert Law, who was given an extra week to put in his answer to Edward Archer's petition in May 1641.[36] Bartholomew Jey had the case against him thrown out in June 1642, when the plaintiff had still not proceeded past the original petition of February 1640.[37] However, the complaint of William Chappell, bishop of Cork, was not looked upon as kindly by the Commons. Their response to the Lords was 'to have patience', despite it being five years since the original complaint against the bishop was presented.[38] These are extreme examples however, and the petitioning process could be, and generally was, a reasonably fast one.

Petitions could also have an effect on cases outside parliament. On 11 July 1644, an order was passed in the Commons to prevent parliament being used as a device to slow up cases in the normal courts.

> Upon report of the grand committee, it is ordered (by the unanimous assent of the house) that no petitions for abating of rents shall be hereafter received into this house, until this house shall give further order therein; and that all persons against whom any such petition is already preferred in this house, be at liberty to prosecute their suits by them commenced, or to be commenced in any of his majesty's courts of justice, for recovery of their said rents, notwithstanding any proceeding upon any such petition, or any order thereupon formerly conceived in this house, the privilege of this house saved. And the members of the long robe of this house are required by the house, to consider of a course against the next session, whereby a general remedy may be provided concerning abatements of rents.[39]

It is difficult to estimate at what stage in the business of the day petitions were read. If we take it that the order of business in either house was laid out in the journals, it does not indicate any particular time of day. The only exception to this was when they were forwarded on to a committee which sat on particular days at particular times. Frequently during the restoration parliament, the House of Commons held that matters of public concern were so urgent in nature that private petitions were put to one side.[40] Indeed, the secondary position of the private petition to legislation can be seen when, in July 1641, 'Mr Robert Byse moved that the report on the bill for inclosures might be forborn, till the house were fuller, and thereupon they proceeded to petitions'.[41]

Gradually, standing orders became established as precedents for future parliaments. During the course of the week of 20–27 May 1661, the Lords were asked by the Commons to be careful in deciding cases relating to the redistribution of land during the first, abortive, Court of Claims in 1660–61. The Lords responded that they would indeed be careful as to what was admitted to them, 'but if any complaint be made of any injustice done, this house being the highest and supreme court of judicature of this land, cannot deny the complaint right'.[42]

In May 1662, the Commons ordered that in future all petitions made by members of their house had to be directed to the Commons only. This related to the case of Archibald Stewart, MP for Tallow in Waterford, who had forewarned tenants in the barony of Carey and island of Rathlin in Antrim not to pay rents to Sir Ralph King, MP for Rathoath in Meath, upon order from the House of Lords.[43] The resultant order was that William Mackerrell, king's servant, was to be allowed collect rents unmolested, and that Stewart, being a member of the House 'ought not to have made application to the House of Lords in a case, wherein another Member of this House was concerned, but should, if there had been any cause or reason for the same, have acquainted this house with his complaint, and have abided their order and pleasure'.[44] While this may not be explicitly referred to as a standing order, it certainly is a reference to how it was felt such matters should have been dealt with.

On 17 June 1662, on the submission of a petition by Edward Davys, presented by an unrecorded member of the House, it was established that no one could present a petition to the House if he still had a warrant outstanding against him.[45] In such a case, the accused would have to surrender himself and then petition the House from his confinement, which was obviously far more expensive as the petitioner would also have to pay the various fees to the clerk for his liberty after the case and also the fees to the gaoler. There would also be expense in his coming to Dublin if he did not reside there, as well as probably having to spend an uncomfortable time lodging in one of the city's jails.

Although, in general, poverty was a bar on petitioning and beginning legal proceedings, there was one occasion where fees were not collected and what was essentially free legal aid was provided. On 3 March 1645, the Lords recorded that

> Upon consideration of the petition of Waldgrave Clopton; It is thought fit and so ordered by the lords, that the said Waldgrave Clopton (taking his oath before the right honourable the lord chancellor, that he is not worth five pounds) be admitted to prosecute his suit in this house, against Mr Baron Hilton, in *forma Pauperis*; and Mr Brent is hereby assigned to be his counsel: And it is further ordered, that Mr Baron Hilton, in the said petition complained of, do make answer to the said petition, by the first day of the next session of parliament.[46]

There were alternative sources of financial assistance upon petition. In August 1641, a petition was made by twenty-eight poor prisoners, and the order was passed that every knight of the shire was to pay two shillings and every burgess one shilling to their cause.[47]

In the aftermath of Blood's plot, Robert Shapcote successfully argued for his right to have his petition read in the House despite the fact that he had been accused of high treason. After an unnamed MP handed the petition to the clerk, others opposed the reading and the house divided, with a majority (sixty-one as opposed to fifty-three) in favour of the reading.[48] Shapcote claimed that a letter of the king pardoned him, so that may account for the right to petition from his seat, despite the fact that he had been suspended from the Commons.[49] The petition was ultimately unsuccessful and he was expelled a few days later.[50]

As an interesting aside, it is surely more than a coincidence that Carey Dillon, MP for Bannagher in King's County, offered his petition against the claims of Dean Blood in November 1665. Dillon successfully petitioned for privilege against Blood for disturbing him in possession of lands in the Glaminagh, in the barony of Burren in County Clare.[51] It happened that this day marked the height of collective enmity of the House against all of those involved in Blood's plot. There were two Neptune Bloods who held the deanery of Kilfernora Cathedral in County Clare.[52] It is not apparent whether the father or the son was dean at this time, but he was either first cousin or uncle to the notorious Thomas Blood, probable leader of the plot two years earlier for which Shapcote and six others were suspended and later expelled, and this surely did Dillon's petition no harm.

Petitioners were on occasion allowed to adapt petitions that had been deemed unsuitable. On 6 August 1643, the Lords ordered that due to the petition of Alderman Edward Jans being 'extravagant, he shall have the liberty to withdraw the same, and if he thinks fit, to prefer another one'.[53] The Commons allowed the same to William Jenkins, 'in all such parts' of his petition 'as are unbeseeming the gravity of this house'.[54] Jenkins' failure to recognise the 'gravity of the house' is probably explained by the fact that he was a stranger to the kingdom, landing the tobacco which was confiscated by customs officials at Kilrush in Clare, after the merchant had been blown off course when heading for Beaumaris in Wales. In order to sustain his crew, Jenkins' captain sold 'a roll or two' of tobacco, which had, unfortunately for the captain, brought him to the attention of Robert Pattershall, a customs official of Limerick.[55]

Lord Conway was allowed to amend his petition in February 1666, on the simple basis that some offensive words were found in his original: 'they judge those words to proceed from mistake or ignorance in the clerk, that wrote the said petition'.[56] This petition was made during one of many rifts between the two houses at the end of the restoration parliament, and despite the Commons' best efforts, a significant row broke out between the two houses. It is not clear what the offence in the petition was, but it is an open question whether the clerk had really made an error or if Conway actively chose to push the Commons into a quarrel.

Sometimes, the House was not prepared to consider certain petitions for a variety of reasons. It is unknown why Juliana Merles' petition was referred to the House of Commons from the House of Lords in June 1662. For whatever reason, she did not then present her petition to the Commons, although the Lords' allowance for her to amend if she saw fit may provide a clue.[57] On another occasion, the Commons refused to pass judgement on the application for enlargement of Henry Porter in March 1662, and decided to leave his petition to the due course of law outside parliament.[58]

Finally, the House might reject petitions outright without reading. This was disastrous for a supplicant, as parliamentary rejection made it exceedingly difficult to go anywhere else since the Lords was the highest appellate court within the kingdom. Nicholas Darcy's 1661 case was rejected when the Lords ordered that it 'be thrown out of this house, it being a scandalous petition'.[59]

Little is known of the petitioner, although he did try the Lords several times later in the parliament, and made it as far as the Standing Committee of Privileges and Grievances.[60] The contents of the petition itself are unknown. It is therefore difficult to know exactly what constituted a 'scandalous' petition. In most likelihood, it was one which was directly offensive towards a member, or against parliament in general. The petition of William and Ellen Malone against the protection of the servant of Thomas Price, bishop of Kildare, was ordered to be 'thrown out of doors'.[61] On another occasion, the petition of James Brien against 'Sir Arthur Loftus and three other members of this house, and against William Hore, esq., and read, and upon serious debate thereof had, is absolutely rejected this house, and by the clerk of this house, with the vote of the same, is torn into pieces and not suffered to remain'.[62] In as much as we recognise the importance of the theatre of parliament, the symbolism of a petition been torn into pieces will not be lost. Of the 1,664 petitions presented, only twenty-nine failed outright.[63] Only three of this total of the rejected were made by peers or MPs. There is no clue as to the nature of either the earl of Clanrickard's petition or of Edward Fitzharris's.[64] One indication as to why James Brien's was 'suffered to be torn into pieces' could be because Sir Arthur Loftus and the other three members were influential.[65]

STATISTICAL ANALYSIS

Summaries of petitions are recorded quite frequently in the journals of both houses. On the days when the houses sat, reference to some petition was almost always made. Lords and Commons combined, there were 1,303 days' worth of records of parliament sitting. During that time, 1,664 petitions were presented.[66] Because of the state of the records, it is difficult to say whether all petitions made to parliament were actually recorded in the journals. It is reasonable to suggest that given the frequency with which they are mentioned most, if not all, petitions made to the House were recorded in some shape or form. This allows for quantitative study in order to provide a more accurate picture of processing of petitions in both houses. It may also indicate who was most likely to petition which house and with what success. Tabulated representations of the evidence has been located at the end of this chapter (Tables 2.1–2.25, pp. 43–51) in order to preserve the flow of the text and to make comparison for the reader easier.

The following analysis draws on all the extant journals, whether printed or in manuscript. As a process of judicature, both first instance and appellate, it grew massively in the seventeenth century (see Table 2.1). This shadows the English experience where the process waned at the end of the middle ages, but revived with a flourish from the 1620s onwards.[67] The spurt in the early 1640s is probably also due to deep dissatisfaction in Ireland with the government of the earl of Strafford and his ecclesiastical servant, the bishop of Derry, John Bramhall. This spike would seem to have been gently encouraged by the commons in particular, who led the impeachment proceedings.[68]

By way of attempting to access more insightfully this sprawl of information, it has been necessary to break down the 1,664 recorded petitions into more defined categories (Tables 2.2 to 2.9). Many different categories could be employed here. When planning this chapter it was necessary to be practical and realistic about what could be garnered from the corpus of petitions. A number of categories suggest themselves: success rates and with special attention to members' petitions; comparisons between male and female petitions; and the general categories of issues upon which petitions were based.[69] What follows is what makes most sense from this author's point of view, and which will hopefully make the information more manageable.

Frustratingly, the 'unknown' category is the largest (see Tables 2.4 and 2.25). This represents recordings of petitions where the petitioner is known and perhaps the defendant, but not the issue at hand. For example, on 27 October 1614, Sir Walter Butler of Kilcash, knight of the shire for Tipperary, entered a petition. The journal is less than helpful in its lack of detail. 'Sir Walter Butler delivered in a petition in the behalf of Midmory O Relye.'[70] There is no more information provided in the journals than this rather sparse statement. As such this petition is being recorded as 'unknown' in two regards: the issue that gave rise to the petition is not revealed in the record, nor is it known as to whether the petition led to a successful outcome from the point of view of the petitioner.

Altogether, there are 437 petitions where the record of the journals in terms of issues petitioned upon is insufficient (see Table 2.25). There is no obvious spike and it is unlikely that the record in this case is dependent upon the style of keeping records. The highest percentage is to be found in Wentworth's first parliament in the House of Commons at 52% with the lowest in the same parliament in the House of Lords at 0%.[71] It would seem a little unfair to blame this lack of information on the clerks, as, in general, they kept the journals of the house under the supervision of a committee of that house. However, it does remain a mystery as to why most petitions (74% of the overall total) would have the detail of the petition recorded, yet we are left with a significant minority for which we have no idea as to what the issue was.

Petitions for 'absence' relate to members or servants of the Commons or the Lords looking to take leave from their parliamentary duties or else retire altogether (see Table 2.10). This is not a very common occurrence, but obviously it is a necessary one, particularly in the longer parliaments such as 1640–48. In most cases, reasons given are pressing affairs regarding business or family or, in some cases, ill-health. For instance, in June 1641, the Commons 'ordered, that Mr Peter Hill, serjeant at arms, upon his humble petition to this house, shall have leave to go into England upon his urgent occasions'.[72] On another occasion, the Lords did not see fit to grant the earl of Thomond his request for leave.[73]

The breakdown of these statistics is interesting. There is one in the Commons in 1634, ten in the Commons in 1640–48 and two in the peers' house in the same period. All of them come from the earlier part of this parliament, before the outbreak of rebellion in October 1641. It is not apparent why this is the case. One would expect that there would be a stronger reason for being absent from parliament during a civil war. We can come to more conclusions from these statistics. For instance, the fact that there are no petitionary applications for the right to stay away from parliament, yet there are several cases of members being fined for non-attendance. Generally, the numbers of members when the house divides would also suggest that there were many members not frequenting the interior of their chamber as often as they should have been. It would seem then that for whatever reason, perhaps the Commons and the peers, at this stage, no longer deemed petitions of this nature to be necessary, although there is no record of such a standing order.

'Appellate' marks a petition whereby an attempt was made to overturn a previous ruling by one of the courts in Ireland, whether common law, equity, or prerogative courts (see Table 2.11). In total, there are thirty-five petitions which ask for justice on the basis that it had not been provided by an alternative court. All forms of justice in Ireland in the seventeenth century are questioned in this process – all of the common law and equity courts of Common Pleas,[74] King's Bench (also known as Chief Place),[75] Exchequer,[76] and Chancery.[77] It is particularly interesting that petitions were made and successfully prosecuted against judgements made in the Court of High Commission,[78] Court of Castle Chamber,[79] and the first Court of Claims (1660–61), which was really as much of an ad hoc and non-permanent commission as it was a court in the traditional sense,[80] but also judgements made at Council Board by the lord deputy.[81] There are also several instances whereby an inferior court was ordered to halt proceedings in a case until it had been considered by one of the houses.[82]

The House of Commons took the lead in this kind of action, as it dealt with twenty-seven cases, and the Lords with just eight. The Commons undertook such jurisdiction not just with regards to their own members, but also as an appeals court for individuals with no connection. This marks a sharp distinction to the judicial responsibilities of the English Commons, who only had competence in disputes concerning members.[83] Admittedly, there is no mention of the Commons having competency, nor does any individual defer to them in the first two parliaments (1613–15, 1634–35) and in the restoration parliament there are only four cases which they undertook to consider. In all likelihood, the rebellion and pre-rebellion parliament of the 1640s provided the unstable political and judicial climate which allowed the House of Commons to 'take the initiative'.[84] In such a climate, where it was common knowledge that a serious renegotiation of the balance of power in all three of the Stuart kingdoms was becoming more likely, the judgements in particular against the Court of High Commission, the Court of Castle Chamber, and against judgements at the Council Board had more to do with scoring political points and pointing to the perceived 'unjust' nature of prerogative justice in Ireland.

'Debt' is a category which occasionally comes up in the journals of both houses (see Table 2.12). In all cases, the petitioner was the individual looking to recover the debt. It would seem from the information available that this avenue was used as a quick and relatively cheap way to recover sums owed. Petitioning parliament avoided the costly journey through the common law courts, and in many cases attorneys appear not to have been used in the House.[85] If the case was clear, then it only took as long as the reading and perhaps a quick debate (if there was to be a debate) and oral vote. Frequently, when MPs were being sued for debt, it was necessary to go through the House in order to avoid claims of privilege and hence either delay or kill the action, as Lord Justice Mayart did when he petitioned for the right to sue Lord Dunsany, then a prisoner, but still a peer.[86] In Ireland during this period, if a civil action was to be taken against an MP or his protected servants during a session, or forty days before or after, and the action failed, it could never be taken again; after 1635, it was only disallowed for the length of the session.[87] This, for instance, was the reason why Theobald Bourke, knight of the shire for Mayo, petitioned for recovery of debt against John and Walter Stanley.[88] The Commons ruled that

> it is ordered, that John and Walter Stanley, merchants, shall satisfy and pay to Sir Theobald Bourke, knight, a member of this house, the sum of three hundred and five pounds twelve shillings and two pence, on or before Saturday next, or else they shall lose the benefit of the privileges of this house allowed to them as against the said Theobald Bourke only.[89]

Richard Head, vicar of Antrim Village (and father of the pornographer of the same name), along with Alexander Forrester, petitioned the House of Commons for tythes to be paid to the parish clergy in the diocese of Connor (in County Antrim).[90]

The fact that thirty-eight petitions out of the total of seventy-two were not committed verifies the speed with which debt could be recovered. Debt recovery petitions also had a very high rate of success. Only four of the total of seventy-two foundered in parliament, with another eighteen where the outcome is not clear. The large number of petitioners attempting to recover debt was probably due to the unsettled nature of Irish politics and the economy in the heated days of 1640–41. Of this overall total of seventy-two, some thirteen are against James Watson and Philip, his son. They were from a merchant family in Dublin and are frequently listed in petitions alongside John Watson, Abraham Rickesis, Thomas Hookes, and Thomas Partington, all of whom were also merchants.

'Elections' refer to disputed elections which come before the House of Commons only (see Table 2.13). In almost all cases, they were made by individuals or groups of burgesses who had a gripe with the election of an MP and brought the issue to the House of Commons, who had, for the most part, exclusive control over the election of members to their House, and they had the power to overturn returns from the shires and boroughs and hold elections a second time. In October 1644, John Harrison presented a petition to the House of Commons against the election of Arthur White for the borough of Newcastle in Co. Dublin.[91] Four weeks later, the House sat as a grand committee, and after reporting, it 'ordered, upon question that the writ whereupon Arthur White, esquire, was elected and returned burgess for the borough of Newcastle in the county of Dublin, unduly issued, and that the election of Mr. White is void'.[92] A petition of John Blennerhasset at the beginning of the restoration parliament asked the House of Commons to reconsider the election of Richard Chute as knight of the shire for Kerry.[93] The House, after advice from the Committee for Privileges, agreed that Chute had been illegally returned and that his brother-in-law, Thomas Crosby, the sheriff and returning officer, had acted improperly and ordered that

> he do there raze out the name of Richard Chute, esq; in the indenture, returned by him of knights of the shire for the said county, and insert therein the name of John Blennerhasset senior, esq; who was, and is adjudged by this house to be duly and legally elected to serve in this present parliament as one of the knights of the said shire.[94]

Altogether, disputed elections make no more than 1% of the overall total of petitions presented to either house. There were three such petitions to the Commons in the 1640s and another eleven in the early and mid-1660s. It is difficult to say why there were none in the 1634–35 parliament. There were massive irregularities in the elections held in advance of the 1613 opening of James I's parliament. This was, however, dealt with at negotiations at Westminster, directly held between the king and the Catholic lobby, made up primarily of MPs and peers.[95]

'Enlargement' is the category where people jailed by either house begged forgiveness and freedom (see Table 2.14). John Morton was jailed on 17 April 1634 on the accusation by the lord primate, James Ussher, on the basis that he had blocked up a doorway into a house on Merchant's Quay in Dublin known as the White Hart. This lease belonged to the archbishop and prevented access to the tenant. On his arrest and appearance before the house, Morton claimed 'that his wife hath made up the door, and that there is rent due unto him, which is unpaid, and that he did petition lately unto his lordship for it'.[96] Morton was put into custody and had to petition the next day

> declaring, that he hath opened the door or passage going into the house on the Merchant's Quay, commonly called the White Hart, and that he had humbled himself to the lord primate, who complained of the stopping up of the door or passage; it is this day ordered, by the lords spiritual and temporal in this present parliament assembled, that the said John Morton shall be enlarged and discharged, paying his fees.[97]

Frequently, enlargement would only be granted on the basis of an apology to the wronged person. In almost all cases, unless the jailed person had been imprisoned in a manner or for a reason that was deemed unfair, the enlargement would only be granted upon the payment of fees to the clerks and gaolers.

In total, we have recorded a total of eighty-three petitions moved in both houses over the century. This represents just under 5% of the overall total. Nine petitions from custody were made by members to either house. Generally, they tend to have been jailed for offensive words, such as Paul Sherlock, MP for Waterford City. He was imprisoned by the Commons after he attempted to bribe Thomas Jones, archbishop of Dublin and lord chancellor, with 40 angels in an effort to get the archbishop to reverse a judgement made in Chancery in the Michaelmas sessions of 1610, regarding the ownership of an estate in Waterford.[98] After he was jailed, Sherlock petitioned his own house for enlargement, which was granted after apology to the lord chancellor and distribution of the original amount of the bribe to the poor.[99]

This case is interesting for several reasons. The first of these is that the lord chancellor did not see fit to petition his own house. Later in the century, it became normal for the aggrieved party to petition his own house. Because the Lords' journals are not extant, we do not know why exactly the Lords did not take on the lord chancellor's case. The fact that he was speaker as well as a spiritual peer in his own right may perhaps have affected the treatment of the case. Second, this is one of the very few instances where the report of the committee has been preserved in its entirety.[100] Finally, in the discussion that followed the report of the committee, there is one of the very few mentions of *scandalum magnatum* – the speaking of scandalous or abusive words against a peer.[101] There were similar episodes throughout the seventeenth century, but the term is almost never mentioned and the crime usually came under the general label of 'breach of privilege'.

Another case of a member petitioning for release from prison was that of Patrick Plunkett, baron of Dunsany, who had been imprisoned and tortured after the outbreak of rebellion in autumn 1641.[102] On two different occasions he petitioned parliament not as their prisoner, but as a prisoner of the administration.[103] Almost all other prisoners who petitioned for their freedom were those who had been imprisoned on the basis of offence caused to either house or to one of its members.

Petitions relating to 'fees' were almost always made by servants of the house looking to supplement their income with extra fees on services provided to members and non-members (see Table 2.15). Altogether, there were a total of fifty-two instances where petitions were made to either house requesting payment of fees. The vast majority of these were made by servants of the house, although in a few instances they were made by outsiders. For instance, in July 1661, the examiners in Chancery petitioned the House of Lords for better salaries, which was recommended to the committee sent over to the king later that summer.[104] In another instance, Lady Ryves petitioned the Lords for recompense for her dead husband's service to that house, as he took over duties of speaker when impeachment proceedings had been made against the previous incumbent.[105]

In most other cases, petitions claiming fees were made by servants of the house. Interestingly enough, even though there was financial support given to speakers and other senior servants, it is the more junior figures who made applications to their respective houses for compensation for services provided who were in fact subcontracted to senior servants rather than being directly employed by parliament.[106] This might indicate that the more powerful easily collected their earnings, but those of more modest influence found it more difficult and had to resort to petitioning. In general, satisfaction was given to these junior servants by recommending their pleas to Dublin Castle.

'Fines' refer to petitions by members making excuses for absence without permission in the hope of having their house-imposed fines remitted (see Table 2.16). In all, there were just thirty-six such petitions, making up just over 2% of the overall total. They were all made by members and they were uniformly successful. In most cases where an excuse for non-attendance was given, it was usually illness. However, on occasion there were less generic excuses. In April 1635, William Wiseman, MP for Bandon in Cork, asked for his fine for £20 to be taken off 'by reason he was employed about his majesty's affairs, being clerk of the crown and peace in the counties of Corke and Waterford; and returning for to do his service to this house, in his way being informed of the sudden death of his wife, did occasion him to return back again'.[107] Roger Southerby avoided his fine of £10 by explaining to the House that his route to Dublin had been blocked by the 'great floods, which hindered his repair hither out of the County of Wicklow'.[108]

Petitions relating to what has been classed as 'government' were usually made by petitioners complaining against sheriffs, civil servants, and revenue collectors (see Table 2.17). There were also some petitions made by such tax receivers and sheriffs. In total, there are just thirty-two petitions regarding this type of complaint, and as such this makes up just under 2% of the total. There does not seem to be a particular time when complaints become more prevalent. It is difficult to know how to judge the spike in Strafford's parliament in the Commons, as the total in the Commons at this time is so small. As has been mentioned, most complaints were against the agents of the government in the localities. There were many against collectors demanding excessive taxes and charges, such as the petition of the corn sellers in Dublin, who were being overcharged in the quantity taken by the scavenger of Dublin.[109] Francis Talbot, eleventh earl of Shrewsbury, despite holding one of the highest honours in the kingdom – the title of lord high steward of Ireland – and also being earl of Waterford held no estates in the kingdom, and as such reckoned that he should not have been assessed for £18 for the tax raising ordinances of the early restoration period.[110] There were also petitions made by the sheriffs as well as against them. For instance, on 9 July 1661, Richard Perkins, Henry Waddington, Tobias Poynes, William Davys, John Ruxton, and William Hancocke all submitted petitions that they were all appointed sheriffs during the interregnum, but

> during all that time they durst not presume to act as sheriffs, neither kept they any courts, or had the execution of any writs, or received any profits by their said employments; and though the petitioners have little or nothing to accompt for ... and as such should not have to pay fees on passing such an account.[111]

Petitions regarding 'legal practice' can mean many things, but most frequently it is relevant to matters of legal procedure, the right to introduce counsel, revocation of protections, and other legal matters (see Table 2.18). There was a considerable number of such petitions made to both houses during the course of the century, particularly to the Lords in the 1640s, where they make up over a quarter of all petitions. Interestingly, all four of the Jacobean House of Commons' petitions regarding legal practice were made by subjects asking for the right to introduce counsel to argue their case.[112] In the Commons in the 1640s, the most frequent reason for a petition which has been categorised as 'legal practice' was that of asking permission to sue an individual who was a protected person. The Lords also received several similar petitions in the same period.

In most of the other periods that parliament sat, there was a hodgepodge of issues which came before either house; such as in the Lords in July 1661, when Donagh MacCarthy, first earl of Clancarty, petitioned them to overturn his outlawry, upon which the House advised that a writ of error was the best way to proceed.[113] Also in the House of Lords, John and Elinor Morton petitioned for, and won the right to, sue the earl of Thomond for replevin for his distraining of goods.[114] In November 1665, when Philip Carpenter, serjeant at arms to the Commons, petitioned the House that one of his prisoners, Philip Hardinge, on order of the House of Commons was to be delivered to the Court of King's Bench upon a writ of *Habeas Corpus*, he looked for instruction from his House as to how to proceed, the House of Commons having already ordered his imprisonment.[115] Such a writ was not common from an inferior court, but the circumstances were exceptional. Hardinge had been committed to the serjeant at arms by a warrant of 13 April 1663, upon the proceedings against him by three MPs, Sir Hans Hamilton, Randolph Clayton, and Alexander Piggott, all of whom were trustees for the 1649 officers, for his distrainment of goods in lieu of rent on the house marked by the sign of the Catherine wheel on High Street, Dublin.[116] The petitioners claimed to be in possession of the lease, and as such claimed breach of privilege. Soon after his imprisonment, parliament was prorogued by Ormond and Hardinge was to stay incarcerated on the orders of the House of Commons until parliament reconvened in late October 1665. This in itself creates an interesting legal question as to whether the orders of parliament were to become dormant during their prorogation, and it would seem in this instance that they were not. It is not known whether Hardinge made any application for his liberty during the thirty-month prorogation he remained in custody of the serjeant at arms. In any case, it is not certain whether the serjeant at arms would have released the prisoner without recourse to the House of Commons, although there are precedents for the serjeant to take bail from a prisoner without recourse to the House.[117] Either way, such a case highlights the dangers of being in custody when the future of a session of parliament was not clear.

Some petitioners saw fit to petition the respective houses of parliament about prospective 'legislation' (see Table 2.19). The fact that only 1.75% of all petitions are in this category, may go some way to illustrate the relative unimportance that members of the public attached to parliament as a law-enacting assembly as opposed to a court or as a representative assembly. Of these twenty-nine petitions, there are eleven made by members to their respective houses. Interestingly, there are two instances, both in the Jacobean parliament, where spiritual peers petitioned the House of Commons. This is commented on elsewhere as interesting in the context of other petitions taking a similar route.[118] One of the other petitions to the Commons in 1614 was by the daughters of the earl of Desmond, appealing to the Commons to positively acknowledge receipt of their petition and a recommendation by the king, through the English Privy Council, to be followed by the Irish Council's transmission of a bill for their restitution in blood.[119] It is curious that consideration of such an obvious aristocratic interest should be moved in the Commons. It is not known whether such an issue was forwarded to the Lords in their house: the imperfect index to the journal of the Lords does not indicate such a consideration.[120] Again, it is not clear why the petition of the bishop of

Waterford tried to suspend or withdraw the act as it then passed through its second reading in the lower house,[121] although it is almost certainly connected to his title to the manor of Lismore and his dispute with Sir Richard Boyle.[122] Nor is it clear why the bishop of Dromore petitioned the Commons, and indeed it is more strange that the Commons ordered that 'the lord Bishop of Dromore shall make a draft of a new bill for the restitution of the possessions of the said Bishoprick, and shall present it to the grand committee, to whose consideration his lordship's petition was referred'.[123] In the restoration parliament, the most common issue was, unsurprisingly, the land settlement. There were twenty-four petitions altogether for the restoration parliament, fifteen of which were made in regard to the bill of settlement and the bill of explanation. All that remain were in relation to trade. One related to the potting of butter, made by the exporters of butter.[124] This was probably a success, as there is record of a heads of bill being drafted for the exportation of butter, and it was later recommitted.[125] The heads of bill for 'preventing the great fraud used in the packing of butter' re-emerged in March 1663, again being recommitted to the Committee of Trade.[126] The remaining petitions all referred to the various acts for raising money either through the bill for licensing those retailing alcoholic beverages (all made by groups of vintners and distillers) and also the tonnage and poundage bills.

What has been termed 'miscellaneous' are those which do not sit comfortably within any other group of petitions (see Table 2.20). There are quite a few petitions on money matters among this number. For instance, in May 1641, Thomas Cromwell, first Viscount Lecale, petitioned the House of Commons for monetary compensation for a bridge he had built at the Portullagh and Quoil ferry in Down.[127] In this case, the Commons was the appropriate house, they having had supremacy over the Lords in all matters relating to the raising of public finance. In May 1662, a group of inhabitants of Dublin successfully petitioned the House of Commons regarding the

> tottering condition of the gate, called the Blind-Gate, standing upon the entrance of the said green next unto Dammaske-Street; and taking notice themselves, that the said gate is much decayed, and being very sensible of the ill consequences which may happen by the fall thereof to the adjoining inhabitants, and to other persons, that at such a time may be going by that place about either publick or private affairs; and considering also, that the said gate is no strength or ornament to the city, and is very incommodious.[128]

Petitions referring to 'property' were usually an attempt at first instance judicature process on property and refer to non-members only (see Table 2.22). There are some exceptions to this rule, such as when, for instance, the earl of Drogheda petitioned for lands on behalf of the security for the 1649 officers.[129] In all, there are only forty petitions of this nature in the records of parliament in the seventeenth century. As is to be expected, three quarters of these are to be found submitted to the House of Commons in the restoration period. This group shows a relatively high failure rate for their petitions. Up until the middle of the century, half of these petitions failed, with an increase in the House of Commons in the restoration but not in the House of Lords in the same period.

'Privilege' is *the* big issue in petitions to the Irish Parliament in the seventeenth century (see Table 2.21). As such, it makes it easy to portray this parliament as a self-obsessed group of individuals far more concerned with preserving the benefits they had accrued as members, rather than dealing with other issues. It deals with disturbance of property of members, breach of protection of their servants, and also worked against anybody who slandered the House or their members or otherwise breached privilege, for instance on the petition of the Viscount Ranelagh,

> Connel Molloy, as well by his own confession, as by the depositions of several witnesses taken in this cause, is guilty of the forgery, complained of by the said petition: And it is therefore humbly offered unto the house, as the opinion of the committee, that the said Connel Molloy shall be made exemplary, by being put to stand in the pillory, in Corn-Market, Dublin, from the hour of ten in the morning till the hour of twelve, for three market-days, and there to have his ears nailed to the said pillory, and his crime to be written in paper, to be fixed upon his breast, and to be imprisoned during the pleasure of the house[130]

There is another useful example in the House of Commons in May 1615, as the individual petition and the deliberations that followed have been recorded entirely.

> This day, the reverend father in God, the lord archbishop of Cashell, preferred a petition to this house, in *haec verba*, viz.,
> The humble petition of Milerus, lord archbishop of Cashell,
> To the knights and burgesses of his majesty's most honourable House of parliament,
> Shewing unto your wisdoms, that whereas on Gerald Nugent, esq., and one of this honourable house, did, within these few days last past, at St. Pulchres, in the house of the right honourable lord chancellor, and in the presence and hearing of his lordship, and of many others, gentlemen of great quality and quality condition, utter and speak to one of your petitioner's sons, named James, these words following, viz., *that he was a base priests chit, and a scald priests son*; which words he repeated very often, without any respect to your suppliant's person and calling. Now, for that the said injury doth not only extend to the petitioner alone, but it is a very great wrong and contempt of all archbishops, bishops, and clergy of the kingdom, whose function and calling all his majesty's loving and loyal subjects ought to have in due reverence and respect, as well in regard of their duties to almighty god, whose embassadors on earth the clergy are, as likewise in respect of his majesty, the

estate, and the laws and statutes established in this kingdom; the breach and contempt whereof, in so high a point, touching all the clergy of the kingdom, cannot but, in some degree, reach his majesty, to whose godly and zealous care, to maintain God's church and the ministers thereof, in their due respect, it well know to the most of this honourable house, and for that the privilege of the said Mr Nugent, being a parliament man, doth not extend to free him from the censures of this honourable house, the petitioner doth therefore appeal to your wisdoms for justice in so high a wrong, most humbly beseeching, that some heavy punishment may be inflicted on the said offender, according to his demerit, whereby all his highness's subjects may take notice, by his example, how far he hath offended.

Mr Nugent, thereupon, alledged for himself, that he spake not those words, but that he said, *he was a paltry fryar's son.*

And Mr Speaker informed the house, that the lord chancellor gave him notice, how that a member of this house carried a challenge from the said James McGraffe to the said Mr Gerald Nugent.

Mr Edmond Nugent. To see the malice of this man, that was not content to send him a challenge, but to prefer a malicious petition against him.

Sir Robert Digby. Not only these things, but to scandalize the archbishop, therefore, that Mr Edmond Nugent should to the bar.

Mr Bryan McDonogh. The member of this house confessed the carriage of the letter, but vowed, that he knew not that it contained a challenge.

Hereupon Mr Gerald Nugent, the party challenged to speak the words in the petition, fell down into a trance, his senses being for a season taken away, being troubled with falling-sickness.

It was alledged, in Mr Gerald Nugent's defence, that he suing James McGraffe for some monies delivered by the wife of the said Nugent to the said McGraffe; McGraffe to the face of the said Nugent, very unworthily told him, that his wife gave it him for a lewd purpose, alledged to be done between the Gentleman's wife and McGraffe, which caused the said Mr Nugent to say, he *was a paltry fryar's son.*

Mr Edmond Nugent, upon his oath, which he offered to take, explained himself, that he knew not, that the lord archbishop's name was used in the petition, but son's only; which explanation was held sufficient.

But it was ordered, that the serjeant at arms should presently go for McGraffe.

And the words of Mr Gerald Nugent, mentioned in the petition, were by him denied; but, considering that others as bad were by him spoken in the house, it was thought fit he should be censured.

But lest that by censuring him he, being now come to his senses again, might fall into the same sickness, whereby his life might be endangered, it is thought good by the house to forbear censuring him.[131]

There are a number of interesting aspects to this case. What stands out immediately is that one of the spiritual peers saw fit, presumably with the knowledge of his own house, to petition the House of Commons to preserve his honour and his privilege. This seems very strange, as in later parliaments the house would always protect its own member, and if there were a difference between a member of each house, it would usually be solved by means of a conference between ad hoc committees of both houses. It is possible that it was tactical, in that the lower house had a large minority of Catholics and the archbishop was himself a convert to the established church, having initially studied and been ordained in Rome.[132] It also allows us a glimpse at some of the detail of debate and we have what seems to be the full discussion that follows the reading of the petition, including the recalling of the 'lewd' acts of an MP's wife and the collapse of the aforementioned MP.

However, the petition of the archbishop of Cashel is an extraordinary example. The vast majority of petitions made to either house of parliament were made in the restoration period, where between the peers and the commons' houses, they make up a total of 378 petitions out of the overall recorded total for the century being 454 petitions relating to privilege. This represents just over 83%, which is a huge number. It would be easy to take on board MacCurtain or Beckett's assertions that the restoration parliament was dominated by 'Cromwellians and Presbyterians' and assume that a strong emphasis on privilege was the work of a self-interested group of MPs, little concerned with the commonweal or the king's interest.[133] If we delve below the surface, however, it becomes obvious that with such a high proportion of these petitions being made in relation to disturbance in their property, it should be of little surprise that such a massive confiscation and turnover in land would produce an unsettled climate.

'Church of Ireland', for the purposes of this categorisation, refers mostly to the religious disputes in the late 1630s and early 1640s and the many petitions which complained of John Bramhall, bishop of Derry, William Chappell, bishop of Cork and recently retired provost of Trinity College, John Leslie, bishop of Raphoe, and Richard Boyle, archbishop of Tuam (see Table 2.23). It is not always abundantly clear from the way that the journals record submission of petitions to the House of Commons, but judging by the petition or the fact that they tended to be sent to what effectively became a standing committee to deal with the bishop of Derry, it seems appropriate to deal with all of these under the banner of 'Church of Ireland'. Looking at these forty-nine petitions, they were all presented in the spring and summer of 1641, and also the fact that they are almost all against allies of Strafford and Laud would seem to indicate that there may be connections. As a general rule, the petitions seem to be against 'Laudian' innovations in the Church of Ireland in the 1630s. Bramhall was at the forefront of this move, and the fact that he and Leslie were petitioned against in abundance indicates that the imposition of the Black Oath and general persecution of the Presbyterians in the northern province were particularly unpopular.[134] The work of Chappell, in particular his remodelling of Trinity College, was also petitioned against.[135]

Finally, 'trade' refers again to the late 1630s and early 1640s where monopolies, particularly the tobacco one, were exceedingly unpopular (see Table 2.24). The statistics have an uncanny resemblance to the 'Church of Ireland' category described above. All of the trade related petitions were presented to parliament in the early 1640s.[136] The total they come to is fifty-six; just seven more than 'Church of Ireland'. Virtually all of the known petitions in this group related to the tobacco monopoly and particularly to the enforcers of this, Thomas Little and Joshua Carpenter, both servants of the earl of Strafford.[137] Indeed, it does not take too much imagination to realise that both issues were pushed by the Commons at the same time as part of an overall strategy to bring down Strafford.

Because of their names, women who petitioned parliament are far more easily identifiable than religious or ethnic groups or social strata. In general, females do not really stand out as a group and tended to follow the established trends of parliamentary petitioning. As seen from Table 2.6, there were a total of seventy-eight recorded petitions made by a female, a group of females, or indeed a female and a male, to the Irish Parliament in our period. In keeping with the overall figures, they were most dense in the early 1640s and the 1660s. Altogether, we have a total of thirteen women that were of the aristocracy and were petitioning on the basis of the nobility that they married or were born into, including the widow of a bishop, on whose behalf she was claiming privilege in the Lords.[138] Unfortunately, again, the unknown quantity is disappointing: for forty of the seventy-eight, we have little idea what they are petitioning for or if their petition was a success. For the others that remain, the statistics break down as follows: four females sought to overturn other judicial decisions, one petitioned on legislation, one on trade, three claiming ownership of land, two suing for debt, two for freedom or enlargement from prison, three on the basis of church or religious-related issues, nineteen on legal practice, two for privilege, and one for fees in respect of her husband's work twenty years previous (Table 2.7). Altogether, thirty were successful, with nine being unsuccessful, one was rejected, and thirty-nine being of unknown success. Overall, this puts women at the higher end of the statistics of successful petitions.

Many of the couples that petitioned were more than likely petitioning on land which was left to the female. On one occasion too, the wife of Laurence Lambert petitioned in the Lords against Thomas Johnson, MP in 1644, on an issue which seems to be related to primacy in judicature, but her petition was rejected to be amended and also signed by her husband.[139] A facility which existed in the Lords, but seems not to have been available in the Commons, was the petitioning of the House by wives and relatives of the peers. This happened on four occasions in the House of Lords. It was usually only used when the peer himself was not in a position to petition. For instance, when the marquis of Antrim was still in the tower, the marchioness of Antrim entered a petition claiming that she was disturbed of her lands in Connaught by the earl of Clanrickard. The House of Lords ordered that she be 'quieted in possession until she be legally evicted'.[140]

On occasion it was possible to offset the costs of petitioning by approaching parliament as a group, such as the inhabitants of Ennis did when they petitioned the Commons, complaining that the sheriff distrained them of goods worth £108, 10s. for the salary of Isaac Grainer (their representative in the Commons) 'who on election promised to serve *gratis*'.[141] In this period, borough members earned 5 shillings a day during term, and also ten days before and ten days after. In all there is a total of fifty-two 'group' petitions being made to parliament over the period. Towns and boroughs made up the majority of them, coming to a total of twenty-six. Many of the towns made complaints either against one of their representatives or against the fact that *Quo Warranto* proceedings had been issued against them. The rest are mostly merchant interests relating to monopolies and restrictions or additional duties on their trade. As one would imagine, most of the merchants' and towns' petitions were delivered to the House of Commons. In the Commons in 1613 and the Lords in 1634 there are no group petitions made, but then there are very few of any sort of petitions being made at this time. In terms of their success rates, again the unknown quantity come up as being all too frequent. Twenty is the unknown, with twenty-three being successful, and nine being unsuccessful or rejected.

And, for a final example, we may look at the members of the lords' house. We have records for three parliaments. In the 1634–35 parliament, there were just two peers who petitioned. In 1640–48 there were thirty-six, and in 1661–66 a massive increase to 206, most of these being privilege cases where lords were disturbed in their properties. Altogether, the numbers break down into the following categories: absence 2, debt 6, enlargement 2, legal practice 20, legislation 4, miscellaneous 2, possession of lands 4, unknown 59, and privileges 145. In terms of success rates, we have 18 petitions not faring well, 129 are successful, and for 97 petitions, we are unsure of how the petition ended up. In all the success rate of the total is 53%, which would put them remarkably just 0.9% above the overall average of both houses over the entire period covered.

Petitions, and the logical progression to the study of adjudication of law and public access to, and involvement in, parliament is not something that has been studied in any great depth in Ireland. While not seeking to overturn or drastically change perceptions about how parliament worked, what its functions were or how people may have seen it at the time, the fact that the number of petitions presented to parliament easily dwarfed the number of bills should perhaps make us rethink the amount of time spent by parliament on non-legislative activity. Aside from the issue of MPs' and peers' willingness to hear and judge issues, the community at large also felt, at least to some degree, that parliament was accessible and could be a fruitful avenue of access to both grace and justice.

PETITIONS AND THE ADMINISTRATION OF JUSTICE

Table 2.1 Overall number of petitions

House	Days	Petitions	Av. per day
Commons 1613–15	60	33	0.55
Commons 1634–35	104	25	0.24
Lords 1634–35	73	12	0.164
Commons 1640–48	260	591	2.273
Lords 1640–48	116	140	1.207
Commons 1661–66	424	388	0.915
Lords 1661–66	266	475	1.786
Total	1303	1664	1.277

Table 2.2 Overall frequency of category

Absence	13
Appellate	35
Debt	72
Elections	14
Enlargement	83
Fees	52
Fines	36
Government	32
Legal practice	208
Legislation	29
Miscellaneous	52
Property	41
Privilege	454
Religion	49
Trade	56
Unknown	437

Table 2.3 Number of petitions by members petitioning their own house[a]

House	Petitions	Member's petitions	% of overall
Commons 1613–15	33	6	18.182
Commons 1634–35	25	8	32
Lords 1634–35	12	2	16.666
Commons 1640–48	591	123	20.816
Lords 1640–48	140	36	25.72
Commons 1661–66	388	278	71.684
Lords 1661–66	475	206	43.383
Total	1664	660	39.666

[a] Normally the speaker of the House of Lords, a servant (rather than a member) of the House and not necessarily a peer, would not be included, but as John Bramhall, archbishop of Armagh, was a member in his own right as primate, his six petitions have been included in the figure for 1661–66.

Table 2.4 Success rate of petitions

House	Petitions	Success	No success	Unknown
Commons 1613–15	33	21	5	7
Commons 1634–35	25	8	3	14
Lords 1634–35	12	8	3	1
Commons 1640–48	591	221	39	331
Lords 1640–48	140	73	14	53
Commons 1661–66	388	304	23	61
Lords 1661–66	475	245	49	181
Total	1664	880	136	648

Table 2.5 Number of petitions rejected outright

House	Petitions	Rejected	% of overall
Commons 1613–15	33	2	6.061
Commons 1634–35	25	3	12
Lords 1634–35	12	0	0
Commons 1640–48	591	9	1.523
Lords 1640–48	140	0	0
Commons 1661–66	388	2	0.515
Lords 1661–66	475	11	2.316
Total	1664	27	1.623

Table 2.6 Number of petitions by one or more females[a]

House	Petitions	Petition by females (noble)	% of overall
Commons 1613–15	33	1 (1)	3.03
Commons 1634–35	25	0	0
Lords 1634–35	12	0	0
Commons 1640–48	591	37 (4[b])	6.26
Lords 1640–48	140	9 (2)	6.428
Commons 1661–66	388	2	0.515
Lords 1661–66	475	29 (6)	6.105
Total	1664	78 (13)	0.468

[a] These are inclusive of petitions made by females, groups of females, or males and females together only. For example, on 10 July 1641 a petition has been included in the statistic which was made by 'Nicholas Combe and Jane his wife', but the petition of 'Thomas Quin in the behalf of Joan Quin, Jane, Mary, and Elinor Quin, orphans' has not. *CJ Ire.*, 10 July 1641, 21 October 1641.
[b] This figure includes the widow of a bishop.

Table 2.7 Frequency of categories of female petitioners

House	Petition by females	Category (frequency)
Commons 1613–15	1	Legislation (1)
Commons 1640–48	37	Appelate (4)
		Debt (2)
		Enlargement (1)
		Legal practice (7)
		Possession of land (2)
		Religion (3)
		Trade (1)
		Unknown (17)
Lords 1640–48	9	Legal practice (4)
		Privilege (1)
		Unknown (4)
Commons 1661–66	2	Enlargement (1)
		Legal practice (1)
Lords 1661–66	29	Appelate (1)
		Fees (1)
		Legal practice (7)
		Possession of lands (1)
		Privilege (1)
		Unknown (18)
Total		78

Table 2.8 Frequency of category when peers petition their own house

Lords 1634–35	Privilege	2
Lords 1640–48	Absence	2
	Debt	5
	Enlargement	2
	Legal practice	8
	Privilege	9
	Unknown	10
Lords 1661–66	Debt	1
	Legal practice	12
	Legislation	4
	Miscellaneous	2
	Possession of lands	4
	Privilege	134
	Unknown	49

Table 2.9 Frequency of category when MPs petition their own house

Commons 1613–15	Enlargement	3
	Privilege	1
	Unknown	2
Commons 1634–35	Enlargement	1
	Fine	4
	Legal practice	1
	Unknown	2
Commons 1640–48	Absence	9
	Appelate	5
	Debt	8
	Elections	2
	Enlargement	1
	Fees	1
	Government	4
	Legal practice	7
	Miscellaneous	1
	Possession of lands	1
	Privilege	30
	Religion	5
	Unknown	50
Commons 1661–66	Appelate	1
	Elections	2
	Enlargement	2
	Fees	3
	Fines	32
	Government	6
	Legal practice	19
	Legislation	7
	Miscellaneous	6
	Possession of lands	1
	Privilege	191
	Unknown	10

Table 2.10 Frequency of 'absence'

House	Petitions	'Absence' petitions	% of overall
Commons 1613–15	33	0	0
Commons 1634–35	25	1	4
Lords 1634–35	12	0	0
Commons 1640–48	591	10	1.692
Lords 1640–48	140	2	1.428
Commons 1661–66	388	0	0
Lords 1661–66	475	0	0
Total	1664	13	0.781

Table 2.11 Frequency of 'appellate'

House	Petitions	'Appellate' petitions (plural)	% of overall
Commons 1613–15	33	0	0
Commons 1634–35	25	0	0
Lords 1634–35	12	12	0
Commons 1640–48	591	23	3.891
Lords 1640–48	140	0	0
Commons 1661–66	388	4	1.03
Lords 1661–66	475	8	0.842
Total	1664	35	2.103

Table 2.12 Frequency of 'debt'

House	Petitions	'Debt' petitions	% of overall
Commons 1613–15	33	3	9.09
Commons 1634–35	25	0	0
Lords 1634–35	12	0	0
Commons 1640–48	591	54	9.137
Lords 1640–48	140	10	7.142
Commons 1661–66	388	1	0.257
Lords 1661–66	475	4	0.842
Total	1664	72	4.326

Table 2.13 Frequency of 'election'

House	Petitions	'Election' petitions	% of overall
Commons 1613–15	33	0	0
Commons 1634–35	25	0	0
Lords 1634–35	12	0	0
Commons 1640–48	591	3	0.507
Lords 1640–48	140	0	0
Commons 1661–66	388	11	2.835
Lords 1661–66	475	0	0
Total	1664	14	0.841

Table 2.14 Frequency of 'enlargement'

House	Petitions	'Enlargement' petitions	% of overall
Commons 1613–15	33	7	21.212
Commons 1634–35	25	1	4
Lords 1634–35	12	7	58.333
Commons 1640–48	591	27	4.568
Lords 1640–48	140	13	9.285
Commons 1661–66	388	13	3.35
Lords 1661–66	475	15	3.157
Total	1664	83	4.987

Table 2.15 Frequency of 'fees'

House	Petitions	'Fees' petitions	% of overall
Commons 1613–15	33	2	6.06
Commons 1634–35	25	0	0
Lords 1634–35	12	0	0
Commons 1640–48	591	10	1.692
Lords 1640–48	140	8	5.714
Commons 1661–66	388	7	1.804
Lords 1661–66	475	25	5.623
Total	1664	52	3.125

Table 2.16 Frequency of 'fines'

House	Petitions	'Fines' petitions	% of overall
Commons 1613–15	33	0	0
Commons 1634–35	25	4	16
Lords 1634–35	12	0	0
Commons 1640–48	591	0	0
Lords 1640–48	140	0	0
Commons 1661–66	388	32	8.247
Lords 1661–66	475	0	0
Total	1664	36	2.163

Table 2.17 Frequency of 'government'

House	Petitions	'Government' Petitions	% of overall
Commons 1613–15	33	1	3.03
Commons 1634–35	25	2	8
Lords 1634–35	12	0	0
Commons 1640–48	591	12	2.03
Lords 1640–48	140	0	0
Commons 1661–66	338	10	2.577
Lords 1661–66	475	7	1.473
Total	1664	32	1.923

Table 2.18 Frequency of 'legal practice'

House	Petitions	'Legal practice' petitions	% of overall
Commons 1613–15	33	4	12.121
Commons 1634–35	25	2	8
Lords 1634–35	12	0	0
Commons 1640–48	591	63	10.659
Lords 1640–48	140	40	28.571
Commons 1661–66	388	44	11.34
Lords 1661–66	475	55	11.578
Total	1664	208	12.5

Table 2.19 Frequency of 'legislation'

House	Petitions	'Legislation' petitions	% of overall
Commons 1613–15	33	4	12.121
Commons 1634–35	25	0	0
Lords 1634–35	12	0	0
Commons 1640–48	591	1	0.169
Lords 1640–48	140	0	0
Commons 1661–66	388	19	4.896
Lords 1661–66	475	5	1.052
Total	1664	29	1.742

Table 2.20 Frequency of 'miscellaneous'

House	Petitions	'Miscellaneous' petitions	% of overall
Commons 1613–15	33	0	0
Commons 1634–35	25	0	0
Lords 1634–35	12	0	0
Commons 1640–48	591	15	2.538
Lords 1640–48	140	1	0.714
Commons 1661–66	388	18	4.639
Lords 1661–66	475	18	3.789
Total	1664	52	3.125

Table 2.21 Frequency of 'privilege'

House	Petitions	'Privilege' petitions	% of overall
Commons 1613–15	33	6	18.181
Commons 1634–35	25	0	0
Lords 1634–35	12	3	25
Commons 1640–48	591	43	7.275
Lords 1640–48	140	24	17.142
Commons 1661–66	388	204	52.577
Lords 1661–66	475	174	36.631
Total	1664	454	27.283

Table 2.22 Frequency of 'property'

House	Petitions	'Property' petitions	% of overall
Commons 1613–15	33	0	0
Commons 1634–35	25	2	8
Lords 1634–35	12	2	16.666
Commons 1640–48	591	3	0.507
Lords 1640–48	140	0	0
Commons 1661–66	388	4	1.03
Lords 1661–66	475	29	6.105
Total	1664	40	2.403

Table 2.23 Frequency of 'Church of Ireland'

House	Petitions	'Church of Ire' petitions	% of overall
Commons 1613–15	33	0	0
Commons 1634–35	25	0	0
Lords 1634–35	12	0	0
Commons 1640–48	591	49	8.291
Lords 1640–48	140	0	0
Commons 1661–66	388	0	0
Lords 1661–66	475	0	0
Total	1664	49	2.944

Table 2.24 Frequency of 'trade'

House	Petitions	'Trade' petitions	% of overall
Commons 1613–15	33	0	0
Commons 1634–35	25	0	0
Lords 1634–35	12	0	0
Commons 1640–48	591	56	9.475
Lords 1640–48	140	0	0
Commons 1661–66	388	0	0
Lords 1661–66	475	0	0
Total	1664	56	3.365

Table 2.25 Frequency of 'unknown'

House	Petitions	'Unknown' petitions	% of overall
Commons 1613–15	33	5	15.151
Commons 1634–35	25	13	52
Lords 1634–45	12	0	0
Commons 1640–48	591	222	37.563
Lords 1640–48	140	42	30
Commons 1661–66	388	21	5.412
Lords 1661–66	475	134	28.21
Total	1664	437	26.262

NOTES

1 I wish to thank Paul Seaward and Valerie Cromwell (Lady Kingman) for an invitation to present what were to later become parts of this chapter as a paper to the *Parliaments, Society and Representation* seminar at the Institute of Historical Research, London.
2 C.A. Dennehy, 'The Irish Parliament after the rebellion, 1642–8' in Little (ed.) *Ireland in crisis*.
3 Similar to Edward I's parliaments where 'If we were to subtract the record of judicial business from the parliament rolls of Edward I's reign, we should be left with little else'. G.O. Sayles, *The king's parliament of England* (London, 1975), p. 79.
4 B. Weiser, 'Access and petitioning during the reign of Charles II' in E. Cruickshanks (ed.), *The Stuart courts* (Stroud, 2000), p. 203.
5 G. Dodd, *Justice and grace: private petitioning and the English Parliament in the late middle ages* (Oxford, 2007), p. 279; W.M. Ormrod, H. Killick, and P. Bradford, *Early common petitions in the English Parliament, c.1290–1420* (London, 2017).
6 H. Wood, 'The public records of Ireland before and after 1922', *Transactions of the Royal Historical Society*, 13 (1930), pp. 17–49.
7 *CJ*, 24 May 1641.
8 *LJ*, 12 December 1662.
9 *CJ*, 6 December 1661.
10 Richardson and Sayles, *The Irish Parliament in the middle ages*, pp. 87–92, 307–10.
11 *Ibid.*, pp. 88–89.
12 *Ibid.*, pp. 89–91.
13 *CJ*, 3 March 1641.
14 *CJ*, 5 June 1641. This order was repeated in *CJ*, 13 December 1665.
15 *CJ*, 2 September 1662.
16 *CJ*, 4 September 1662.
17 The Lords never formally made an order on paper petitions, but this is surely because it was already in operation. It seems unlikely that a petition to the highest court in the land would be on paper if an inferior court were accepting petitions on parchment only. As an interesting aside and a reinforcement of their collective opinion on the importance of the use of parchment in legal proceedings, the House of Lords complained of judges making, what they termed, extra-judicial judgements on paper petitions. *LJ*, 15 February 1641.
18 *CJ*, 7 November 1640, 17 February 1641.
19 *CJ*, 22, 26, 28 June 1641, 1, 3, 5 July 1641.
20 *CJ*, 20 July 1641.
21 *CJ*, 7 August 1641.
22 Weiser, 'Access and petitioning', pp. 203–4; Dodd, *Justice and grace*, ch. 9.
23 *CJ*, 13 December 1665.
24 Juxon to Gower, 22 May 1661, *CSPI*.
25 D. Judge, 'Public petitions and the house of commons', *Parliamentary Affairs*, 31 (1978), p. 394.
26 *LJ*, 16 May 1661.

27 Richardson and Sayles, *The Irish Parliament in the middle ages*, p. 92.
28 *LJ*, 24 March 1635.
29 *CJ*, 22 October 1614.
30 *CJ*, 17 November 1635.
31 *CJ*, 17 July 1641.
32 *CJ*, 15, 20 July 1641.
33 *CJ*, 23 December 1665.
34 Irish miles were longer than English ones in the ratio of 14:11. E. MacLysaght, *Irish life in the seventeenth century* (3rd edn, Dublin, 1979), pp. 239–40.
35 Between the 1570s and 1630, cases in the Court of Chancery not only became more complex but also trebled in number. In the early seventeenth century, the amount of cases being heard from Ulster increased from a mere fifty a year up to 715. This is due to increasing recourse to litigation, but also by the incorporation of parts of the kingdom where, before 1603, the king's writ had not extended. R. Gillespie, *Seventeenth-century Ireland: making Ireland modern* (Dublin, 2006), pp. 34–35.
36 *CJ*, 26 May 1641.
37 *CJ*, 23 June 1642.
38 *CJ*, 15 May 1647.
39 *CJ*, 11 July 1644.
40 *CJ*, 3 February 1666.
41 *CJ*, 7 July 1641.
42 *LJ*, 20 May 1661. A claim which was formally (if not for the first time) destroyed by judgement in *Annesley v Sherlock* and the declaratory act of 1720. Victory, 'The Declaratory Act of 1720', pp. 9–29; D.W. Hayton, 'The Stanhope-Sunderland ministry and the repudiation of Irish parliamentary independence', *EHR*, 113 (1998), pp. 610–36.
43 *LJ*, 17, 31 May 1661, 11, 18 June 1661, 6 March 1662, 21 May 1662.
44 *CJ*, 6 May 1662.
45 *CJ*, 17 June 1662. This entry is listed as 17 July 1662, but this is a misprint by the printer of the 1753 edition.
46 *LJ*, 5 March 1645.
47 *CJ*, 4 August 1641.
48 *CJ*, 9 November 1665.
49 *CJ*, 2, 3 November 1665.
50 *CJ*, 14 Nov 1665. Contrary to what Richard Greaves claims, some of the plotters did show up at the House of Commons to defend themselves. R.L. Greaves, *Deliver us from evil: the radical underground in Britain, 1660–1663* (Oxford, 1986), p. 150.
51 *CJ*, 9 November 1665.
52 The first was born on the Irish Sea, fought for the king at Oxford, married three times and, apparently, lived to be one hundred years old. D.C. Hanrahan, *Colonel Blood: the man who stole the crown jewels* (Stroud, 2003); A. Marshall, *Intelligence and espionage in the reign of Charles II* (Cambridge, 1994).
53 *LJ*, 6 August 1643.

54 *CJ*, 15 May 1641.
55 *CJ*, 24 July 1641.
56 *CJ*, 27 February 1666.
57 *LJ*, 27 June 1662.
58 *CJ*, 6 March 1662.
59 *LJ*, 16 May 1661. It is no coincidence that same day the House of Lords established a committee made up of the bishop of Elphin, the earl of Kildare, Viscount Montgomery of the Ards, and Lord Coloney, which was to examine all petitions given to the clerk and then lay aside the scandalous ones, allowing the remaining petitions to be read.
60 *LJ*, 20 May 1661, 2 June 1662.
61 *LJ*, 14 May 1662.
62 *CJ*, 10 June 1641.
63 Only one of these was allowed to be amended and presented later.
64 *LJ*, 9 April 1663; *CJ*, 19 May 1641.
65 *CJ*, 10 June 1641.
66 See Table 2.1.
67 Hart, *Justice upon petition*, pp. 2–3, 22.
68 Clarke, *The old English in Ireland*, p. 141.
69 There are many other possible categories. For instance, if time allowed, it would have been interesting to know what the petitioning rate of members from a particular county or province was. The problem with such a task is that many MPs were not necessarily from the constituency which they represented and in some cases may never even have visited them, despite statute law to the contrary (33 Henry VIII, Sess. II, c. I). A similar problem is encountered with the House of Lords. For instance, a figure such as the duke of Ormond owned a total of 256,408 acres, out of a total of 9.1 million acres in the kingdom as a whole, spread over all four provinces with several residences, so it would be difficult to say which region of the kingdom he 'belonged to'. As such, it would be impossible to tie him to a particular region without knowing the exact content of all of his petitions.
70 *CJ*, 27 October 1614.
71 With only twelve petitions presented to the upper house in 1634–35, this overall figure is too low to allow us to speculate as to whether this suggests anything of note.
72 *CJ*, 10 June 1641.
73 *LJ*, 20 February 1641. Interestingly, although the House of Lords had authority to control attendance in cases such as this, they rarely punished those peers who fail to attend.
74 *LJ*, 23 March 1663.
75 *CJ*, 10 February 1663.
76 *CJ*, 28 July 1641.
77 *CJ*, 18 June 1647.
78 *CJ*, 26 May 1641.
79 *CJ*, 9 June 1641.

80 *LJ*, 17 May 1661.
81 *CJ*, 25 May 1641. Parliament did not sit frequently enough for such bold moves to become thoroughly established procedure, but in the strictest interpretation, parliament and indeed both of its constituent houses were genuine courts of record, and each of these cases were established precedent.
82 *CJ*, 7 June 1641.
83 Smith, *The Stuart parliaments*, p. 177.
84 A. Clarke, 'Ireland and the general crisis', *Past and present*, 48 (1970), pp. 79-99; J. McCafferty, '"To follow the late precedents in England": the first Irish impeachment proceedings in 1641' in D. Greer and N. Lawson (eds), *Mysteries and solutions in Irish legal history* (Dublin, 2001).
85 In a lecture at Trinity College Dublin in November 2010, Bríd McGrath highlighted the role played by professional attorneys who guided many petitions in 1640 and 1641 through the House. While not denying this point, it is important to stress that many petitions in these months were of a political nature, while the majority of those that form the basis of this chapter were not. At the same time acknowledging that an absence of evidence is not always evidence of absence, the journals would in all likelihood have made more mention of their presence. Occasionally there is reference to counsel being admitted, but more often than not, there is none.
86 *LJ*, 18 December 1643.
87 See Chapter 5.
88 *CJ*, 5 July 1641.
89 *CJ*, 21 July 1641.
90 *CJ*, 20 July 1641. R. Gillespie, 'Richard Head's *The Miss Display'd*', *Irish university review*, 34 (2004), pp. 213-28.
91 *CJ*, 3 October 1644.
92 *CJ*, 31 October 1644.
93 *CJ*, 22 May 1661.
94 *CJ*, 11 July 1661.
95 J. McCavitt, *Sir Arthur Chichester, lord deputy of Ireland, 1605-16* (Belfast, 1998), pp. 184-87.
96 *CJ*, 17 April 1635.
97 *CJ*, 18 April 1635.
98 An angel was a coin which was last minted in 1642, probably worth somewhere in the region of 11 shillings a piece in the early seventeenth century.
99 *CJ*, 22, 27, 28 April, 3 May 1615.
100 *CJ*, 27 April 1615.
101 E.R. Foster, *The House of Lords, 1603-1649* (Chapel Hill, 1983), pp. 150-51. The actual law, part of the Statute of Westminster (1275), was a creation of one of Edward I's English parliaments and was revised in the reign of Richard II.
102 M. Ó Siochrú, *Confederate Ireland, 1642-1649: a constitutional and political analysis* (Dublin, 1999), pp. 28, 215.
103 *LJ Ire.*, 11 August, 6 December 1642.
104 *LJ Ire.*, 9 July 1661.

105 *LJ*, 26 March 1663. For details on impeachment, see McCafferty, 'To follow the late precedents of England', p. 51–73. For details on the implications of a possible precedent in this replacement speaker, see C.A. Dennehy, 'The restoration Irish parliament, 1661-6' in C.A. Dennehy (ed.), *Restoration Ireland: always settling and never settled* (Aldershot, 2008), p. 58, n. 27. A more thorough investigation of impeachment in Ireland is not being covered in this book for several reasons. First, it has already been covered in a more than competent fashion by McCafferty. Also, the primary function of this study is to examine how parliament worked through a comparative approach. The very fact that there is only one, incomplete, attempt at impeachment is in itself a sufficient reason not to discuss it in such a comparative study.

106 See Chapter 4; Thomas Preston, Ulster king at arms, surprisingly made application to the House of Commons despite serving in the Lords, *CJ*, 26 January 1641; Peter Hill, serjeant at arms, Richard Warburton, assistant clerk in the commons, *CJ*, 16 February 1663; door keepers and messengers, *LJ*, 7 December 1661; William Craige, keeper of the speaker's chambers, *CJ*, 6 April 1666.

107 *CJ*, 7, 11 April 1635.

108 *CJ*, 30 January, 8 February 1666.

109 *CJ*, 12 June 1662.

110 *LJ*, 5 December 1661.

111 *CJ*, 9 July 1661.

112 *CJ*, 22, 25, 31 October 1614.

113 *LJ*, 3, 5 July 1661.

114 NLI MS 9607, p. 85; *CJ*, 19 February 1641.

115 *CJ*, 24 November 1665.

116 *CJ*, 7, 19, 28 Feb, 23 March, 13 April 1663.

117 At the end of the long 1662 session, the serjeant took bonds from Sir Bryan O Neill, and only informed the Commons after the resumption of parliament in February 1663. The Commons' journals do not betray any censure or disapproval against the serjeant for this. *CJ*, 5 February 1663.

118 See Chapter 5.

119 *CJ*, 17 Nov 1614. A later complaint by the lords highlighted that restitution of blood should come from the upper house, via the monarch. See p. 193.

120 BL, MS Add. 4792, ff. 90–95.

121 *CJ*, 27 October 1614.

122 *CJ*, 25 October 1614. T.O. Ranger, 'Richard Boyle and the making of an Irish fortune', *IHS*, 10 (1957), pp. 257–97; P. Little, 'The Geraldine ambitions of the first earl of Cork' *IHS*, 32 (2002), pp. 151–68.

123 *CJ*, 10 November 1614.

124 *CJ*, 2 July 1662.

125 *CJ*, 28 August 1662.

126 *CJ*, 13 March 1663.

127 *CJ*, 17, 24 May, 9, 15 July 1641.

128 *CJ*, 19 April 1662.

129 *CJ*, 25 June 1666.

130 *CJ*, 24 July 1666.
131 *CJ*, 16 May 1615.
132 J. Barry, 'Magrath, Miler (Meiler)', *DIB*.
133 M. MacCurtain, *Tudor and Stuart Ireland* (Dublin, 1972), p. 164; Beckett made a similar mistake for both the convention and the restoration parliament: J.C. Beckett, *The making of modern Ireland* (2nd edn, London, 1981), p. 124, 118.
134 J. McCafferty, *The reconstruction of the Church of Ireland: Bishop Bramhall and the Laudian reforms 1633–1641* (Cambridge, 2007).
135 *CJ*, 13 July 1641.
136 Although there were some petitions presented to the House of Commons in the restoration parliament that could be described as 'trade' related, the main focus was legislation, and so that is where they have been recorded.
137 Perceval-Maxwell, *The outbreak of the Irish rebellion*, p. 119.
138 *CJ*, 24 May 1641.
139 *LJ*, 18 April 1644.
140 *LJ*, 22 July 1662.
141 *CJ*, 9 April 1666.

3

Making law: bills and acts

THE RELATIVE IMPORTANCE OF LEGISLATION

Without doubt, the over-riding concern of Irish historians who attempt to come to understand parliament and the creation of law is Poynings' Law. One would struggle to find a publication on the Irish Parliament in the early modern period which does not cover it in some detail. Whereas generations of English historians sought to legitimise the role of the English Parliament and later to explain its role, Irish historians have traditionally used their parliamentary history to come to a better understanding of relations between ethnic or religious groups on the island and also understand 'the National Question'. As part of this process, law has figured reasonably well. In particular, the working of Poynings' Law and also the penal laws of the eighteenth century have captured the imaginations of historians and a wider public alike. While, of course, both of these topics are of huge significance in their own right, they also fit perfectly into the study of Irish history in relation to England/Britain.[1] Generally speaking, if we take a look at the historiography of the individual parliaments of the seventeenth century, it becomes clear that there has been no study of legislation from the perspective of the institutional productivity of parliament in the seventeenth century.

James I's parliament, which sat from 1613–15, has been chiefly remembered for the violent breakdown in the House of Commons followed by the withdrawal of the Catholic members of first the Commons and then the Lords.[2] There can be no doubt that this episode is of profound importance. The walkout by a significant minority of both houses represented a real break with the past, and although the idea of Irish Catholics appealing over the head of the chief governor directly to the monarch was a well-worn path for Irish politicians, the fact that this was the first instance of a Protestant majority in the Commons, and also the admittance of many new boroughs for Ulster in particular, meant that their dominance of the Commons (and as a result, of the parliament) would be more likely to extend for the foreseeable future.[3] There has been little mention of legislation specifically other than that as part of Catholic negotiations with James I.[4]

In reinforcing the argument that sometimes the more prolific legislative programmes have received little attention from historians, the first parliament of Wentworth's viceroyalty is a good example. The 1634–35 assembly passed seventy-two acts. That is more than any other seventeenth-century Dublin parliament. Wentworth's skill in disposing easily of a parliamentary 'opposition' has actually eclipsed the legislative achievement.[5] Most studies of this parliament tend to focus on two interrelated matters. The first of these is the failure by the government to pass the graces in their fullest form. These were provisions for, among other things, security of estates in Ireland similar to the (statute of) limitations act in England, and matters of access to posts in government, the judiciary, and the army. These had been agreed to by Charles I in exchange for cash payments in the late 1620s.[6] Once Wentworth showed his hand by putting a bill, which was little more than a mutilated form of the graces, before the Commons in the second session (finance had already been secured in the first), the Catholic MPs broke from supporting the government.[7]

Without a doubt, the parliament given most attention has been that of the 1640s, mirroring English historiography.[8] Wentworth, having managed to upset too many vested interests, fell from power in Ireland once his administration came under the concerted pressure of not just the combined forces of Irish Catholics and Protestants, but also puritan elements within the English Parliament. This parliament is sometimes seen as part of the process that led to the 1641 rising and the expression of some important constitutional assertions.[9] Little attention has been paid to legislation with the exception of a number of bills which were rejected by the Commons as part of this political confrontation.[10] Indeed, one striking aspect of the historiography of the 1640–48 parliament is that as the interests of political historians shift towards the civil wars and particularly the confederate assembly, acknowledgement or even knowledge of the Irish Parliament for the six years after October 1641 is negligible. It is not entirely clear whether they simply do not know or do not want to know of the assembly that sat relatively regularly between 1642 and 1648. What is clear is that the parliamentary historiography of the era concentrates on the political confrontations and the lead up to war. To exacerbate the matter, the fact that the 1645 act for remittal of rents, services, compositions, first fruits, and twentieth parts was not included in the printed *Statutes at large* has contributed to an erroneous belief that no legislation was passed after the outbreak of the rebellion.[11]

The early 1660s have fared little better and to a large extent have featured less due to the relative disinterest in the period in general.[12] Apart from concentrating on the emergence of the restoration land settlement and the residue of Cromwellians to be found among its members, there has been little work on the Irish Parliament of 1661–66.[13] James Kelly is noticeable by the fact that his work on Poynings' Law spends far more time on the progress of legislation, whereas his predecessors on the same project tended more towards the political side of the issue – although it is true that source material is more plentiful for the 1660s than it was for the Tudor or early Stuart period.[14] The history of the land settlement occasionally refers to parliament, but there has not been a comprehensive account of the passing of the two settlement acts in parliament. Arnold's account of the settlement refers to parliament only infrequently, and the journey of the act in parliament is reduced to one sentence; although in fairness, the book is more concerned with the content and application of the settlement acts than the legislative process.[15]

Least attention has been given to the parliament of James II, which sat in summer 1689. There are several reasons for this. The journals were destroyed in the aftermath of the Williamite victory in Ireland, and so there are no known surviving records that are reliable for either the Commons or Lords. Thus we are left with the private correspondences of individuals who may have witnessed events and published records that came after the events, most of which are unreliably Jacobite or Williamite.[16] This parliament was ignored by Kelly in his treatment of Poynings' Law, probably because of its perceived illegality, as were the government preparations for a parliament at the end of the 1670s.

In general, legislation has been used to enlighten readers as to the development of politics in seventeenth-century Ireland rather than being studied in its own right.[17] Laws passed – such as the acts of settlement and of explanation, acts for finance, and also prospective acts that were to remain bills such as the bills against Jesuits (1613), gunpowder (1635), and the raft of bills rejected in the summer session of 1641 – have all been used to illustrate the political history of Ireland.[18] This chapter will attempt to write a parliamentary history of Ireland through the prism of legislative output. It will focus primarily on the legislation that was passed and that was rejected, the theory and practice of how it was passed, and the associated processes and roles played by members and servants of the house. This chapter will not study legislation in its widest sense. It will not study the general operation of Poynings' Law for two main reasons. First, understanding of Poynings' Law is well advanced thanks to the work of Aidan Clarke and James Kelly. The second reason is that the history of Poynings' Law is as much about the office of the lord lieutenant, the king, and the respective privy councils of Ireland and England and their committees as it is about parliament. This chapter will refer to Poynings' Law only when necessary to explain the role of parliament in the passing, and occasionally in contributing to the drafting, of law in Ireland.

Another issue this chapter will not consider in its entirety is the creation of law. There were many ways to create law in Ireland and, on occasion, the Irish Parliament had no input. The lord lieutenant created acts of state (the chief governor simply creating law with the advice of the Privy Council). The Kingdom of Ireland had laws made for it by the English Parliament on a fairly regular basis. These were made both when the Irish Parliament was sitting, adjourned or prorogued, and between parliaments. In 1642, the English Parliament passed the adventurers' acts, which raised money in England for the suppression of the rebellion in Ireland, on the basis that confiscated Irish lands would be used for repayment.[19] Early in the reign of Charles II private acts, such as that for the restoration of the estates of Wentworth Dillon, earl of Roscommon, were passed in the English Parliament.[20] In 1691, the English Parliament also passed legislation regarding the internal procedures of the Irish Parliament by ruling that all MPs had to take the oath of supremacy.[21] This flew in the face of the Irish houses who, by the seventeenth century, had established to their own satisfaction that they were the final court of adjudication as to who was entitled to sit in the Dublin parliament. There was little opposition in the Irish Parliament to any of these acts, but in the face of the outright hostility of Irish parliamentary opposition early in George I's reign, the English Parliament expressly asserted, by statute, that the English House of Lords was the final and sole court of appeal for the Irish legal system and that the English Parliament was competent to legislate for Ireland.[22] Also, the English Parliament, when making a statute that explained or confirmed the common law, obviously had a strong, albeit indirect, influence on law creation in Ireland.

English case law was also taken into account in the Irish Parliament when it acted as a court and also in the regular court system.[23] Judicial precedent had an obvious influence when we consider that the Irish system had no tradition of indigenous law reporting in the period: Davies was probably the first published reporter.[24] Many judges were English in origin and all those who wished to plead professionally were required to spend at least some time in education at the inns of court at London.[25] Donaldson also points to what, despite the protestations of Darcy, Molyneux, and others, seems to be the clear fact that English law could be and was directly applied to Ireland by the methods above and also by application of writ and royal mandate.[26]

While confirming the facts stated in the preceding paragraphs, it is important to acknowledge that the Irish Parliament existed from the mid-thirteenth century until August 1800. Part (but certainly not all) of its judicial function was removed in 1720 and law for Ireland could be created from several sources other than the Irish Parliament. So why then did the Irish Parliament continue in its existence? Surely there is more to it than the Stuarts or any other dynasty having a reverence for the principles of *quod omnes tangit, ab omnibus approbetur*, or that of *plena potestas*.²⁷ While it may be unwise to entirely dismiss these essential principles of Roman law handed down via the medieval church, it would seem likely that they were no longer as applicable in the seventeenth century. Certainly it would seem to be the case that after the 1541 act for kingly title, parliament was, in theory, representative of all the population on all the island, yet it was always an 'apartheid' system: in the medieval period the distinction was ethnic and after the reformation the policy steadily became one of religious discrimination, even if society itself was not nearly so divided.²⁸ Judging by events in the seventeenth century, many of the laws created in Westminster for Ireland, particularly the private acts, were not sufficiently important to cause a problem. When serious issues, such as the adventurers' acts or the act for administering the oath of supremacy, were dealt with by enactments in England, they were legislated upon when there was a perceived danger to both kingdoms. In many ways what is more interesting is what did not happen. In the seventeenth century in more normal times, the English Parliament did not pass legislation for the raising of taxation in Ireland. Nor did it try and settle the difficult or contentious issues of the day, such as the land settlement of the 1660s, even though it might have been more easily done in London where there was a more compliant House of Commons than in Dublin – although it was briefly contemplated with a bill considered.²⁹ While there may have been a nod to parliament's original feudal principles, certain issues were simply of too great an importance to be dealt with outside Ireland or outside its parliament.³⁰

POYNINGS' LAW AND THE IRISH LEGISLATIVE TRADITION

Although there were many differences between the Irish and English parliaments in the middle ages, Irish legislation does seem to have developed in a similar manner to English legislation up until the late fifteenth century. By the end of the fourteenth century, the Irish Parliament had broken into its easily recognisable parts of an upper and lower house.³¹ The upper house was certainly the house with more prestige and greater dignity, but the Commons was, by 1450, generally the instigator of legislation. Richardson and Sayles have demonstrated that by this year (although presumably it was a process that solidified over time), the Commons was putting forward what were in essence petitions for the approval of the House of Lords (although they were not known by this name at the time) and the justiciar or lord deputy.³² Bills that the government wanted were also put forward through the Commons, and presumably the Lords also had a process whereby legislation that suited their purpose could be passed through the Commons. Legislation from the localities, communities, towns, or individuals could also go through the Commons, although the format was adjusted slightly.³³ In most parliaments and great councils, the Commons also petitioned (passed legislation) for certain rights and privileges for the church, the land, and the towns of the kingdom. These acts, which continued well into the sixteenth century, were customary and may be seen in a similar fashion to the customary privileges that the English speaker asked for at the start of each parliament.[34] Despite the fact that legislation formally originated with the Commons, it is important to be cognisant of the fact that the Commons must have been very much controlled by the justiciar and that many administrative, legislative, private, and commonweal bills were proceeded upon by the Commons at the instigation of the justiciar, his ministers, or on occasion a sufficiently important peer: 'the normal relation of the commons to the government was that of willing servants (or coadjutors, if that word be preferred) to authority'.[35]

The end of the fifteenth century saw a significant sea-change in the way that legislation could be passed and is the stage when most historians acknowledge that parliamentary history becomes modern rather than medieval. The historical background is to be found in the over-spill of the wars of the roses into Ireland. In the first instance, the Irish Parliament had shown some streak of independence, described by Curtis somewhat controversially as 'aristocratic home rule' or 'legislative independence'.[36] This was 1460, when it was declared that Ireland 'is and at all times has been corporate of itself, by the ancient laws and customs used in the same, freed of the burthen of any special law of the realm of England, save only such laws as by the lords spiritual and temporal and the commons of the said land had been in great council or parliament there held, admitted, accepted, affirmed and proclaimed'.[37] Later in the war, the earl of Kildare, head of one of the most powerful families in Ireland, bet wrongly on two pretenders to the throne. In the case of Lambert Simnel, Kildare had him crowned with the agreement of parliament as Edward VI in Dublin in May 1487 and proceeded to undertake an invasion of England on behalf of the Yorkists. The resultant Battle of Stoke turned out to be a decisive defeat for Kildare. Simnel took up a position as skivvy in the kitchens of Henry VII and Kildare, perhaps surprisingly, remained as lord deputy and still in effective power in Ireland.[38] By November 1491 a second pretender named Perkin Warbeck, claiming to be Richard, Duke of York, landed in Cork. Although probably not directly involved with Warbeck, many members of Kildare's family were and his lack of action on behalf of the king made the weakness of royal authority in Ireland all the more apparent.[39]

Warbeck departed Ireland by the following spring and although he threatened Ireland again by sea, he did not land. In general, though, the problem remained. Henry VII could not afford to keep a permanent English administration and sizeable army in Ireland and yet repeated experiments brought him to the conclusion that he could not leave Kildare out of its administrative structure. As Steven Ellis has pointed out, Henry's prime motive for the administrative reforms that followed was essentially to ensure that his westerly lordship would give him as little trouble and cost as little money as was possible.[40] Sir Edward Poynings was sent to Ireland as a temporary provision to bring about a reformed administration so that when Kildare resumed the lord lieutenancy of the lordship, he would not be able to intimidate and control parliament as he had during the previous decade. Thus, Poynings' Law was passed as an effort to prevent a lord deputy having too great a degree of control of parliament, especially if he might be at variance with royal policy. The wording of the act follows:

> noo parliament be holden here after in the said land but at such season as the kynges lieutenaunt and Counseill ther first doth certifie the kyng, under the great seall of that land, the causes and consideracions, and all such actus as theym semyth shuld passe in the same parliament. And such causes, consideracions, and actes affermyd by the kyng and his Counsell to be good and expedient for that land, and his licence thereuppon, aswell [in] affermacion of the said causez and actes as to Sommon the said parliament vnder his great seall of England had and optained that don, a parlement to be had and holden after the fourme and effect afore rehersed and if any parliament be holden in that land here after, contrarie to the fourme and prouision aforesaid it demyd voi[d a]nd of noon effect in the lawe.[41]

This act is of massive significance. It is among the first laws that were promulgated in a (relatively) modern English language in Ireland. Up to this point, legislation in Ireland had been generally recorded in archaic Norman-French.[42] The implications of this were of real significance to the making of statutes in Ireland until the 1801 union. Legislation could no longer originate with the Irish Parliament directly. Prospective legislation, along with the reasons for calling a parliament, was supposed to be passed to the king and English Council and, if their approbation was given, the writs could be sent out for elections and parliament called. As Quinn points out, the implications of the act did not allow for the addition of further bills originating in England, the addition of further bills originating in Ireland after the licence had been granted, or the sending of bills to England after the initial transmission to England in advance of parliament.[43] Theory aside, it was not uncommon to have some of the regulations which were set down in 1494 ignored on occasion in the following forty years, which in a strictly legal sense made any particular parliament, and all of its acts, invalid. In most cases, the changes made were not overly objectionable and passed without too much trouble.[44]

For the most part, the application of the law worked reasonably well for the following forty years, but the growth of governmental and religious reform caused stress to the parliamentary system and necessitated amendments. The main change in Tudor government in the sixteenth century was the replacement of Anglo-Irish lord deputies (usually of the Kildare family) with an English-born lord deputy and an increasingly English administration, a process that was largely complete by the start of the Stuart era. In addition to the creation of the Kingdom of Ireland, a religious reformation was also foisted on the island. As the century progressed, it becomes more obvious that loyalty was being judged, partially at least by religion, and the return of continentally-educated Catholics from the last third of the century onwards solidified the sharp divide in the population of Ireland. In addition to the establishment of a reformed Church of Ireland, plantations of English and later Scottish populations were established on lands of failed rebels and also by 'discovery' of title. When these are combined with the exclusion of recusants from central government, the judiciary, and the army by the beginning of the reign of James I, it is quite clear that there was an effect on the Irish Parliament and how it worked.[45] It must have been a strange position for the Old English (as the Anglo-Irish were by the sixteenth century being termed) – they had from the thirteenth century onwards petitioned for a strong English lord deputy and the strengthening and extension of the colony.[46] Although under the circumstances of the fourteenth and fifteenth centuries, the Anglo-Irish expected to still be the colonial, privileged population rather than what, by the early seventeenth century, James I termed his 'half-subjects'.[47]

During the sixteenth century, we find that there were two occasions when Poynings' Law was suspended because the statute was found to be an obstacle to getting parliamentary business completed quickly enough.[48] In the first instance, most of the major pieces of reformation legislation were brought in, and it was considered appropriate to have the option of negotiation and amendment of this legislation available to the lord lieutenant. There was an explanatory act passed later in the reformation parliament, which explained the nature of the suspending act.[49] Interestingly, the suspending act was passed without too much difficulty and there was no sign of anything like an organised opposition in either the Commons or Lords to the ecclesiastical supremacy legislation or the suspension.[50] The only exception was the clerical proctors who were abolished shortly afterwards.[51] The second suspension act came in 1569.[52] This act was passed only after an agreement was reached with the members of the Commons, who it seems were by this stage well aware of the importance of Poynings' Law in protecting them from an over-zealous lord deputy.[53] The agreement was that they would consent to the passing of the suspension act on condition that the planned anti-Catholic legislation was dropped and that in the future no bill for suspending Poynings' Law could be transmitted to London without the prior approval of a majority in both houses.[54] This really was quite a victory for the Irish Parliament. This provision was put to good effect by the Commons when they voted the measure down in 1585. James I refused Chichester permission to suspend the act in 1613 on the grounds that frequent dispensations weaken laws and, if the original law was found faulty, it needed to be replaced rather than suspended.[55] After 1613, there was no request to suspend Poynings' Law.[56]

There was only one occasion before the 'new constitution' of the early 1780s when Poynings' Law itself was amended. This happened during the reign of Philip and Mary.[57] The amending act reduced the role of the English Council, in that the monarch no longer had to consult it on prospective Irish legislation.[58] In all likelihood, the monarch continued to consult with the English Privy Council, and certainly in virtually all cases kings continued to do so throughout the seventeenth century. Chief governors in Ireland were now restricted from holding parliaments until express permission had been granted by way of licence, which had been the case since the original law was enacted, but also from announcing the summoning of parliament or issuing writs for election without licence. It was this proviso that Lord Deputy Falkland was unable to comply with at the end of the 1620s.[59] The amending act of Philip and Mary also allowed for the monarch to adapt proposed Irish legislation, although this was almost certainly happening in London before this act was passed. The major clarification that this act did provide for was the transmission of bills after parliament had begun, which again was probably in use already and so was really just a codification of custom.[60] In less than seventy-five years, this provision had moved from what was originally a short-term fix to an act which was deemed too restrictive and obstructive by the king's governors in Ireland but which was seen as a constitutional safeguard by MPs in Ireland.[61] Until 1615, it restricted the freedom of movement of the lord deputy when dealing with the Irish Parliament.

We now finally move on to the application of Poynings' Law in the seventeenth century. Although the law was neither amended nor suspended in the seventeenth century, it was certainly interpreted in different ways. First we may consider how the executive viewed Poynings' Law. In general, Chichester, who was lord deputy in the first parliament of the century, treated the provisions of Poynings' Law in much the same manner as the Elizabethan governors had. Chichester saw it as a stop on his activities and a barrier in his way, hence his attempt to have it suspended. Later in that same parliament he did allow a certain amount of latitude to the Irish Parliament in initiating legislation, which may give some indication as to how he figured the impact of Poynings' Law on the actualities of doing business.[62] Drastically different circumstances at the end of the 1620s saw the Catholic community on the verge of securing concrete concessions from the monarchy, which would protect their estates and their fortunes into the foreseeable future. These matters of 'grace and bounty', given on the back of financial contributions already collected before parliament was called, were to be enacted by means of statute legislation in a parliament to be held in Dublin. Seemingly under pressure to call parliament and show good faith, Falkland summoned parliament and sent out writs for elections before the official return of the Irish bills from the English Privy Council and the warrant to hold parliament had been procured.[63] The knock-on effect of this meant that what began as a sign of good faith by the administration became suspect in that judicial opinion at the Privy Council in London inclined towards the lack of legality in any resultant parliament and hence the cancellation of what had been due to take place in November 1628.[64]

Wentworth's proclaimed determination to reduce powerful subjects meant that parliament was not called immediately. When it was called in 1634, Wentworth found it necessary to raise funds and also to prevent the Graces being passed *in toto*. The method by which these aims were arrived at was to follow an interpretation of Poynings' Law which was far more beneficial to the administration than parliament. He stipulated that business concentrate on the provisions of supply first, reserving other matters for the later sessions. In the first instance, advance consultation with, or inspection of legislation by, the Old English lords of the pale was refused. He played along with parliament as they framed a bill for the graces to be passed in the second session. Once supply had been achieved, Wentworth attended the House of Lords and explained his interpretation of the law:

> his lordship said he doubted not but that their lordships should have satisfaction in the effect of their desires; but for the manner, his lordship dissents, inasmuch as their lordships by an act of parliament, made in the time of the government of Sir Edward Poynings, are debarred from penning any act, and have power only to move or petition the lord deputy and council, for drawing and transmitting into England such acts as they desired to be passed in the matter.[65]

Later in the same session, he sought to curtail the judicial function of the House of Commons by reminding them that Poynings' Law barred them from proceeding in the attempted impeachment of Vincent Gookin.[66] Wentworth struck another blow in 1640 when, after advance consultations with parliament on the money bill, he inserted a preamble that lauded his role in Ireland since his arrival. As parliament could not amend the bill and did not want to seem to be depriving the king of assistance in his time of need against the Scots, it was passed. Wentworth then departed to London with a legislative record of his own success but a dangerous misunderstanding of the pliability of the Irish Parliament. The Commons assumed the right to declare the means of assessment of the subsidy and later attacked Wentworth's restrictive interpretation of Poynings' Law.[67] The 1634–35 attempt to restrict parliament's competence in judicial affairs was overthrown when, in conjunction with allies in London, the Irish Parliament impeached four members of the administration in Ireland, both as an end in itself, but also in order to prevent their giving assistance to Wentworth at his trial in London.[68]

After the outbreak of rebellion in October 1641, parliament has been generally seen as less relevant and focus is inevitably diverted to the Catholic confederation at Kilkenny. The confederates spent a considerable amount of time in their negotiations with the Dublin administration trying to achieve the suspension of Poynings' Law as a way of securing their long-term position within the Irish body politic and the preservation of their estates, despite the provisions of the adventurers acts of 1642.[69] Any conclusion was made redundant by the presence in Ireland of Cromwell and the New Model Army in 1649.

Poynings' Law obviously had no relevance once Ireland was represented in the union parliaments of the 1650s.[70] Once the kingdom was returned to its previous status with the restoration of monarchy in the early 1660s, the government attitude towards Poynings' Law changed. Both the lords justices and Ormond tended towards compromise and moderation in dealing with parliament and the constitutional position of the houses in relation to developing the heads of bills – essentially a recognition of the right of either house to, in some element, initiate legislation.[71] Certainly the net result of the 1660s parliament was one that saw a beneficial supply package for government, far in excess of anything that Wentworth would have hoped for.[72] Admittedly, the executive held out the prospect of withholding the royal assent for the land settlement as a way of convincing parliament to partake in provisioning a supply, which was more than enough to guarantee their participation.[73] Ormond further extended his consensual approach to the creation of law in Ireland, when, in anticipation of a parliament at the latter end of the 1670s, he produced legislation in advance for, what was essentially, a semi-public consultation process.[74]

Finally, we must discuss the only attempt by a parliament to extinguish Poynings' Law in its entirety. The Jacobite parliament's status is questionable under the provisions of Poynings' Law. Under the terms of the original 1494 act, it was stated that permission and the returned bills had to be certified under the great seal of England. When James II fled England, his seal was lost to the bottom of the Thames. James had another seal created while in France and so bills could be certified under the seal of England, although the sealing act took place in Ireland. The second objection is that the first paragraph of the 1556 amending act stipulates that parliament could not be called until the requisite materials had returned 'declaring their [Philip and Mary's and their heirs and successors] pleasure, eyther for the passing of the said acts, provisions, and ordinances, in such form and tenour as they shall be sent into England, or else for the change or alterations of them, or any part of the same'. Obviously, in 1689, bills were not 'sent into England' as the king was already in Ireland. Does this make the Jacobite parliament automatically illegal?[75] While acknowledging this, there were several examples in the first few decades after the enactment in 1494 where historians have strongly suggested that the law was not implemented in full.[76] If such a strict interpretation applied to the Jacobite parliament, then surely those of the early sixteenth century might also be declared void and illegal?

Such an argument may not end there. There were several other occasions when the failure to comply with statute law which regulated parliament should have made parliaments void in their entirety. For example, in 1478 the Irish Parliament passed 'An act that the governors of Ireland not to call parliaments to meet, etc., at any places save Dublin and Drogheda'.[77] For reasons of safety and security, it was deemed necessary to restrict the holding of parliament to the eastern coastal towns. The stipulation did not apply if parliament was being convened by a chief governor who was a member of the English peerage. This law was not repealed until 1542.[78] In the time between these two acts, several parliaments were convened in Naas (1480), Limerick (1483), Trim (1485), and Castledermot (1499, 1509), which according to a strict legal interpretation should be considered 'quashed, voided and of no effect in law'. In the same respect, there were regular infringements of the laws that regulated the property and residential qualification for voters and candidates.[79] The legality of the parliaments where such infringements took place was subsequently declared by the same act used to repeal the act stipulating the legal location of parliament.[80]

Finally, there is one other aspect of Poynings' Law that needs to be considered with regards to the legality of the parliament that sat in the summer of 1689. A close reading of the law of 1494 will show that it was necessary 'at such season as the kynges lieutenaunt and Counseill ther first doth certifie the kyng, under the great seall of that land, the causes and consideracions, and all such actus as theym semyth shuld passe in the same parliament'.[81] James II landed at Kinsale on 12 March 1689 and was later met by Tyrconnel at Cork. As such, sometime between his making landfall in Ireland and meeting Tyrconnel, where presumably the sword of state was surrendered to the king, Tyrconnel was no longer lord lieutenant nor was he replaced by a chief governor of any sort until the king departed the kingdom in the aftermath of the Battle of the Boyne.[82] While the king was in Ireland and in control of the administration, there was simply no position of lord lieutenant, and so it was impossible for the provisions of Poynings' Law to be carried out. The Jacobites lost at the Boyne and at Aughrim and so their parliament was always going to be deemed null and void, just as legislation of the commonwealth in England was after the restoration of the monarchy. The Williamite point of view was that James II had abdicated his throne and, as the Irish crown was 'united and knit to the imperial crown of the realm of England', he had effectively abdicated his rights in regard to his western kingdom also.[83] Hence all actions taken after he fled from England were null and void, including summoning of parliament and giving assent to legislation.[84]

There was an attempt in the parliament of 1689 to restructure the entire relationship between the Irish Parliament and the monarchy and the Irish kingdom and the English kingdom. In the first instance, there was the successful introduction of an act declaring that the parliament of England cannot bind Ireland, and against writs of error and appeals to be brought for removing judgements, decrees, and sentences, given in Ireland, into England. This act essentially pre-empted the 1720 declaratory act which provided for the exact opposite: legislative and judicial dependence upon Britain. This act declared that 'no act of parliament passed, or to be passed, in the parliament of England, though Ireland should be therein mentioned, can be, or shall be any way binding in Ireland, excepting such acts passed, or to be passed in England, as are or shall be made into law by the parliament of Ireland'.[85] It is mainly due to this act that this parliament is still called by the title given to it by Thomas Davis, 'The Patriot Parliament'.[86] There was also an attempt to repeal Poynings' Law. It was discussed in council before parliament sat, but James, always an English king first and a Catholic king with some sympathies for the Irish second, was reluctant. He had for the same reasons been reluctant to agree to the declaratory act, but the precarious nature of the royal finances necessitated his capitulation. On the issue of Poynings' Law, he agreed, it seems, to a measure which would allow the proposed legislation to be scrutinised by the chief governor in Ireland, but not to be sent to England. A bill of some sort seems to have been introduced into the commons on 15 May but was delayed and only reported by 21 June, when the court informed the house, through a member, that the bill was displeasing to the king, and the subsequent re-committal meant it was lost by the end of the session.[87] Both of these issues were prevalent in the later seventeenth century and naturally came up as an issue in the Jacobite parliament, especially when there was a royal presence in Ireland. It was also particularly important to press both issues, especially when one considers that the chances of wringing concessions from the king were highest because of his difficult predicament.

INTRODUCING LEGISLATION

We may now turn our attention to the procedure for passing legislation in the Irish Parliament in the seventeenth century. The process, in general, was fairly similar to England. However, as we shall see below, the Irish Parliament had its own peculiarities, some of which occurred organically while others were there by design. It makes sense to start at the beginning. As has been mentioned above, legislation returned to Ireland after approval had been granted, and was sent to the executive at Dublin Castle rather than to parliament. The bill was then sent on to parliament. It is not entirely clear who carried it. In most cases when there was an official message from the head of the executive to parliament it was not delivered by the person of the lord deputy, but by a member of the Privy Council. The first mention of a bill in parliament is when it received its first reading. If there was any solemnity to the delivery of the bill, it would surely have been recorded in the journals and, since it is not, it is probably indicative that bills were delivered with no particular ceremony, either by a member who was a privy councillor or possibly by a regular messenger. The privy councillor is the more probable. Alternatively, the clerk may have collected bills from the Castle.[88] Bills generally stayed in the possession of the clerk of the particular house where it was until it was passed on to the other house for its readings there.

The vast majority of bills read in the Irish Parliament in the seventeenth century started in the House of Commons and Table 3.1 illustrates this point statistically. We need to be careful with the conclusions drawn from these figures. The vast majority of bills began their journey in the House of Commons but it is not clear why this is. It is important to remember that all English legislation started in the house of its promoter. In Ireland this was not a possibility, as all legislation was, in theory at least, promoted by the lord deputy and the Privy Council, and they then chose whether to put it before the upper or lower house. What may have driven them in one direction or another is not clear. It is probably fair to assume that Dublin Castle would prefer to see legislation move through parliament as quickly as possible. If legislation was still lagging in a house and a prorogation became necessary, it would have to go through both houses again in one session (see footnote 93). There was just one exception to this rule. A naturalisation bill for the children of Colonel Thomas Preston was read twice and ordered to be engrossed on 13 February 1635.[89] The bill seems to have been then forgotten about as it was not read a third time before Wentworth prorogued parliament on 21 March 1635. This is in itself a little strange as in the prorogation order arrangements were made to reconvene parliament only three days later.[90] After parliament did reassemble, the bill for Preston's childrens' naturalisation was read the third time in the Commons on 15 April 1635 and sent to the Lords the following day.[91] In the Lords it was read three times and passed to the lower house and was the last bill to receive the royal assent before dissolution.[92] The Commons had almost four weeks between the beginning of the new session and when they sent the bill up to the Lords, so there would have been plenty of time. Private bills tended to be short and rarely took up much time, if debated at all. The only conclusion might be that private bills were not sufficiently important to arouse anybody's indignation at this violation of constitutional convention.[93]

There is nothing obvious to suggest that the movement of bills through one house would be quicker than the other. For although the Commons had a strong tradition of lawyers in the house in the early modern period, the

Table 3.1 Bill starting point

Year[a]	Number of bills[b]	Commons (%)	Lords (%)
1613	40	25 (62.5)	15 (37.5)[c]
1634	104	99 (95.19)	5 (4.81)
1640	81	64 (79.01)	17 (20.99)
1661	85[d]	83 (97.65)	2 (2.35)[e]
Average	77.5	67.75 (87.42)	9.75 (12.58)
Total	310	271 (87.42)	39 (12.58)

[a] The Jacobite parliament has not been included in this statistic. As has been mentioned several times, without the parliamentary journals it is very difficult to gauge with any accuracy whether bills began their journey in the Lords or the Commons.

[b] These bills include duplicate bills that had to be passed through one or both houses again because the original process was discontinued due to a prorogation. For example, the bill for punishing the vice of buggery proceeded through the Commons with little trouble in the first session of the 1634–35 parliament up to the committee stage. While at this stage, a prorogation was issued by the Lord Deputy Wentworth, and the bill was killed. It had to begin through all stages again the following November, passing through the Lords in the same month and receiving the royal assent several weeks later.

[c] A series of assumptions had to be made regarding the bills, dates, and number of readings for the House of Lords in James I's parliament. Because of the deficiencies in journals, the information had to be garnered from a manuscript index, published as V. Treadwell, 'The House of Lords in the Irish parliament of 1613–1615', *EHR*, 80 (1965), pp. 92–107. Using the published *Commons journals for the Kingdom of Ireland* as a check along with the published index, despite the necessity of filling in the blanks with informed assumptions, we can be reasonably confident of these figures.

[d] I have included in this figure, four 'declarations' issued in the period before a general agreement of finance in return for the land settlement had been arrived at. These are described in greater detail later, but for the moment, it suffices to explain that, as such, these were temporary tax raising measures dealing specifically with the pressing needs of the army arrears and demobilisation. They were proceeded upon in the same manner as bills and had the same effect as a short-term finance bill. The only real difference was that they were not called bills and they did not go through the same pre-parliamentary process as Poynings' Law demanded bills did.

[e] This figure includes two bills (a bill for the duke of Albemarle and a bill concerning marriages) that had proceeded through the Commons in the normal fashion but died in the Lords due to a sudden prorogation in the spring of 1663. The bill started afresh in the Lords in 1665 and was sent down for processing in the Commons after.

lords had the lord chancellor present on the woolsack, the rest of the judiciary present on the judicial benches, and, in theory at least, should have had the services of the attorney general, solicitor general, and the prime serjeant at law – although as the century progressed these officers were regularly permitted to sit as elected MPs in the Commons. A cursory glance at the dates of respective readings indicates that there was real difference in the amount of time the Lords took to pass a bill compared with the Commons.

When the bill was introduced to a house it was generally delivered in handwriting on paper. Clerks working in Dublin Castle were of course capable of error and on several occasions there were discrepancies between the engrossed parchment copy of the bill, which had been returned to Dublin from England, and the paper one which had been copied from the transmiss. In October 1614, the House of Commons appointed four members as a standing committee to 'examine the copies of bills in paper with the original'.[94] In Charles I's first parliament, there were two occasions (both were subsidy bills) when the clerical errors were noted between the parchment transmiss and the paper copies put before the House of Commons.[95]

An interesting episode took place in the Commons in 1662. When presented with several bills from Dublin Castle they refused to read any of them until they discussed possible precedents as to 'whether the original transmission of bills out of England, treated upon in parliament in this kingdom, were not to be brought and lodged with the clerk of the house, before any proceedings were made in parliament thereupon, which the house conceived was their privilege'.[96] Ormond, seemingly content to go along with the demand, conceded that the Commons 'were very good judges of their own privileges; that he thought it fit they should have those transmissions, and would cause the same to be sent unto them'.[97] It seems, from the sources available to us, that the transmisses from London normally resided with the executive and, if anything, the Commons were creating a precedent. The issue does not seem to have come up again in the seventeenth century.

READINGS

Ideally, all bills had to be read three times. The origins of this tradition were medieval. In a pre-printing world with relatively low levels of literacy, in order to have the chance to fully understand and perhaps mull over a prospective statute, it was thought necessary to read the bill aloud three times.[98] The tradition became a feature in English parliaments sometime in the first half of the fifteenth century and almost certainly the norm in the second half, and it probably became common in Ireland around the same time or soon after. There were certainly plenty of occasions in seventeenth-century Ireland when bills were not read three times, or at least not recorded as having been read three times. It is quite possible that the clerk simply forgot to record that there were times when the bills were read, but it is also a real possibility that some bills simply did not receive a full complement of readings. Some of the bills that may either have had less than three readings or were not reported include the bill for ale-house keepers to be bound by a recognisance (April 1635),[99] a follow-up bill for punishing those who break the law regarding ale-house keepers in County Dublin (June 1640),[100] the bill against carnal knowledge of women-children (June 1640),[101] the bill of explanation (December 1665),[102] the bill for the confirmation of marriages (November 1665),[103] and the bill for establishing an additional revenue upon his majesty (December 1662).[104] If the Commons' clerk showed signs of inability when it came to record keeping, the Lords' clerk was more exact. He has left exact records in June 1640 of the passing of five bills, each of them receiving only two readings. Interestingly, all bills were private, and this fact is what probably allowed their passing after just two readings.[105] Robert Digby, Lord Geashill, objected, claiming 'that he conceived, by the orders of the house, they ought to receive three readings'. The record follows: 'Agreed by the house to be put to the vote, and with unanimous consent, are passed as laws'.[106] All five bills received the royal assent two weeks later.[107]

Once the bill was in possession of the clerk of the House of Commons or the clerk of parliament, as the clerk in the House of Lords was called, it was usually the role of the speaker to provide the initiative and momentum to get the bill through its various stages.[108] In so far as we can see, the speaker, probably assisted by the clerk, set the agenda for any particular day and it was generally up to him as to when the issue of the bill came up. However, it is also important at the same time to acknowledge that the speaker was a tool of the house, and if the house chose to, it could very easily change the order of business or give instructions for making a particular bill a priority.[109] It was not common for the speakers' agenda to be disrupted and it is probably fair to assume that the speaker was well attuned to the sensibilities and priorities of the members of his house. Rules of the House of Lords stipulated this arrangement at the end of the seventeenth century (and again amended and added to at the beginning of the eighteenth), but from observing procedures as described in journals over the seventeenth century and earlier rules, it is clear that these were the codifications of a longstanding arrangement. The second rule states that:

> The Lord Chancellor, when he speaks to the House, is always uncovered; and is not to adjourn the House, or to do any thing else as Mouth of the House, without consent of the lords first had, excepting the ordinary things about Bills, which are of course, wherein the lords may likewise over-rule; as for preferring of one Bill before another, and such like: And in case of difference amongst the lords, it is put to the Question ...'.[110]

Once agreement had been made, the bill would be read by the clerk, standing up at his desk between the bar and the chair or woolsack.[111] Generally, this was a straightforward affair and aroused little excitement. The first reading was a matter of course and usually there was no debate of the bill at that point. Indeed, the vice-treasurer, Sir Thomas Ridgeway, was adamant 'That it is against all the rules of parliament, to speak to a bill at the first reading'.[112] However, just a few months later, the Commons' journals states that 'any man may speak to a bill at the first or second reading, if they will, but it is unusual'.[113] The House of Lords had a similar provision: 'For Bills they are commonly let pass at the first reading without speaking to, unless Motion be made against the second reading in order to throw them out.'[114] There is no regular record of debate on the first reading. There are certain instances where breaches of the rules did occur; such as in February 1666, when the House of Commons read for the first time the bill for the punishing of several offences in the Court of Castle Chamber. Immediately after the reading:

> several members took exceptions unto the said bill, and, having spoken largely thereunto, desired the same might be rejected by the house; others insisted upon the usefulness and conveniency thereof; but, the time of the day being far spent, the ensuing order was conceived:
> Ordered upon question, that the debate upon the bill, entituled, an act for punishing several offences in his majesty's court of castle chamber, be adjourned, until Thursday next in the afternoon at three of the clock; at which time the king's councel at law, and the gentlemen of the long robe, who are members of this house, are to give their attendance.[115]

It is obvious from this excerpt that the house occasionally might debate after first reading.

As such, then, the first reading was generally a mundane affair. With little or no debate and many bills being but a few paragraphs in length, the process must have taken only a few minutes.[116] Debate usually came after the second reading when the bill could be committed for further discussion. There were at least a few occasions when a bill was rejected without discussion immediately after the first reading. In all, there were eleven bills that we know of rejected on the first reading, with one rejected before it was read.[117] The latter, having been already read and rejected once, had been put before the House of Commons a few months later and 'appears to agree *verbatim*' with the former bill.[118] The issue of bill rejection will be discussed in greater detail below.

Once the first reading had been completed, the process moved onto the second reading. On occasion, a motion would be passed for the bill to be read on a specific day in the near future. This was not always the case, and more often than not the journals would not record such a motion, and so it appears that without particular instruction, the speaker usually brought the second reading in some days following the first reading. Whereas it was not rare for the first two readings to take place on the same day, strictly speaking, the third reading should never have taken place on the same day as the first two. In the 1613–15 parliament, an issue seems to have arisen over the passing of a bill for the amending of highways and cashes. The bill was read twice and discussed in committee on 3 May 1615. In what seems to have been an attempt to rush a bill through parliament when numbers were good for those supporting it, Sir Christopher Plunkett moved that 'that no one bill shall be read thrice in one day'. The house agreed to the motion that the restriction 'be for ever henceforth observed for a rule'.[119] As with most of the Commons' permanent rules, the lower house was more than willing to break them on occasion. During the restoration parliament, MPs passed in a single day bills such as the bill for joyful recognition of his majesty's undoubted title,[120] the bill for £30,000 for the duke of Ormond,[121] and the bill for the grant of eight subsidies by the clergy.[122] In 1613, the bill of joyful recognition passed in one day[123] and there are many other examples of this in the 1634–35 and the 1640–48 parliament.[124] The House of Lords had no formal rule that bills had to be read on at least two separate days, but in general they behaved like the Commons: usually reading on two separate days but, on occasion, could read a bill three times in one day.

The first reading of the first bill also had some importance for the lords' house. All of the sets of rules of the House of Lords mention the reading of a bill as the first business to be undertaken by the lords:

> The first work commonly either at the beginning of a parliament or of session (after prayers are said) is, that some bill *pro forma* be read, and then a motion is to be made for a committee to be chosen out of the house, which shall stand all the session, to review the orders of the house, and see from time to time that they be duly observed.[125]

This is a little strange in the context of the seventeenth-century Irish parliaments, as so many bills went through the Commons first and it is unlikely that any bill would have been available to read in the first few days in the Lords. There are two possibilities: one is that the word 'bill' here is being used to describe any sort of official business that comes before the House of Lords that may invest them. Another possibility is that the rules which were settled upon in July 1634, and very closely followed in November 1692 and again in the eighteenth century, were in fact just another recitation of rules of the House of Lords that had been settled upon before 1634. In these pre-journal days there may well have been a bill waiting to be read as soon as parliament began. Either way, we can be certain that, where journal evidence survives, no bills were read in the House of Lords within the opening week or so.[126]

Once the house moved to the second reading, it ran in a similar fashion as the first. The speaker, with the approbation of the house, would direct the clerk to give the bill a second reading. Normally the bill was read through without interruption. When reading through the bill of explanation (1665), it was moved that the bill 'should be read in paragraphs, and that any member, as he saw occasion, might speak unto every paragraph', but this motion failed after 'arguments [were made] against the precedency thereof, it was, by consent of the house, ordered to be read through, before any liberty should be given to speak for or against the said bill, or to debate any of the clause therein mentioned'.[127] Obviously the reading of an exceptionally long bill, such as the bill of settlement (1662), would be interrupted by the need to break for the day and then resume the following morning. There are only a few snippets of evidence as to how debates took place. The Commons' journals for 1613–15 provide the most useful illustrations as Edmond Medhop then took a more detailed account of discussions. Here is the debate in October 1614 on an act for the bishop of Lismore:

> Bill for the bishop of Waterford and Lismore ... second reading.
> Mr Justice Sibthorp, Mr Crewe, Mr Dr Reeves, and Mr Crooke, to have the bill committed.
> Two persecutions: *Dioclesianus occidit presbyteros* and *Julianus presbyterium*
> Sir John Everard, to have it rejected.
> Sir Christopher Nugent, to quash the bill.
> Mr Bolton, to reject it *in jure humano* lands, *in jure divino* titles. If the law afforded the bishops power to receive lands, the same law doth not restrain them to part with them. The bishop capable of himself to receive, to the use of the church, but cannot part with it, without the dean and chapter.
> The petition of the bishop of Waterford was this day read, desiring a suspending or withdrawing of the act.
> Sir John Everard, not to withdraw the bill.
> Sir Oliver St John, to pause upon the petition, and not to put the bill to the question.
> Mr Justice Silthorp, to the same purpose.
> Mr Treasurer, touching the precedent of baronet Seymour's committee.
> Sir Oliver St John, that the bill may not be disgraced.
> 1st question. Whether the bill should be put to the question? And resolved it should.
> 2nd question. Whether it should be committed? Resolved, No.
> 3rd question. Whether it should be engrossed? Resolved, No.[128]

This level of detail is otherwise rare. A report in the state papers of the debate that raged in the Lords over the explanatory bill in December 1665 illustrates the point:

> Dublin, 27 December 1665
> Sir Winston Churchill to Secretary Arlington,
> We have had stormy weather both out of doors and within. "When the bill stuck in the birth some tried to rip it untimely out of the womb, others were as ready to assassinate it while but half born. In fine on Saturday last was sevennight, the humour was most virulent, the members confronting each other with swords half drawn and with words sharper than they: some being heard to say that the lands they had gotten with the hazard of their lives should not now be lost with Eye's [sic] and No's. In this distraction 'twas yet more dismal to see how little my Lord of Orrery could prevail, much less my Lord Anglesey, both at the same time tormented in their feet, but more in their heads, who keeping their chambers as I did my cabin in the late great storm, dreaded the effects of every wave, I mean of every vote; some whereof were so violent that in despite of all our pilots they made

the bill leak (as your lordships will find by the exceptions, which I suppose your lordship will have from another hand) neither was it in the power of any man's single reputation but the Duke's only to have kept if from sinking; who by an eloquence (peculiar to himself) seemingly unconcerned, but certainly extemporary, so charmed their fears and jealousies that they that were most displeased with the bill were yet so pleased with the overtures he had made them that when it came to pass it had only one negative.[129] On Saturday last it had the Royal assent which hath put an end to all our fears and made us merrily begin our Epinicia with that noted Cantilene *Per varios casus, per tot discrimina rerum*, being confident of such a peace to be established here upon that we shall need to fear no war but what we have with Heaven, and that I hope will cease. If it please God to stop the plague, I doubt not but His Majesty will by Easter find the people of this Kingdom is so good a temper and so settled a posture that they may be very considerable in his service."[130]

While it is certainly a pleasure to have parliamentary reports full of allegory and quoting Virgil's *Æneid*, it tells us little about the process of debate or rules that may or may not have been followed. There is little detail about how readings, debates, or votes took place. As for how long debate took, again there is no firm indication. Obviously for bills of some importance, the debate could take place over several days, while for the formulaic bills, bills pertaining to the royal title (which was never opposed), or local or private bills, the debate could be very short or sometimes non-existent.

COMMITTALS

The next step in both houses was normally committal. Development of committees and their work is an indication of a growing efficiency in dispatching business, rather than a move by the Commons to 'take the initiative' and negate Privy Council influence within either house.[131] The many conventions that regulated and, in particular, restricted the debates of the two houses made it increasingly difficult to expedite the ever-increasing work-load. The solution was an ad hoc committee, appointed from among members of the house in question, to evaluate the proposed legislation, and then to recommend, through the committee chairman, a particular course of action. Of course it is possible that the committee may have been used on occasion to reduce the influence of the speaker, who was almost always a government appointee, but its regularity suggests that its use was for practical rather than confrontational purposes in the seventeenth century.

Usually, when a motion was made for the committal of a bill, it was duly committed. In only one instance was the call rejected by the house. In March 1640, Lord Netterville called in the Lords for a committal which was rejected on the advice of the lord chancellor who advised that the act touching the finding of offices before escheators was 'beneficial to all the subjects in general;

prejudicial to none'.[132] Many legal figures within the House, including the lawyers (regularly referred to as members of the long robe), were instructed to attend the committee discussing a bill to lend their knowledge. In the Lords, at least some of the judges were expected to attend as was the lord chancellor if he were called upon.[133] It was one of the interesting aspects of committee work that the speaker of either house could indeed be called to attend as a member of the committee, but not as speaker, and would take a seat as a regular member. Any member at any time could, if he wished, attend a committee he had not been appointed to, but not vote. This is unlikely to have happened very often, as many committees had a quorum established which was significantly lower than the number of members, which suggests that the committees were not very well attended. This leads to a conclusion that committees were run by a relatively small number of MPs or peers and as such were not a political battleground. The following entry for the House of Commons in November 1662 illustrates the point:

> Ordered upon question, that the committee, unto whom the bill, entituled, an act enabling ecclesiastical persons to make leases for sixty years for the encouragement of planters, was referred, be revived; who are to meet, in the afternoon at three of the clock, in the speaker's chamber, and with all convenient speed to report their proceedings therein to the house; their quorum to be reduced unto three, and Captain Evans and Mr Weaver to be added unto the said committee.[134]

If committees were cockpits then they would have been better attended and the reports from the chairman would surely have been disputed more often.

Chairmen were appointed, at least some of the time, by the house. Occasionally the journals mention a bill referred to an ad hoc committee with special reference to a named individual. Usually this was someone particularly concerned with the bill. For example, Sir Paul Davys or Sir George Lane (two of the more senior privy councillors in the House of Commons in the restoration) were frequently chairmen of committees dealing with finance bills. An order of November 1662 committed a bill for the granting of wine licences to a committee and 'the care of this business is particularly recommended to Sir George Lane'.[135] On other occasions there was no chairman named at the time of committal. This may be a clerical omission and a chairman had been appointed. It may have been possible for the committee to vote in its own chairman when the house failed to give direction. The role of the chairman was to guide the committee through its discussions and present the report. Committee reports or discussions are very rarely printed in the journals. Usually the fact that the chairman read the report is recorded, sometimes with the main points paraphrased, followed by a vote. There is an interesting motion from November 1614:

it was agreed by the house, that if a gentleman should mis-report from the committee, one of the same committee may stand up, and acquaint the house, and, till the house be fully thereof satisfied, the gentleman is to deliver in the bill and amendments (if any be) and then he is to stand by the clerk's table, and read first all the strikings out, and then all additions.[136]

Despite the apparent need for this order, the process worked quite well. Committees took a lot of pressure off the house. Reports were probably penned by the chairman with advice from members. On occasions when the report of the committee was not thought to be sufficient, a matter could be recommitted, and this was also the case with committees formed to deal with prospective legislation. Table 3.3 refers to re-committals and shows that this was not a regular occurrence. For example, many parliaments were concluded with no re-committals recorded in the Lords.

If a bill were of sufficient importance, the Grand Committee or Committee of the Whole House, as it was sometimes referred to, was used. The Grand Committee was the metamorphosis of the house into a committee. It stayed in the same room, sometimes the speaker remained in place as a chairman, sometimes he was replaced by another member. All members of the house were automatically members of this committee. The Grand Committee elected their chairman. It was a way for either house to free themselves from their usual debating constraints and create a more efficient way of processing the bill. For example, in the regular house, a member could not speak more than once on the same issue other than to clarify some point he may have made earlier, whereas in a committee or the Grand Committee, they could speak freely and regularly. Usually a bill had to be of importance to merit a committee of the whole house. Peers never used the Grand Committee as much as the Commons. This may have been a consequence of the far smaller size of their house. Both the highest and the second highest number of bills to pass through a house were matched by the greatest number of Grand Committees.[137]

Tables 3.2 to 3.5 give a good idea of the rate at which bills were committed. All three groups of statistics come with the usual caveat that the statistics are based on the available information that can be deducted from the journals of both houses. It is quite clear that the Lords tended to send more bills to committee than the Commons. It is also clear that committal of bills was by no means the norm. With the notable exception of the peers' house in the first Caroline parliament, less than a third of all bills were committed. It also seems that there was no set procedure as to why bills might have been committed. There were some bills that were not committed as a matter of course, such as the formulaic bills for royal title.[138] The spike for both the House of Commons and the House of Lords in 1634–35 is interesting. With regards to legislation,

Table 3.2 Committal of bills

House	Year	Bills	Committed	%
Commons	1613–15	34	9	26.47
Lords	1634–35	78	57	73.08
Commons	1634–35	103	39	37.86
Lords	1640–48	35	11	31.43
Commons	1640–48	77	16	20.78
Lords	1661–66[a]	58	23	39.66
Commons	1661–66	85	23	27.06
Average		67.14	25.43	37.87
Total		470[b]	178	37.87

[a] Table 3.2 includes tax raising declarations in the figures for both the Lords and the Commons in the restoration parliament

[b] The 'Total' number of bills refers to the legislative journey of each bill through each house. As such, many bills are counted twice – once in the Commons and once in the Lords. The figure also refers to a bill sometimes processed more than once through a house, such as the bill for Albemarle, which went through the Commons in 1663 but, due to a sudden prorogation, had to be read again three times in 1665 when parliament resumed.

Table 3.3 Re-committal of bills

House	Year	Bills	Re-committed	%
Commons	1613–15	34	2	5.88
Lords	1634–35	78	0	0
Commons	1634–35	103	10	9.71
Lords	1640–48	35	1	2.86
Commons	1640–48	77	1	1.3
Lords	1661–66[a]	58	0	0
Commons	1661–66	85	3	3.53
Average		67.14	2.43	3.62
Total		470[b]	17	3.62

[a] Table 3.3 includes tax raising declarations in the figures for both the Lords and the Commons in the restoration parliament.

[b] The 'Total' number of bills refers to the legislative journey of each bill through each house. As such, many bills are counted twice – once in the Commons and once in the Lords. The figure also refers to a bill sometimes processed more than once through a house, such as the bill for Albemarle, which went through the Commons in 1663 but due to a sudden prorogation had to be read again three times in 1665 when parliament resumed.

Table 3.4 Committal of bills to a grand committee

House	Year	Bills	Grand committee	%
Commons	1613–15	34	1	2.94
Lords	1634–35	78	1	1.28
Commons	1634–35	103	7	6.78
Lords	1640–48	35	0	0
Commons	1640–48	77	3	3.7
Lords	1661–66[a]	58	3	5.17
Commons	1661–66	85	7	8.23
Average		67.14	3.14	4.68
Total		470[b]	22	4.68

[a] Table 3.4 includes tax raising declarations in the figures for both the Lords and the Commons in the restoration parliament.

[b] The 'Total' number of bills refers to the legislative journey of each bill through each house. As such, many bills are counted twice – once in the Commons and once in the Lords. The figure also refers to a bill sometimes processed more than once through a house, such as the bill for Albemarle, which went through the Commons in 1663 but due to a sudden prorogation had to be read again three times in 1665 when parliament resumed.

Table 3.5 Bills per days sitting

House	Year	Bills	Days	Bill per day
Commons	1613–15	34	60	60
Lords	1634–35	78	73	
Commons	1634–35	103	104	104
Lords	1640–48	35	116	
Commons	1640–48	77	260	260
Lords	1661–66[a]	58	226	
Commons	1661–66	85	424	424
Average		67.14	180	0.373
Total		470[b]	1263	0.373

[a] Table 3.5 includes tax raising declarations in the figures for both the Lords and the Commons in the restoration parliament.

[b] The 'Total' number of bills refers to the legislative journey of each bill through each house. As such, many bills are counted twice – once in the Commons and once in the Lords. The figure also refers to a bill sometimes processed more than once through a house, such as the bill for Albemarle, which went through the Commons in 1663 but due to a sudden prorogation, had to be read again three times in 1665 when parliament resumed.

that parliament was overall the most productive in that both the number of bills read and the number of acts passed are the highest of all. The statistic is further reinforced when we compare the number of bills read and acts passed with the number of days sitting.[139] In short, it shows that committees correlate higher workload, which mirrors the English experience.[140] That fact that the heightened frequency of the committee was when parliament was under the tightest executive control further reinforces this argument. Other parliaments not as busy with bills may have deemed many committees unnecessary.

Second committals were uncommon. They were usually used to demand further information on the bill or to reinvestigate some matter discussed at the initial committal. For example, in July 1634 the House of Commons committed a bill for the prevention of buggery, and once the committee reported difficulties, it was re-committed for recommendations on possible amendments.[141] In the restoration Commons, a secondary committee was formed to pick up the slack left by the previous committee's inability to get its work done:

> Whereas the former committee, unto whom the bill, entituled, an act for the building of a bridge over the river of Blackwater at Cappoquin, in the county of Waterford, was referred is discontinued, and several of the said committee are now absent; it is ordered upon question, that for the more speedy dispatch of the said bill, it be, and is hereby referred to the under-named persons, who are to withdraw into the speaker's chamber in this house, and, having considered of the said bill, are forthwith to make report thereof what they conceive fit to be done therein, for further consideration.[142]

Most of the time, though, recommittals are unexplained.

ENGROSSMENT

If a positive report was received from the committee and agreed by the house, a motion was made to have the bill engrossed. Engrossment of a bill was a simple transfer of the paper form to parchment. The movement from paper to parchment was largely a symbolic one. Exactly when this took place can be difficult to ascertain. Usually, but not always, there was a space between the report stage and the third reading, and so it is most likely that engrossment took place in the afternoon after the report was made. It is also possible that the clerk sent out the paper copy to his office outside and had it copied while the house continued to sit. The old paper copy remained in the office of the clerk who engrossed.[143] The only example of a bill being read in parchment before the third reading was a bill for granting eight subsidies by the prelates and clergy. This 'received its [only] reading in the engrossment'.[144] Usually engrossment took place after the second of the three readings.[145] There is one anomaly in the process of engrossment in May

1662, when after the second reading of the Bill for the Perpetual Anniversary and Thanksgiving on 29 May (the date of Charles II's birth and restoration), the order for engrossment was given and 'upon motion made that the said bill was already engrossed by the clerk of this house, it is ordered, that it shall be read in the engrossment this day'.[146] The bill seems to have been rushed through. It received all three readings in both the lords and commons on 24 May (possibly in an effort to have it passed by both houses before 29 May).[147] It was probably the speed of the bill that prompted the clerk of the Commons to have the bill engrossed in advance. Like the bills confirming royal title in 1613 and 1661, there was no chance whatsoever that any member would speak against such a bill or impede its progress. However, such a rush job may have produced the mistake that was spotted when the engrossed version made its way to the Lords. When committed, the bill was noticed to have a mix-up between the words 'satisfying' and 'sacrificing'. The committee had the bill brought down to the Commons to have the original wording in the paper bill compared with the parchment. Once rectified, a third reading was given, and it was deemed passed.[148] Interestingly the Commons' journal makes no record of Sir John Skeffington delivering up the bill to the Lords (which they normally would), nor does it record the issue of the mistake made in copying to parchment.

There is also an indication towards the end of the restoration parliament of an engrossment before the second reading. On 11 July 1666, 'It being moved, that the bill, entituled an act of free and general pardon, indemnity, and oblivion, might be read, some were of the opinion, that it should be read in the engrossment; some, that it should be read in paper; whereupon it was resolved, that it should be read in the paper copy'.[149] There is no reason given as to why some members wished to have it read in the engrossment. It is possible that the bill was engrossed early to speed the process up as it was coming to the end of the parliament.[150] It would seem that at least some members wanted the bill passed quickly, although in the end it failed at the committee stage.[151] It is likely that a team of clerks would have been engaged in the engrossment of some of the more substantial bills, such as the bills of settlement and explanation in 1662 and 1665 respectively. Engrossment was a very good indicator that a bill would pass. Which is not to say that there were no fierce debates nor bills that failed on the third reading.

Once engrossed, the bill moved onto the third reading, usually at least a day after the second reading. The process followed the form of the second reading quite closely. The bill was read aloud for the third time by the clerk, followed by debate. From this point a motion would be made for a question to be put, and if the motion passed, the question would generally be put whether the bill in question should pass in the positive. If the majority (whether by an oral vote or by a more formal division) were in favour, the bill would be deemed to have passed. Only on a handful of occasions was there a division. In 1613, there was one on whether to engross a private bill for Piers Lacye, which was rejected and 'so the bill was dashed' (eighty-two to sixty-four against).[152] The sole recorded occasion of a bill formally dividing the house on third reading was when that for enabling ecclesiastical persons to make leases for sixty years for the encouragement of planters was voted worthy of committal (forty-eight to forty in favour).[153] This was plainly an unusual course to take and since the membership of the house was quite low, it appears that enemies of the bill (or at least aspects of it) took the opportunity to have it recommitted 'in order to amendments to be made therein, and to be reported to this house for further consideration'.[154]

TRANSFER TO THE OTHER HOUSE

As seen in Table 3.1, over 87% of bills processed by the Irish Parliament made their appearance first in the Commons and were then, if successful, transferred to the peers' house. This was usually a straightforward affair. The Commons always used one of their own members to carry messages and bills to the Lords. Normally, one individual was appointed along 'with such others of the members of the house as please to accompany him'. Frequently, this individual was the moving force behind the piece of legislation. Government MPs, particularly privy councillors, delivered up bills that had strong Castle support, such as a finance bill. In other instances, it was the chairman of the committee to whom the bill had been committed. The manner of approaching the Lords was set down in detail in 1634:

> XIII For meeting with any of the lower house, it is either upon occasions of message, which they send up, or upon conference when they come up. The manner is this: After the lords have notice given them by the usher of the house that they have sent unto the lords, they attend until the lords have put that business to some end, wherein they are; and the lords sitting, all covered, send for them in, who stand all at the lower end of the room, and then the lord chancellor, with such as please, rise, and go down to the middle of the bar; then the chief of the committee in the midst of them, and the rest about him, come up to the bar, with their courtesies, and deliver their message to the lord chancellor, who, after he hath received it, retires himself to his former place; and the house being cleared and settled, he reports it to the lords, who help his memory, if any thing be mistaken; and after the lords have taken resolution (if business require any answer) they are called in, an approaching to the bar, with their courtesies as before, and the house sitting in order and covered as before; the lord chancellor sitting on the wool-sack, covered, doth give them their answer in the name of the house; or else, if the resolution be not speedy, the lords send them word by the usher, that they shall not need to stay for the answer but that their lordships will send by some express messenger of their own.[155]

The House of Lords, on the relatively rare occasions when they sent bills down to the Commons, sent them by servants rather than members. The judges were always almost selected to pass messages, including bills, to the House of Commons. When a delivery was made to the Lords, the lord chancellor went to the bar of the House and collected the bill from the members of the Commons. It is not abundantly clear what the machinery was when a bill was moving the other way. In both cases, the clerks of either house held custody of the bills until they were proceeded upon. Deliveries would have taken little more than a few minutes since the houses were separated by no more than a few metres.[156]

Once the second bout of readings began, usually in the upper house, there was just as vigorous a process of reading, debate, and committals as when first read. Table 3.2 shows that the rate of committals in the upper house was consistently higher than in the lower. This indicates that, despite the fact that the Commons had pored over many of the bills and on occasion discussed them at great length, the Lords debated and committed many of the same bills a second time (Table 3.6).

ROYAL ASSENT

Once legislation had been through the second house, it was ready for the attention of the third part of the parliamentary trinity. The role of the monar-

Table 3.6 Bill committed in both houses/one or the other

Year[a]	Number of bills[b]	Both	One/other
1634–35	104	16	81
1640–48	81	2	24
1661–66	85[c]	7	31
Average	90	8.33(9.26%)	45.33(50.37%)

[a] The Jacobite parliament has not been included in this statistic. As has been mentioned several times, without the parliamentary journals it is very difficult to gauge with any accuracy whether bills begun their journey in the Lords or the Commons. The Jacobean parliament has also been omitted as the House of Lords data is incomplete and so there is a difficulty in coming to anything close to an accurate figure for committals in the Lords between 1613–15.
[b] These bills include duplicate bills that had to be passed through one or both houses again because the original process was discontinued due to a prorogation. For example, the bill for punishing the vice of buggery proceeded through the Commons with little trouble in the first session of the 1634–35 parliament up to the committee stage. While at this stage a prorogation was issued by the Lord Deputy Wentworth and the bill was killed. It had to begin through all stages again the following November, passing through the Lords in the same month and receiving the royal assent several weeks later.
[c] I have included in this figure four 'declarations' issued in the period before a general agreement of finance in return for the land settlement had been arrived at.

chy had, by the seventeenth century, been reduced to largely symbolic appearances at the opening sessions, an occasional speech to the combined houses, and the giving of the royal assent, usually at the end of the session.[157] The royal assent provided for the change from a bill to an act – the ink and parchment did not change. Once assent was given, the bill became law. This was the most ceremonial aspect of the parliamentary event along with the opening. As such, the giving of the royal assent provided for the temporary re-emergence of the medieval parliament of the king-in-parliament, along with a uni-cameral assembly.[158] What follows is a typical report from the Lords' journals of the arrival of the king's representative in the house:

Hora secunda post meridiem ejusdem Diei
Prayers read.
Lord chancellor acquaints the house, that he hath received a message from his excellency the lord lieutenant, signifying that it is his pleasure, that his lordship, the earl of Kildare and the earl of Thomond go to attend his lordship to the house: Whereupon the house is dissolved into a grand committee, during pleasure, and the said lords go to attend the lord lieutenant's excellency.

The lord lieutenant, in the royal robe, comes in, attended by the lord chancellor and the officers of arms; the earl of Thomond bearing the sword; the earl of Kildare, the cap, Colonel Chichester, son and heir to the lord viscount Chichester, captain Cary Dillon, brother to Earl of Roscommon, and captain Richard Lambart, bearing the train.

The lord lieutenant ascends the chair of state, and afterwards beckons the lord chancellor, who presently attends him, on his knee.

The lord lieutenant whispers to him, and afterwards he makes obeisance, and repairs to his seat, on the right hand of the lord lieutenant; and then calls to the gentleman usher aloud, and tells him, 'tis the lord lieutenant's pleasure he forthwith repair to the house of commons, and command them to come to his said excellency.

The speaker and commons approach to the bar, with three courtesies. The lord lieutenant beckons the lord chancellor again, who attended him as formerly, and so repairs back to his seat.

Lord chancellor commands the clerk to read the act for remitting to his majesty's protestant subjects, and their adherents, all arrears of rent, services, compositions, first fruits and twentieth parts, due to his majesty at Michaelmas 1641, ever since, and at Easter 1645; which being done, his lordship [the lord chancellor] declares the royal assent.

Lord chancellor commands the clerk to read the instrument of prorogation, which was done.
Ormond.
James marquis of Ormond, earl of Ormond and Ossory, viscount Thurles, baron of Arklowe, lord lieutenant general and general governor of Ireland, and chancellor of the University of Dublin: To the lords spiritual and temporal and to the commons in this present parliament assembled, greeting: For certain reasons us moving, as well for his majesty's service as for the good of the subjects of this

kingdom in general, we have thought fit to prorogue this present parliament, and do by these presents prorogue the same, until the twentieth day of this instant May, on which day our purpose is to hold the same at this his majesty's castle of Dublin. Given under our seal, at his majesty's said Castle of Dublin, the sixth day of May, Anno Domini one thousand six hundred forty five, and in one and twentieth year of the reign of our Sovereign lord King Charles of England, Scotland, France, and Ireland.

The lord lieutenant returns to the preference, and the whole house attend him in order, the puisne judge first, and the lord lieutenant last.[159]

There is much of interest in this episode. First and foremost, the Commons play a very minor role. On occasions when there was a finance related bill, the Commons presented it to the lord deputy, from below the bar and via the lord chancellor.[160] The Commons held the finance bills in their house until the time of the royal assent. Other than that, they were spectators in the same way as the lords were but the event took place in the lords' house and the speaker of the Lords played an important role, in that the lord deputy never spoke aloud but simply whispered in the ear of the speaker and the speaker then communicated it to the assembled parliamentarians. One unique aspect of the royal assent in Ireland is that it was, in a roundabout sort of way, unnecessary. Poynings' Law stipulated that legislation was acceded to by the royal council in Dublin and the monarch in advance of being laid before the Irish Parliament. Of course the royal assent was required legally to provide the final stage of the legislative journey, but royal assent, as such, had been given to all bills in advance. This raises a question about bills which had passed both houses but failed to get the royal assent when put before the king's representative. For example, in December 1634 some twenty-seven acts were presented to the lord deputy for the royal assent, yet one was not assented to by Wentworth despite the fact that he, his council, and the English Privy Council along with the monarch had agreed on the bill before it was presented to the Commons earlier that month.[161] The exact content of the bill of several charges imposed upon the lands and persons of *Cestui que Use* is unknown, but it remains a mystery as to why Wentworth refused to give his consent in the Lords. One possibility is that such a bill might have been twinned with another and if one had not passed both houses, the other would not get the royal assent. However, this could not have been the case this time as all bills put before parliament in that session and the previous one had been passed without problem. It is possible then that circumstances had changed and the effect of the law would have been deemed counterproductive to the government's intentions.

Granting of the royal assent was frequently followed by prorogation or dissolution of parliament. As mentioned above, parliament was primarily called by government for the purposes of passing legislation, and in theory it should have ended on the assent being given to legislation in accordance with the provisions of Poynings' Law. The passing of a specific bill to prevent immediate dissolution on granting of royal assent was necessary throughout the seventeenth century.[162] The exact timing of the assent seems to have been in the power of the lord deputy but was not jealously guarded. On many occasions, the Commons, but more often the Lords, sent word to Dublin Castle that there were bills waiting in parliament for royal assent. As a general rule, the chief governor waited until the end of the session to give the assent and so it was followed by a prorogation; but on occasion, particularly if there were a finance bill that needed assent as a matter of urgency, it might be given at any time. This was the case in late 1661 and early 1662 when royal assent was given to two bills, both for raising money for army pay and for the continuance of customs and excise for a finite period of time.[163] When assent was given, the particular phrase used to record the fact in the journals was 'Le Roi le veult'.[164] 'Le Roi remercie a touts ses loyaux Sujets, accepte leur Benevolence, ainsi le Roi le veult' was used by the lords justices to give the royal assent to the bill for speedy raising of money for his majesty's service.[165] 'Le roi remercie a tous a ses loyaux Sujets, accepte leur recognition, ainsi le vault' was used giving the royal assent to the act of recognition in June 1661.[166] 'Soit fait comme desire' was used by the lords justices when giving the royal assent to a bill presenting £30,000 to the duke of Ormond for his services to the monarchy in the previous two decades.[167] In all likelihood, such a phrase was probably spoken each time the assent was given, but it has only been recorded in the journals for the restoration House of Lords.

Once the royal assent had been proclaimed on a particular bill, turning it into an act, the legislative journey was over. But there was some aftercare by parliament. The first was the printing of some acts. It is clear where the power or responsibility for printing lay. When the House of Commons decided to have acts printed after passage, they usually sent a deputation to Dublin Castle to ask the chief governor to have them published, as happened in 1615, 1661, and 1662.[168] However, when the peers considered printing, they frequently made stronger recommendations:

> Lord chancellor acquaints the house, that there be several acts of parliament passed since the beginning of this parliament, and that the greater part of them are general acts; and said, that the judges and subjects in general (for aught known) have erred, and may hereafter err, for want of knowledge of them; and therefore moved, that a command be laid on the clerk of this house, to have then inrolled, whereby they may be printed.
>
> It is ordered by the lords, that the clerk of this house do get such general acts of parliament as have been passed since this parliament began, inrolled, and do deliver the same to the clerk of the rolls, whereby they may be printed.[169]

Early in the first session in May 1661, on the third reading of the Bill for the Confirmation of Judicial Proceedings, a word had been transcribed twice by accident by the clerk, whereby the Lords made an order for the printed version to omit the repetition.[170] In March 1663, the Lords also gave an order for the printing of the act for £23,500 for parliamentary expenses.[171] After the bill had become an act, although there is only brief mention of it in the parliamentary journals, it appears that the engrossed parchment copy was normally sent to the clerk of the rolls, who worked under the master of the rolls and was responsible for preserving the official copy.[172]

INFLUENCE ON THE CREATION OF LEGISLATION

As mentioned at the start of this chapter, legislation is one of the few functions of parliament that has been given considerable attention by historians of the Irish Parliament in recent decades.[173] As has been described at length by Edwards and Moody and Clarke, the three early Stuart parliaments were almost entirely unsuccessful in their attempts to initiate legislation, with only one successful recorded attempt at creating law by statute originating in the Commons between 1613 and 1641.[174] After October 1641, everything had changed, and it becomes obvious that the use of the word 'restoration' is a misnomer: it was impossible for the kingdom to turn the clock back to the late 1630s. Government figures in the Castle and in London were more than aware that the delicate nature of politics in Dublin, and indeed in the three kingdoms as a whole could not bear a 'brute force and ignorance' approach, as undertaken by Wentworth. Both the lords justices (especially Orrery) up to the summer of 1662 and Ormond thereafter were willing to allow the Commons and the Lords to draw up legislation. Some of this made it into the rolls. Most politicians realised that the constitution had been stretched beyond what were reasonable limits in the 1630s in both kingdoms, and were keen to return to a more balanced, almost consensual relationship.[175] However, this should not be taken as a sign of weakness, but more an acute realisation of the hard facts of politics as they emerged in the early 1660s. The three kingdoms were, in reality, given back to Charles II, and many believed that they could be taken away if he did not govern moderately and appropriately. That approach was largely justified by its success. Despite his initial gains, Wentworth's house of cards collapsed in spectacular fashion in the early 1640s. In the 1660s, Ormond was presented with a situation far more daunting, a task far more arduous, but he managed to put together a (albeit far from perfect) land settlement that promoted and preserved Protestant ascendancy and provided the monarchy with an eventual exchequer surplus, something which early modern Ireland had seldom, if ever, experienced.[176] This is not to suggest for a moment that the fortunes of the early and late Stuart monarchy revolved around the Irish Parliament's ability to initiate legislation, more that Dublin Castle's attitudes towards initiation of legislation fitted with a general *politique* approach during the 1660s.

The Irish Parliament in the seventeenth century took a role in initiating or attempting to initiate legislation: 1661 is a dividing line between success and failure in this respect. Before 1661, the two houses of the Irish Parliament, especially the House of Commons, proposed legislation in two ways. The first of these was non-contentious and indeed was the manner prescribed by Wentworth when he lectured the lords on Poynings' Law: 'inasmuch as their lordships by an act of parliament ... are debarred from penning any act, and have power only to move or petition the lord deputy and council, for drawing and transmitting into England such acts as they desired to be passed in the matter'.[177] As such, then, according to this interpretation, the formal drafting of any bill would have to be performed by the council with the assistance of anyone they desired to include in the process, but either house could make a suggestion of what bills they might like. Throughout the lifetime of all the parliaments in this study, regular messages were sent to Dublin Castle to this effect. In 1615, the Commons made application to Chichester for the transmission of a host of new acts and also for the amendment of some that had already come before them.[178] In cases where the commons asked for amendment and got it, twelve lawyer MPs (both Catholic and Protestant) were included in the drafting committee employed by the Privy Council. Of the fresh bills, some were actually drafted in the Commons. For example, the bill for making 5 November a day of remembrance was drawn up by the speaker by order of the Commons.[179] The remaining thirty-two bills may well have been the fruit of the labour of a joint committee of privy councillors and MPs, a course recommended by the Commons in a message to the lord deputy in November 1614.[180] Interestingly, it was the Lords rather than Dublin Castle which objected to the lower house's actions, when they claimed to be:

> not a little grieved, that the house of commons do challenge to themselves an absolute power and authority to propound laws to the royal assent, and to this effect have made discourses before the state, not once making mention, but omitting quite the consent of the lords of the upper house, as though they were called to none end, to endure and bear such charges as their attendance in parliament doth require, and they, in duty to his majesty do perform, but that the sole authority of propounding of laws, reforming of abuses, disorder, and wrongs, resteth solely in them during the time of parliament.[181]

In reality, the Lords need not have worried, as these suggestions were made on the last full day of sitting, and the proposed later session never materialised. The government was not too perturbed by the prospect of the Commons initiating legislation. When legislation was proposed in the House of Commons, it was frequently drawn up by the very same individuals that were drawing up bills on behalf of the council, such as Sir John Davies for the bill for 5 November above, or Justice Sibthorp for a bill for the trial of murders in an earlier session.[182] After that stage, they still had a double-lock mechanism to keep less desirable proposals from the rolls. Bills would still have to proceed through the privy councils in Dublin and London where they could be adapted, rejected, or indefinitely shelved.

Keeping this in mind, and also the fact that no parliament-initiated legislation made it onto the rolls, it appears that Wentworth's slap-down of any initiative in the second session of the 1634–35 parliament was more about principle and power-politics than a practical necessity to secure any royal freedom of action, although it also inadvertently had the effect of preventing any delay or adding to the Commons' negotiating strength. Putting to one side, for a moment, the relative importance of Wentworth's announcement in parliament of the restrictions on its actions, the practical application of that declaration is not always immediately apparent in the field of legislation. Just as in 1614 and 1615 (and possibly in the previous century), the Irish House of Commons continued to make submissions for prospective legislation to Dublin Castle and they appointed committees to draw up apparent heads of bills, such as in November 1634 when a committee was appointed to 'draw up an act for restraining the converting of arable lands into pastures, and to bring it into this house, to be viewed and considered of'.[183] In the following parliament, the Commons took up where they had left off. Early in the first session they appointed a committee to 'advise of, and draw up a bill for pulling and breaking down such weares, and all other impediments'.[184] During the sessions after Wentworth's departure for London in 1640, the opposition in parliament highlighted the importance of reforming Poynings' Law.[185] That aside, the House of Commons continued to act in the same fashion as it had done in the 1634–35 parliament; that is, to occasionally either approach the executive with general suggestions for bills or to sometimes go a step further and appoint a committee to formally draw up a heads of bill, usually with the cooperation and assistance of some of the kingdom's legal officers who were members. This was the case in April 1640 when a large committee was appointed to consider and 'draw and prepare bills' that 'tend to the better settling of the common wealth, and the remedying of such abuses and inconveniencies'.[186] In 1642, the Commons went a step further when they invited the Lords to join them in their endeavours to present a heads of bill for the part-suspension of Poynings' Law 'concerning acts to be passed to abolish popery, and to attaint rebels'.[187] As in the 1613–15 parliament, their efforts were largely in vain, as none of these were engrossed on a parliament roll. The one partial exception to this general rule was in the case for the act for remittal of rents, services, compositions, first fruits, and twentieth parts where the Lords and Commons discussed the content they would like to see in the bill, and then directly applied to the king to have a bill created.[188]

There was nothing new about heads of bills emanating from the Irish Parliament in 1661. The Commons particularly, but also the Lords, spent an increasing amount of time drafting legislation formally and also making representations to Dublin Castle. The process worked in a similar fashion as before the mid-century break, in that both houses took it upon themselves to appoint committees, containing judges and other royal legal officers, to draft what was a bill in all but name and present that to Dublin Castle for transmission to London. On one occasion, after initial drafting of the heads of bill of explanation in summer 1662, the lords read each paragraph several times, although this was almost certainly to have a more thorough understanding of the contents rather than a formulaic three readings as if it were real legislation, as was to become standard procedure at the end of the century.[189] Indeed, the heads of bill for an explanatory act in the summer of 1662 were proceeded upon independently by both houses and presented to the lords justices separately.[190] The critical difference in the proceedings in the matter of heads of bills was not the actions of either house, but the willingness of the executive to accept those heads and effectively establish a legislative relationship with both houses of the kind that Wentworth was not prepared to countenance some twenty years earlier. Indeed, not only was the executive prepared to accept legislative initiatives from either house, but in the case of the explanatory heads of bill mentioned just now, the lords justices promised to invite a committee of the Commons to join with the Privy Council if their assistance were needed, and also invited them to submit further clauses if this became necessary.[191] Two days later, the lords justices sent a message to the Commons concerning the method of drafting and improvements they felt could be made.[192] The fact that this bill was returned to the Commons the following spring, only to be rejected on the first reading, indicated that open channels of communications and a willingness to interact between executive and parliament was not an automatic recipe for success.

STATISTICAL ANALYSIS: PRODUCTIVITY

Considering the many bills that came before the Irish Parliament, we can certainly look at the legislation to try and come to some conclusions on how this process worked. We may first look at the number of bills that made it to royal assent. The statistics in Tables 3.7 and 3.8 illustrate the number of bills passed and the number of days the Commons sat.

What can be deduced from these statistics? The first observation is that the 1634–35 parliament of Charles I was far more productive than all others. It is difficult to ascertain why this was so. It is quite possible that the close

Table 3.7 Acts per parliament in the House of Commons

Year	Days sitting	Acts	Average acts per day
1613–15	60	10	0.166
1634–35	104	76	0.73
1640–48	260	29	0.112
1661–66	424	47	0.111
1689	57[a]	35	0.614

[a] This is an informed estimate. Dennehy, 'An administrative and legal history of the Irish Parliament', p. 132, n. 207.

Table 3.8 Acts per parliament in the House of Lords

Year	Days sitting	Acts	Average acts per day
1613–15	------[a]	10	
1634–35	73	76	1.041
1640–48	------	29	
1661–66	266	47	0.176
1689	------	35	

[a] Because of the incomplete nature of the Lords' journals, it is not possible to quantify how often they sat.

supervision of parliament by Wentworth, both in his provision of his placemen in the Commons and his stipulation as to what functions they could and could not perform, was part of the reason.[193] In addition, many of the bills in this parliament were enactments of legislation already in force in England, and so they were for simple adoption. In the Commons, the 1640s parliament stands out as being particularly unproductive in terms of the ratio of legislation passed as compared with days sat, but there were good reasons for this. There was a deep crisis in government and Dublin Castle only brought forward a handful of bills. After October 1641, the government only placed ten bills before the Commons, five of which made three readings and only one of which was processed in the Lords to become an act. Again in the restoration parliament, the low ratio of bills to days sitting in both houses cannot be read as a sign of discord between parliament and executive. The unique circumstance of calling a parliament in a post-revolutionary setting, with a vacuum of power in Dublin Castle, meant that both Lords and Commons took an active role in the shaping of the settlement that followed. Therefore, despite the fact that the raw statistics show a relative inability to process legislation as quickly as the 1634–35 parliament, once we take into account the nature of how the settlement was devised, and also keep in mind the fact that parlia-

Table 3.9 Acts as a percentage of bills read in the House of Commons

Year	Acts	Bills	%
1613–15	10	32	31.25
1634–35	76	104	73.099
1640–48	29	77	37.665
1661–66	47	85	55.309
1689	35	-------	

Table 3.10 Acts as a percentage of bills before the House of Lords

Year	Acts	Bills	%
1613–15	10	-------[a]	
1634–35	76	77	98.72
1640–48	29	44	65.91
1661–66	47	62	75.81
1689	35	-------	

[a] Because the Lords' journals for the 1613–15 and 1689 sessions are not extant, it is not possible to count the numbers of bills that might have gone before the house.

ment undertook a great deal of work in terms of petitions received, compared to a smaller number in the 1634-35 parliament, its record does not appear quite so poor.

A cursory glance at the figures in Tables 3.9 and 3.10 for both houses immediately indicates that the Lords had a much higher completion rate of bills put before them, but again it would be an error to assume that this means either the House of Commons was unable to complete the scheduled work put before it or was a house that was less amenable to handling by the executive, although there may be a little bit of truth in both statements. However, the Lords was a smaller body, with fewer speakers and a professional corps of legal advisors, and so, as such, management of legislation would have been easier. In all likelihood, a Lords committee of eight peers would come to a conclusion on a committed bill faster than a Commons committee of forty members. There were also times when the Commons was being particularly obstreperous and many bills were thrown out not necessarily because they were bad, but because they wished to make a political point.[194] The main reason, though, why the Lords have a higher completion rate is because the Commons acted as a filter, weeding out poorly drafted, unpopular or otherwise undesirable legislation.

NOTES

1 Kelly, *Poynings' Law*, pp. 1–14. Interestingly, at the launch of Kelly's 2008 book in the old House of Lords at College Green, the then minister of justice, Michael McDowell, bemoaned the fact that Poynings' Law was no longer taught in primary schools.
2 J. McCavitt, *Sir Arthur Chichester*, ch. 10, 11; 'An unspeakable parliamentary fracas: the Irish house of commons, 1613', *Analecta Hibernica* (hereafter *AH*), 37 (1995–96), pp. 223–35; B. Jackson (ed.), 'A document on the parliament of 1613 from St Isidore's College, Rome', *AH*, 33 (1986), pp. 47–58; T. Ó hAnnracháin, 'Imagining political representation in seventeenth-century Ireland' in R. Armstrong and T. Ó hAnnracháin (eds), *Community in early modern Ireland* (Dublin, 2006).
3 For some impressions of how this episode can be viewed within the general history of the Irish Parliament, see C.A. Dennehy, 'Dependency and subservience: The Irish Parliament as a "small-state parliament"', *Czasopismo prawno-historyczne*, 61 (2009), pp. 99–112.
4 A. Clarke and D. Edwards, 'Pacification, plantation, and the Catholic question, 1603–23' in T. W. Moody, F.X. Martin, and F.J. Byrne, F.J. (eds), *A new history of Ireland, vol. 3: Early modern Ireland, 1534–1691* (Oxford, 1976) (hereafter *NHI*), vol. 3, pp. 215–16. Interestingly, despite the continual growth of a Protestant presence in parliament, including an exclusively Protestant Commons in 1661, no new expressly anti-Catholic penal legislation made it onto the statute books until 1695. English legislation in 1691 forbade Catholic attendance in parliament (3 William & Mary, c. II [Eng.] – An act for the abrogating the oath of supremacy in Ireland and appointing other oaths). There was other legislation that was to hurt the Catholic population more, but this is the first anti-Catholic act, by strict definition, of the seventeenth century.
5 *NHI*, vol. 3, p. 251.
6 21 James I, c. XVI[Eng.]; A. Clarke, *The graces, 1625–41* (Dundalk, 1968); '28 November 1634: a detail of Strafford's administration', *Journal of the Royal Society of Antiquaries of Ireland* (hereafter *JRSAI*), 93 (1963), pp. 161–67; *The Old English in Ireland, 1625–42* (2nd edn, Dublin, 2000); A. Clarke and D. Fenlon, 'Two notes on the parliament of 1634', *JRSAI*, 97 (1967), pp. 85–90; H.F. Kearney, *Strafford in Ireland, 1633–41: a study in absolutism* (Manchester, 1959); C.V. Wedgewood, *Thomas Wentworth, first earl of Strafford, 1593–1641: a revaluation* (London, 1961).
7 'Wentworth admitted in a frank letter to Laud that he had lost control of affairs for five or six days and that by the "extreme perversity" of the Papist party the parliament was "in great danger to have been lost in a storm."' Kearney, *Strafford in Ireland*, p. 59.
8 What follows are just some of the examples of recent publications on the 1640s parliament: A. Clarke, 'Colonial constitutional attitudes in Ireland, 1640–60', *Proceedings of the Royal Irish Academy* (hereafter *PRIA*), 90 C (1990)' pp. 357–73; 'Historical revision XVIII: the history of Poynings' Law, 1615–41', *IHS*, 18

(1972–73), pp. 207–22; 'Ireland and the general crisis'; 'Patrick Darcy and the constitutional relationship between Ireland and Britain' in J. Ohlmeyer (ed.), *Political thought in seventeenth-century Ireland: kingdom or colony* (Cambridge, 2000); McCafferty, 'To follow the late precedents in England'; B. McGrath, 'Parliament men and the confederate association' in M. Ó Siochrú (ed.), *Kingdoms in crisis: Ireland in the 1640s* (Dublin, 2001); 'The Irish elections of 1640–1' in Brady and Ohlmeyer, *British interventions in early modern Ireland*; J.H. Ohlymeyer, 'The Irish peers, political power and parliament, 1640–1' in Brady and Ohlmeyer, *British interventions in early modern Ireland*; C. Russell, 'The British background to the Irish rebellion of 1641', *Bulletin of the Institute of Historical Research*, 61 (1988), pp. 166–82.

9   Ó Siochrú, *Confederate Ireland*.
10 Clarke, *The Old English*, p. 140.
11 Dennehy, 'The Irish parliament after the rebellion'.
12 Dennehy (ed.), *Restoration Ireland*, p. vii.
13 Most of the earlier work was contained in largely unpublished theses. C.A. Dennehy, 'Parliament in Ireland, 1661–6' Unpublished M.Litt. thesis, University College Dublin, 2002; S. Egan, 'Finance and the government of Ireland, 1660–85', Unpublished Ph.D. thesis, Trinity College Dublin, 1983; F.M. O'Donoghue, 'Parliament in Ireland under Charles II', Unpublished M.A. thesis, University College Dublin (1970); M. Twomey, 'The financial and commercial policy of the English administration in Ireland, 1660–1670', Unpublished M.A. thesis, University College Dublin, 1954. Recent developments have been the publication of: Dennehy, 'The restoration Irish parliament, 1661–6'; Kelly, *Poynings' Law*; Clarke, *Prelude to restoration in Ireland* has two superb chapters on the Irish convention, which while not in the purest sense a parliament, shared many similarities with the institution.
14 Kelly, *Poynings' Law*, pp. 17–46; R. D. Edwards and T. W. Moody, 'The history of Poynings' Law: part I, 1494–1615', *IHS*, 2 (1940–41), pp. 415–24; Clarke, 'Historical revision XVIII'.
15 'It passed both houses of the Irish Parliament in May and was given the royal assent on 31 July 1662'. L.J. Arnold, *The restoration land settlement in County Dublin, 1660–1688: a history of the administration of the acts of settlement and explanation* (Dublin, 1993), p. 47.
16 The likely reason for the production of so little secondary material for some time is that the work of Simms generally on this parliament appears to be difficult to surpass, although there has been some notable improvement of late. J.G. Simms, *Jacobite Ireland* (London, 1969); *The Jacobite parliament of 1689* (Dundalk, 1969); J. Bergin and A. Lyall (eds), *The acts of James II's Irish Parliament of 1689* (Dublin, 2016); E. Kinsella, '"Dividing the bears skin before she is taken"': Irish Catholics and land in the late Stuart Monarchy, 1683–91' in C.A. Dennehy (ed.), *Restoration Ireland*; *Catholic survival in Protestant Ireland, 1660–1711: Colonel John Browne, landownership and the Articles of Limerick* (Woodbridge, 2018).
17 With the exception of Kelly on Poynings' Law, and even there the publication

is focused sharply on Poynings' Law and its procedures rather than the general legislative output: Kelly, *Poynings' Law*. Although not concentrating on the seventeenth century, some useful comments are passed upon legislation in general in Ellis, *Reform and revival*.

18 Although rejected by the Commons, the gunpowder bill was converted into an act of state by Wentworth while parliament was sitting, leaving no uncertainty as to where he saw the place of both parliament and his own office in the constitution.

19 Although always referred to as the adventurers' act, there were, in fact, several pieces of legislation passed which set up the scheme. 17 Charles I, cc. XXXIII-XXXV, XXXVII [Eng.].

20 12 Charles II, c. XVIII [Eng.]; *The journals of the House of Commons*, 30 August, 15 November, 11 December, 17 December 1660; *The journals of the House of Lords* (hereafter *LJ Eng.*), 18 August, 20 August, 23 August, 24 August, 30 August 1660. There were also private acts, generally for the restoration of estates in Ireland passed in England for the marquis of Ormond (12 Charles II, cc. VII, XV [Eng.]), the earl of Inchiquin (12 Charles II, c. III [Eng.]), Sir George Hamilton (12 Charles II, c. XX [Eng.]), Sir George Lane (12 Charles II, c. VI [Eng.]), Thomas Radcliffe (13 Charles II, Sess. I, c. III [Eng.]), and Viscount Scudamore, which related to the endowment of churches in Ireland (14 Charles II, c. XII [Eng.]).

21 *CJ*, 21 June 1642.

22 6 Geo. I, c. V [Eng.]; Victory, 'The making of the 1720 Declaratory Act'.

23 A.G. Donaldson, *Some comparative aspects of Irish law* (Durham NC, 1957), p. 27.

24 J. Davies, Le primer report des cases in les courts del roy (Dublin, 1615), translated as *A report of cases and matters in law resolved and abridged in the king's courts in Ireland* (Dublin, 1762).

25 W.N. Osborough, 'Puzzles from Irish law reporting history' in P. Birks (ed.), *The life of the law: proceedings of the tenth British legal history conference, Oxford 1991* (Rio Grande, 1993), pp. 89–111; F.E. Ball, *The judges in Ireland, 1221–1921* (2 vols, Dublin, 1993), vol. 1, 231–307. The act determining that Irish lawyers should be at least partially educated at London is known as the statute of jeofailles (33 Henry VIII, Sess. II, c. III).

26 A.G. Donaldson, 'The application in Ireland of English and British legislation made before 1801', Unpublished Ph.D. thesis, Queen's University Belfast (1952), pp. 189–222; *Some comparative aspects of Irish law*, p. 41.

27 Roughly translated (respectively), they are the principles of 'what touches all shall be approved by all' and 'full power'. It was necessary in Ireland, as in all medieval European countries, that consent was required for changes in the law and also that when representatives arrived at parliaments and great councils, they would have to have plenipotentiary powers to votes taxes on behalf of their constituents. M.A.R. Graves, *The parliaments of early modern Europe* (Harlow, 2001), pp. 7–14; Marongiu, *Medieval parliaments*, pp. 33–37; G. Post, 'Roman law and early representation in Spain and Italy, 1150–1250', *Speculum*, 18 (1943), pp. 211–17; '*Plena postestas* and consent in medieval assemblies: a study in Romano-canonical procedure and the rise of representation, 1150–1325', *Traditio*, 1 (1943), pp. 355–408;

B. Tierney, 'Freedom and the medieval church' in R.W. Davis (ed.), *The origins of modern freedom in the West* (Stanford, 1995), pp. 85–86.

28 33 Henry VIII, c. I.
29 Parliamentary Archives, HL/PO/JO/10/1/298B.
30 As Aungier put it, the declaration of 30 November was 'only an act of state [and] is no safe and justifiable rule to walk by in the disposing of men's estates'. Aungier to Ormond, 27 April 1661, the Bodleian Library, University of Oxford (hereafter Bodl.), Carte MS 31, f.151.
31 Richardson and Sayles, *The Irish Parliament in the middle ages*, pp. 183–86. From the literature of the Irish Parliament in the medieval period, it is still not abundantly clear what the role of the proctors was.
32 Richardson and Sayles, *The Irish Parliament in the middle ages*, pp. 196–226.
33 *Ibid.*, p. 207.
34 *Statute rolls of the Irish Parliament, Richard III – Henry VIII* (Dublin, 2002) ed. by P. Connolly, p. xvii; Smith, *The Stuart parliaments*, p. 65.
35 Richardson and Sayles, *The Irish Parliament in the middle ages*, p. 202.
36 E. Curtis, *A history of medieval Ireland* (Dublin, 1938), pp. 292–325; 'Richard duke of York as viceroy of Ireland, 1447–1460', *JRSAI*, 62 (1932), pp. 158–86.
37 32 Henry VI, c. 6. For recent work on this declaration, see A. Cosgrove, 'Parliament and the Anglo-Irish community: the declaration of 1460' in A. Cosgrove, A. and J.I. McGuire (eds), *Parliament and community: historical studies XIV* (Belfast, 1983); J.F. Lydon, 'Ireland corporate of itself: The parliament of 1460', *History Ireland*, 3 (1995), pp. 9–12; S.G. Ellis, 'Parliament and community in Yorkist and Tudor Ireland' in Cosgrove and McGuire (eds), *Parliament and community*.
38 S.G. Ellis, *Ireland in the age of the Tudors: English expansion and the end of Gaelic rule* (Harlow, 1998), pp. 84–87; M. Bennett, *Lambert Simnel and the Battle of Stoke* (Gloucester, 1987).
39 I. Arthurson, *The Perkin Warbeck conspiracy, 1491–1499* (Stroud, 1994); Ellis, *Ireland in the age of the Tudors*, pp. 87–88.
40 Ellis, *Ireland in the age of the Tudors*, p. 88.
41 10 Henry VII, c. 4 *(Statutes at large)*. There does seem to be some confusion about this act. As an exercise, 'poynings law' was entered into an internet search engine. Most UK-based websites assert that Poynings' Law is in fact the act for passing all English public legislation, previous to 1494, in Ireland (usually printed as 10 Henry VII, c. XXII). To further the confusion, some historians list the act as 10 Henry VII, c. IX (which seems to be the enrolled chapter), whereas the printed *Statutes at large* (Dublin, 1756) list it as chapter four. This simply highlights the messy nature of recording statutes. The fact that the collection of statutes as rolls has not always been well kept and at times has been split up means that the recording of statutes under particular chapter numbers has not always been consistent. For example, the printed *Statutes at large* record the act for the English order, habite, and language as 28 Henry VIII, c. 19, yet in her publication of the last unpublished parliament roll of 1537, Philomena Connolly published it as she found it: 28 Henry VIII, c. XXX. Neither can be deemed more correct than the other, but this is of little comfort to the reader who may be referred to the same

law listed entirely differently by different authors. It is difficult to decide what the solution may be. Perhaps it may be useful, as we know of no more manuscript sources, to publish a new, all-encompassing list of Irish legislation from the earliest form to 1800, with a revised chaptering system. The Irish legislation project based at the history department in Queen's University, Belfast would probably be the logical home for such a project (www.qub.ac.uk/ild). Publications of Irish statute law are listed in the primary sources bibliography under Statutes. For additional information on the process of collating and printing the statutes, see: D.B. Quinn, 'Government printing and the publication of the Irish statutes in the sixteenth century', *PRIA*, 44 C (1943), pp. 45–129; 'The bills and statutes of the Irish parliaments of Henry VII and Henry VIII', *AH*, 10 (1941), pp. 108–15; C. Benson and M. Pollard, '"The rags of Ireland are by no means the same": Irish paper used in the statutes at large', *Long Room*, 2 (1970), pp. 18–35; W.N. Osborough, 'The legislation of the pre-Union parliament' in *The Irish statutes revised edition: 3 Edward II to the union, AD 1310–1800* (Dublin, 1995). See Donaldson, 'The application in Ireland of English and British legislation', pp. 166–69.

42 Richardson described it as a 'lifeless, conventional, ungrammatical French, rendering the English vernacular word for word, innocent of the idiom of France': H.G. Richardson, 'The Irish parliament rolls of the fifteenth century', *EHR*, 58 (1943), pp. 448–61. There were rare occurrences when ecclesiastical legislation was recorded in Latin. It would seem likely from the inference that the recorded Norman-French was translated directly from the English language in which the original petition/bill was presented in. *Statute rolls of the Irish Parliament*, ed. by Connolly, p. xviii.

43 D.B. Quinn, 'The early interpretation of Poynings' Law, 1494–1534', *IHS*, 2 (1940–1), p. 247; E. Curtis, 'The acts of the Drogheda parliament, 1494–5, or "Poynings' Law"' in A. Conway (ed.), *Henry VII's relations with Scotland and Ireland, 1485–98* (Cambridge, 1932).

44 Quinn, 'The early interpretation of Poynings' Law', pp. 248, 250–52; Edwards and Moody, 'The history of Poynings' Law', p. 417.

45 For a general history of Ireland in the sixteenth century, see C. Lennon, *Sixteenth-century Ireland: the incomplete conquest* (Dublin, 1994); Ellis, *Ireland in the age of the Tudors*; S.J. Connolly, *Contested island: Ireland 1460–1630* (Oxford, 2007).

46 Cosgrove, *Late medieval Ireland, 1370–1541* (Dublin, 1981); J.F. Lydon, *The lordship of Ireland in the middle ages* (Dublin, 1972).

47 Quoted in J. Silke, 'Primate Lombard and James I', *Irish theological quarterly*, 22 (1955), pp. 131–33.

48 28 Henry VIII, c. IV; 11 Eliz., Sess. II, c. I.

49 28 Henry VIII, c. XX.

50 B. Bradshaw, 'The opposition to the ecclesiastical legislation in the Irish reformation parliament', *IHS*, 16 (1969), pp. 285–303.

51 28 Henry VIII, c. XII. It is not abundantly clear whether this statute was brought in as a result of their failure to support the reformation or whether it was just a part of bringing the Irish constitution into line with the English one. It would be

most likely the former. Despite the splendid work undertaken by the historians of medieval Irish parliaments, there still does not appear to have been a successful explanation of exactly what role the proctors had in the Irish Parliament.

52 11 Eliz., Sess. II, c. I.
53 Most historians of the period speak of 'the opposition'. I would deem it best practice not to use the term. Although there was certainly concerted opinion and action on certain issues within the House of Commons and perhaps the Lords, there was no organisation of opposition in the modern sense. Using the term 'opposition' creates an impression of a well-organised national movement, akin to the developed parties of later Stuart England, whereby there could be a developed policy on many issues, as well as a party machine which included newspapers, dining-clubs, etc. T. Harris, *Politics under the later Stuarts: party conflict in a divided society, 1660–1715* (Harlow, 1993); N.E. Key, '"High feeding and smart drinking": Associating Hedge-Lane lords in exclusion crisis London' in J. McElligott (ed.), *Fear, exclusion and revolution: Roger Morrice and Britain in the 1680s* (Aldershot, 2007).
54 11 Eliz., Sess. II, c. VIII; Edwards and Moody, 'The history of Poynings' Law', p. 420.
55 Edwards and Moody, 'The history of Poynings' Law', p. 421; T. Moody, 'The Irish Parliament under Elizabeth and James I: a general survey', *PRIA*, 45 C (1939–40), pp. 56–57. The suspending acts were usually used so as to get private acts for the benefit of individual Catholics MPs to ensure the passing of possibly contentious religious acts.
56 Suspension had been suggested to Wentworth from London, but he turned down the offer. Clarke, 'The history of Poynings' Law, 1615–41', p. 211.
57 3 & 4 Philip & Mary, c. IV.
58 This is interesting in that it may be one of the few instances of Irish legislation affecting the competence of the English Privy Council on certain matters.
59 Clarke, 'The history of Poynings' Law, 1615–41', pp. 208–10.
60 Edwards and Moody, 'The history of Poynings' Law', p. 419.
61 Quinn, 'The early interpretation of Poynings' Law, 1494–1534', p. 242.
62 Edwards and Moody, 'The history of Poynings' Law', p. 422.
63 V. Treadwell, *Buckingham and Ireland, 1616–1628: a study in Anglo-Irish politics* (Dublin, 1998), p. 292.
64 Kearney, *Strafford in Ireland*, pp. 28–29.
65 *LJ*, 2 August 1634.
66 Clarke, 'The history of Poynings' Law, 1615–41', p. 213.
67 *Ibid.*, pp. 215–122.
68 McCafferty, 'To follow the late precedents in England'.
69 Ó Siochrú, *Confederate Ireland*; 'Catholic confederates and the constitutional relationship between Ireland and England, 1641–1649' in Brady and Ohlmeyer (eds), *British interventions in early modern Ireland*, pp. 216–17.
70 P. Little, *Lord Broghill and the Cromwellian union with Ireland and Scotland* (Woodbridge, 2004); 'The first unionists?: Irish Protestant attitudes to union with England, 1653–9', *IHS*, 32 (2000), pp. 44–58.

71 Kelly, *Poynings' Law*, pp. 44–46.
72 Dennehy, 'The restoration Irish parliament', p. 68.
73 *CJ*, 25 June 1662. N. Johnston, 'State formation in seventeenth-century Ireland, 1660-62', *Parliaments, estates and representation*, 36 (2016), pp. 115–36.
74 NLI, MS 802, [n.p.] Ormond to _____, 27 June 1678. 'The bill of confirmation of Estates has been Exposed to y^e perusall of the Irish Lawyers, & yesterday they were heard as long as they would speake, & many observations they made ag^t it, of which I think some are reasonable & materiall, & others directly contradictory to y^e generall Scope of the Bill: They were required to reduce all their discourses to Writing by Friday & what shall be found fitt & possible to satisfy them in shall be admitted, that his Matie when the Bill shall be transmitted may not be troubled wth their Applications there, or his Service delayed by hearings, which if once begun in one Case will Introduce many.'
75 By a strict interpretation of the law, pre-conditions were attached to the legislative process by Poynings' Law which insisted on the sending of transmissions to the king, the sending of legislation to England specifically, and the use of the Great Seal of England (presumably by none other than the lord chancellor, lord keeper or a commission for the seal) in certifying the returning bills and the warrant giving permission to hold parliament. Poynings' Law spelt out that 'if any parliament be holden in that land here after, contrarie to the fourme and prouision aforesaid it demyd voi[d a]nd of noon effect in the lawe'. 10 Henry VII, c. IV.
76 Quinn, 'The early interpretation of Poynings' Law', p. 250; Edwards and Moody, 'The history of Poynings' Law', p. 417.
77 18 Edward IV, Sess. IV, c. VIII.
78 33 Henry VIII, Sess. II, c. I; Bradshaw, *The Irish constitutional revolution of the sixteenth century*, pp. 240–41.
79 16 & 17 Edward IV, c. LVI; 18 Edward IV, Sess. IV, c. VII; 18 Edward IV, Sess. V, c. II.
80 33 Henry VIII, Sess. II, c. I.
81 10 Henry VII, c. IV.
82 Simms, *Jacobite Ireland*, pp. 62–63, 152–55.
83 33 Henry VIII, c. I.
84 7 William & Mary, c. III.
85 5 James II, c. X. Obviously, as the Jacobite parliament was subsequently declared illegal, this act never received an official chapter in the records, and so it seems best to follow the most authoritative listing as found in Bergin and Lyall (eds), *The acts of James II's Irish Parliament of 1689*. The exact text of this statute as well as that of 'an act concerning tithes and other ecclesiastical duties' can be found as Appendices B and C in Simms, *The Jacobite parliament of 1689*, pp. 27–28. Further texts are located in T.O. Davis, *The patriot parliament of 1689* (3rd edn, Dublin, 1863), pp. 43–136.
86 Davis, *The patriot parliament*. There were also other 'patriotic' acts passed such as an act prohibiting the importation of English, Scotch, or Welsh coals into this kingdom (5 James II, c. XXI).

87 Simms, *The Jacobite parliament of 1689*, p. 9.
88 Which is certainly a possibility as several of the clerks held posts in the executive also and may have had regular contact with Dublin Castle. For example, Sir George Lane (although probably rarely performing the role personally) was clerk of parliament and also a privy councillor and personal secretary to the duke of Ormond (as well as holding a host of other positions) during the restoration parliament. From 1628–66, Philip Ferneley was clerk of the House of Commons, but also 'doubled-up' as chief remembrancer of the Exchequer and also served Ormond during the confederate wars. Edmond Medhop was assistant clerk and later clerk of the House of Commons from 1613 to 1615; and was also a clerk of the Court of Common Pleas and attained the post of clerk of the commons' house when the previous clerk, William Bradley, became so sick that he could no longer execute his office. Medhop's wife was a niece of Lettice Perrot, the wife of Sir Arthur Chichester, the lord deputy, and he probably owed his many professional positions within the administration to him. *Patentee officers in Ireland, 1173–1826, including high sheriffs, 1661–1684 and 1761–1816*, ed. by James L.J. Hughes (Dublin, 1960), pp. 49, 77, 89; NLI, MS 8646 / 1; Armagh public library (hereafter APL), MS P001497118, f. 1 v.
89 *CJ*, 13 February 1635.
90 *LJ*, 21 March 1635.
91 *CJ*, 15, 16 April 1635; *LJ*, 16 April 1635.
92 *CJ*, 17 April 1635; 17 & 18 Charles II, c. V.
93 Having just made this suggestion, it will still need to be acknowledged that many other bills were repeated properly in the same house, including Albermarle's bill in the restoration parliament. *CJ*, 30 March, 3, 10 April 1663, 20 December 1665; *LJ*, 14 April 1663, 16, 18, 20, 23 December 1663.
94 *CJ*, 13 October 1614.
95 *CJ*, 25 July 1634, 20 February 1635.
96 *CJ*, 25 August 1662.
97 *CJ*, 28 August 1662.
98 R.H. Fritze and W.B. Robinson, *Historical dictionary of late medieval England, 1272–1485* (Westport, CT, 2002), p. 408; A.F. Pollard, *The evolution of parliament* (London, 1920), pp. 239–30.
99 *CJ*, 9 April 1635.
100 *CJ*, 6 June 1640.
101 *CJ*, 6 June 1640.
102 *LJ*, 18 December 1665.
103 *LJ*, 27 November 1665.
104 *LJ*, 9 December 1662.
105 These statutes are not numbered in the *Statutes at large*, received the royal assent on 17 June 1640, and are the Act concerning the lord archbishop of Dublin and Sir William Usher, knight, the act for securing of three messuages or houses, with their gardens and one orchard, the Act for securing several and respective estates to William Bulhely, priest, the Act for securing of certain lands in the county of Wexford, from Nicholas Loftus, to George, Lord Bishop of Ferns, and the Act

for the settlement of divers lands and rents in the lords archbishops of Elphin. Interestingly, the bill regarding William Bulhely does not appear, in the journals at least, to have received a first reading in the Commons, but again, this is probably a clerical error.
106 *LJ*, 4 June 1640. It is difficult to see how the vote could have been unanimous, considering Digby's protestations. It seems more likely that the clerk was confused between 'unanimous' and *'nemine contradicente'* (without opposition, which allowed for abstention).
107 *LJ*, 17 June 1640.
108 The clerk in the House of Lords was generally known as the clerk of parliament, a throwback to the medieval parliament when the lords, clergy, and commoners sat in the one house and only one clerk was necessary. For an excellent account of the clerks, see O.C. Williams, *The clerical organisation of the House of Commons, 1661–1850* (Oxford, 1954).
109 As Speaker Lenthall pointed out when Charles I arrived to arrest the five members in England, 'I have neither eyes to see, nor tongue to speak, in this place but as this House is pleased to direct me, whose servant I am here'. Quoted in Smith, *The Stuart parliaments*, p. 70.
110 NLI, MS 2091; *LJ*, 2 November 1692: Rule 2: Speaker's Office; *LJ*, 23 July 1634. Rule II.
111 This is described as such in the *CJ*, 1 June 1640. It is not usually stated in the journals of either house who reads the bills, but considering the roles of clerks in other Irish courts and in the English Parliament, it is safe to assume that the clerk did all of the reading aloud.
112 *CJ*, 4 May 1615. He is described in the House of Commons' journals as 'Mr Treasurer'. Although he may have acted more as a treasurer, the post of treasurer was usually reserved for a significant peer, for whom the post was largely symbolic.
113 *CJ*, 18 October 1614.
114 NLI, MS. 2091; *LJ*, 2 November 1692. Rule 6: Proceedings on Bills; *LJ*, 23 July 1634: Rule V.
115 *CJ*, 26 February 1666.
116 It does seem to be possible to at least tentatively estimate how long it would take to read a bill. A casual entry in the Commons' journals in November 1665 mentioned, when questioned about the continuing of the reading of the bill of explanation into the later afternoon and evening, 'the speaker gave notice, that the clerk wanted not above seven or eight skins of reading the same through, which will be done in an hour's time' (*CJ*, 28 November 1665). We know from this entry that the last eight pages of the bill took an hour to read. Some eighteen days earlier, when coming to the end of the first reading of the same bill, the House of Commons applied to the lord lieutenant to have the bill printed to better facilitate the second reading and debating of the contents of the bill, citing that bill contained 'near six hundred sheets of paper' (*CJ*, 10 November 1665). The piece of detail allows us to compare the length of the explanatory bill in its paper form, which contained 'near six hundred sheets', to that of the printed version found in the *Statutes at large*,

which comes to a total of 135 pages (*Statutes at large*, vol. 3, pp. 2–136). From this example, we can deduce that, in this instance, it took an hour to read eight handwritten pages. This is the equivalent of 1.82 pages of the printed *Statues at large*, and so hence it would, going by these figures, take about 74 hours 10 minutes to read the entire bill through. Obviously such a figure is by no means certain, as it is based on just one example. Some bills surely would have needed no debate nor a forensic attention to detail, such as a bill for confirming the monarch of the kingdom or the bill for the continuance of the session after the giving of the royal assent, but even a very approximate figure may be of some use (examples of such are 11, 12, 13 James I, c. I, and 13 Charles II, c. IV). An hour to read just under two printed pages from the *Statutes at large* seems to be a reasonably slow pace. It might indicate that the clerk read quite slowly on at least the second and third readings so as to give the MPs time to digest the detail of the bill, although in this case they all had a printed copy by the beginning of the second reading.

117 These are: the bill for the freedom of working the materials in this kingdom into manufactures, within the said realm (*CJ*, 17 April 1635); the bill concerning the importation of tobacco; the bill that men in cities, boroughs and towns, which be clearly worth forty pounds in goods, shall pass trials in murder; the bill that lessees in years, being worth in leases for years and moveable goods and substance, to the clear value of fifty pounds sterling, shall pass in trials; the bill for explaining a statute made in the tenth year of Henry the 7th, entitled, an act, whereby murder of malice pretensed is made treason (*CJ*, 17 June 1641); the bill to take away the benefit of clergy from stealers of cattle or sheep; the bill to take away benefit of clergy from some kind of man-slaughter; the bill to take away benefit of clergy from accessaries, where the principal is excluded there from; the bill to take away benefit of clergy from such, as rob shops and rooms of merchandize; the bill to take away benefit of clergy from cut-purses and their assistants (*CJ*, 18 June 1641); the bill of settlement (*CJ*, 5 February 1663).

118 Bill for Punishing Several Offences in his majesty's Court of Castle Chamber. *CJ*, 5 March, 30 May 1666.

119 *CJ*, 3 May 1613.

120 *CJ*, 15 May 1661.

121 *CJ*, 1 May 1662.

122 *CJ*, 23 September 1662.

123 *CJ*, 13 October 1614.

124 *CJ*, 18 November 1634, 4, 5 December 1634, 21, 26 March 1640, 22 October 1640.

125 NLI, MS 2091; *LJ*, 2 November 1692: Rule 4: Beginning of Parliament; *LJ*, 23 July 1634. Rule IV.

126 In 1634, the first bill was read fourteen days after the opening, in 1640 it took eight days, and in 1661 it took a total of nine days to read the first bill.

127 *CJ*, 27 November 1665.

128 *CJ*, 27 October 1614.

129 Interestingly, in the Lords' journals, the record states that the explanatory bill passed *nemine contradicente* (*LJ*, 27 December 1665). It is apparent that the official record is more reliable. Churchill, as he states himself, confined himself to his

lodgings at the time and in any case he was forbidden from attending the House of Lords unless attendance was demanded, as were all other non-members. The clerk was less likely to have mistaken a vote in the Lords as they voted orally, aloud, and singularly. NLI, MS 2091; *LJ*, 2 November 1692, Rule 7: Order of Speaking and Votes, Rule 10: Respect to the House, Rule 17; *LJ*, 23 July 1634, Rule VI, IX.

130 Churchill to Arlington, 27 December 1665, *CSPI*.
131 There is much that has been written on committees and their role in parliament, but unfortunately not on the Irish Parliament. For good work and up-to-date approaches of scholars working on early modern England, see C.R. Kyle and J. Peacey, J. (eds), *Parliament at work: parliamentary committees, political power and public access in early modern England* (Woodbridge, 2002). Footnotes in this work will lead readers to more specific published works of Chris Kyle, Sheila Lambert, and Elizabeth Read Foster.
132 *LJ*, 30 March 1640. The House of Lords, by the end of the century, had established as a rule that once any peer demanded that the house be put into committee, it should be done. NLI, MS 2091; *LJ*, 2 November 1692: Rule 34: Committee of the House.
133 NLI, MS 2091; *LJ*, 2 November 1692: Rule 12: Committees of the House; *LJ*, 23 July 1634, Rule XII.
134 *CJ*, 10 November 1662. This bill was originally committed to twenty-four members. Hence, the work of the committee was valid with 87.5% of its members absent.
135 *CJ*, 19 November 1662.
136 *CJ*, 2 November 1614.
137 Between 1634 and 1635 there were seven Grand Committees in the Commons relating to 103 bills and the same number are found in the Commons in 1661–66 for eighty-five bills. See Table 3.4.
138 11, 12, & 13 James, c. I; 13 Charles II, c.I.
139 See Table 3.5 and Table 3.7.
140 M.A.R. Graves, *The House of Lords in the parliaments of Edward VI and Mary I* (Cambridge, 1981), pp. 6–8.
141 This is an interesting example, as it may point us towards the conclusion that the House of Commons felt they had the power to consider amendments to bills and to have committees draft such amendments. Wentworth, in his famous speech to the Lords on 2 August 1634, refused any involvement in the initiation of law except via the lord deputy and his council. It is not clear whether changes were taken into account by the council and deputy, but a bill for the prevention of buggery did pass both houses in the second session in November 1634. *CJ*, 23, 25, 28 July 1634; 4, 6, 10 November 1634; *LJ*, 2 August 1634, 15, 18 November 1634; 15 December 1634. 10 Charles, Sess. II, c. XX.
142 *CJ*, 13 June 1666.
143 *LJ*, 20 February 1641.
144 *CJ*, 17 March 1635.
145 It seems a possibility that the copy read might have been transferred over from

convocation (convocation of the Church of Ireland and parliament sat concurrently in Ireland until 1666).
146 *CJ*, 24 May 1662.
147 *CJ*, 24 May 1662; *LJ*, 24 May 1662, 31 July 1662.
148 *LJ*, 24 May 1662.
149 *CJ*, 11 July 1666.
150 Orders for new heads of bills were being prepared as late as four days before the dissolution on 7 August 1666. *CJ*, 3 August 1666.
151 *CJ*, 3 August 1666.
152 *CJ*, 10 November 1614.
153 The total possible membership of the House during this parliament was 256.
154 The bill was recommitted several times during the winter of 1662–63 and eventually passed in its original state on 2 March 1663, which is a little strange in that it passed some five months after its third reading. It later failed in the House of Lords, much to the disappointment of John Bramhall, speaker and primate. The problem with the bill seems to have been the particular detail rather than the general issues. The Lords also set up a committee to create a heads of bill for a new bill after it had rejected the original. It does not seem to have reported, although there is later, in 1666, a private act passed enabling the precentor and treasurer of the cathedral church of St Patrick's Dublin, and the arch-deacon of Dublin, to make leases of part of their yards and gardens for sixty years. *CJ*, 23, 27 September 1662, 4, 10, 13 November 1662; *LJ*, 19 March 1663, 1 April 1663. 17 & 18 Charles II, c. XIV.
155 NLI, MS 2091; *LJ*, 2 November 1692: Rule 13: Conferences; *LJ*, 23 July 1634. Rule XIII.
156 The parliament, although by law obliged to sit in Dublin or Drogheda, was still itinerant within Dublin. It sat in several locations within the city, but as far as it is known, the two houses always sat quite close within the same complex of buildings, usually closer than the Lords and the Commons at Westminster. During the restoration, the distance in Dublin between the houses was eleven feet, six inches. P. Hunneyball, 'Note on the conjectural plan of the palace of Westminster' Westminster' in Kyle and Peacey (eds), *Parliament at work*, pp. xii-xiii; Johnston-Liik, *History of the Irish Parliament*, vol. 1, pp. 323–26; C. Lennon, *Dublin, part II: 1610–1756* (Dublin, 2008), plate 2a, 2e, Map 7; P. McCarthy, 'A favourite study': building the king's inns (Dublin, 2006), pp. 3, 5.
157 For some idea of the importance of symbolism and ceremony, see the excellent D. Shaw, 'Restoration through ritual in Ireland: The celebrations of 1661' in M. Potterton and T. Herron (eds), *Ireland in the renaissance, c.1540–1660* (Dublin, 2007), pp. 325–36; 'Thomas Wentworth and monarchial ritual in early modern Ireland', *History journal*, 49 (2006), pp. 331–55.
158 There is just one occasion where there is no record (in either journal) of the Commons attending to witness the royal assent, which was normally the case. There is a slight possibility that the clerk in the House of Lords forgot to mention the attendance and that as a prorogation was initiated immediately after the royal assent, the Commons may have not returned to their house, and as such the clerk

may have not recorded anything in that house either. This would be quite a coincidence. What is even stranger on this occasion is that there is a bill for charging taxes upon the absentee aristocracy and also a bill for eight subsidies, albeit granted by the clergy and prelates. This almost certainly came from convocation as it was read only once in each house and did not belong to the Commons in the same way as other finance bills did. *LJ*, 21 March 1634; *CJ*, 21 March 1634; 10 Charles, Sess. III, cc. XXI, XXIII.
159 *LJ*, 6 May 1645.
160 Finance bills are described in greater detail below.
161 *LJ*, 15 December 1634.
162 An act that this session of parliament shall not determine by his majesties royal assent to some bills. This is explained in further detail below.
163 *LJ*, 10 September 1661, 6 March 1662. 13 Charles II, Sess. II, c. I; 14 Charles II, Sess. III, c. I.
164 *LJ*, 12 June 1661.
165 *LJ*, 10 September 1661.
166 *LJ*, 12 June 1661.
167 *LJ*, 15 May 1662; *CJ*, 14 May 1662. Interestingly, the journals of both houses give conflicting evidence for the date of the giving of the royal assent.
168 *CJ*, 6 May 1615, 19 June 1661, 18 November 1662.
169 *LJ*, 17 March 1645.
170 *LJ*, 31 May 1661.
171 *LJ*, 23 March 1663. Interestingly, when this executive order was made, the word used in the Lords' journals is 'bill' rather than 'act' even though the bill became an act some four months earlier when it received the assent on 20 December 1662.
172 *LJ*, 17 March 1645.
173 Clarke, 'The history of Poynings' Law, 1615–41', pp. 207–22 ; Kelly, *Poynings' Law*; Edwards and Moody, 'The history of Poynings' Law: Part I', pp. 415–24.
174 Clarke, 'The history of Poynings' Law, 1615–41', p. 213.
175 Clarendon, although always anxious to steer clear of intense involvement in the minute detail of the settlement, was particularly influential on Ormond in the 1650s and 1660s and had begun his political career in the early 1640s in opposition to royal government in the House of Commons. R. Ollard *Clarendon and his friends* (New York, 1987), pp. 56–60.
176 Dennehy, 'The restoration Irish parliament, 1661–66'; Johnston, 'State formation in seventeenth-century Ireland'.
177 *LJ*, 2 August 1634.
178 *CJ*, 21 April, 13 May 1615.
179 *CJ*, 4, 23 November 1614, 13 May 1615.
180 *CJ*, 29 November 1614.
181 *CJ*, 13 May 1615.
182 *CJ*, 20 October 1614.
183 *CJ*, 19 November 1634.
184 *CJ* 30 March 1640.
185 For details of this, see Clarke, 'The history of Poynings' Law, 1615–41', pp. 207–22.

186 *CJ*, 1 April 1640.
187 *LJ*, 6, 9 August 1642.
188 20 Charles, c. I; *CJ*, 6, 9, 10, 13 April 1644, 17, 18 March 1645; *LJ*, 6 May 1644, 18 March, 6 May 1645.
189 Kelly, *Poynings' Law*, p. 95; *LJ*, 3 July 1662.
190 *CJ*, 23, 26 June 1662; *LJ*, 3, 7 July 1662.
191 *CJ*, 26 June 1662.
192 *CJ*, 28 June 1662.
193 Kearney, *Strafford in Ireland*, p. 45–52; Clarke, 'The history of Poynings' Law, 1615–41', p. 213.
194 *CJ*, 18 June 1641.

4

Officers and servants of parliament

THE SPEAKERS: BACKGROUND, TRAINING, AND EXPERIENCE

The Irish speaker was similar to his English counterpart. He, with assistance from the clerk, organised day-to-day business, chaired meetings, and was on formal occasions the mouthpiece of the house. Since the speaker in the Lords was usually lord chancellor, he had additional responsibilities, being both the head of the legal arm of the kingdom in the House and the chairman of the highest court. The incumbent was usually a loyal servant of the government of the day.[1] There was no selection process when the lord chancellor was available, but, when not, the government decided the matter. The king had a strong part in recommending Sir William Ryves in 1640, but in 1661 the lords justices were permitted to select the speaker.[2] The situation in the Commons was a little different. Theoretically, the speaker could be chosen from any of the members, but the government almost always exerted influence. As Wentworth pointed out in 1634,

> it was not worth their [the Commons] contention, considering the power of allowance was undeniably in the King, and that if he rejected, they were still to chuse another, and another, till his Majesty approved thereof; and that it would be taken as an ill presage of some waywardness or forwardness of Mind reigning in them, if they should go about to deny such for their speaker as should be recommended by his Majesty's Privy Council.[3]

Yet there is no instance of a chosen speaker being rejected. As in England, in reality, Dublin Castle chose the preferred candidate and he was normally the one elected. In 1634, 1640, and 1689 there was no competition.[4] In 1613, the Catholics had put forward their own candidate, Sir John Everard, whose defeat prompted a (probably pre-arranged) walkout.[5] In 1661, there was another competition. The king's candidate Sir William Domville only commanded minority support. Orrery and Mountrath encouraged the king to yield to the wishes of the Commons.[6] This is an important event in the history of parliamentary privilege, as it is the only time in the seventeenth century, and perhaps the first time in the history of the Irish Parliament, that the speaker of the Commons, Sir Audley Mervin, was not the king's choice. Charles surely regretted this as Mervin has been seen as obstructive to the government programme.[7]

In addition to Domville and Everard, one other was left disappointed. James Barry, Lord Santry, the lord chief justice of the King's Bench, considered himself suitable for the speakership of the restoration House of Lords but failed.[8] Lord Chancellor Eustace had suggested him for the woolsack at the council table in advance of the 1661 meeting of parliament, but was overruled by Lords Justices Mountrath and Orrery in favour of Archbishop Bramhall. Orrery said that it would be 'for the betterment of the established church after the miseries the 1640s and 1650s had brought' and also cited his experience, Bramhall being 'a person well known in ye rules & proceedings of ye Howse[,] have two passte sat'.[9] Santry had a decent claim, being the next senior legal figure after the lord chancellor, and the appointment of Sir William Ryves, a judge, as speaker in 1640 had established a precedent, as had the appointment of Sir James Ley in England replacing the disgraced Francis Bacon as speaker, but not as lord chancellor.[10] Feeling slighted, he entered a protest to the Privy Council, but the council viewed it as an affront and had him 'severely chastis'd and confined to the Castle' for two days until he relinquished his claim.[11]

The position of speaker was invariably political. The speaker was expected to influence the house as much as was possible, within the rules of his office, in favour of the government. But while political subservience was important, so too was the legal training and experience. Government patronage was vital in securing the position, along with family connections, religious outlook, racial or ethnic background. A study of the men who were appointed and elected to the position may also tell us much about what was expected of them.

Such a study has been taken in much greater detail elsewhere.[12] In all, the speakers from the earliest journal records in 1613 to the point where parliament became a more permanent institution in the 1690s had several common traits. Training in the law, coupled with legal and administrative experience, was normally required. However, the ethnic and religious affiliations of the various speakers of both the House of Commons and the House of Lords mirrored the outlook and vision of the prevailing administrations then resident in Dublin Castle, for despite the fact that parliament undertook many judicial, legislative, and administrative functions, in the religiously and ethnically divided and highly politicised Ireland of the seventeenth century, political reliability was absolutely essential.

SPEAKER OR LORD CHANCELLOR

Before we can ascertain what the responsibilities and privileges of the speakers were, we first need to treat the roles separately. We must note that the two houses, although part of the same institution, had very different functions. This applies to most areas, but especially representation in that the Lords represented themselves directly whereas the Commons represented towns, cities, and counties; legislation, in that the Commons had pre-eminence in raising of public finance; and also in regard to the judicial functions of parliament, in that the Lords were the apex of the judicial system.

We may begin with the speaker of the House of Lords. For the sake of consistency and simplicity in this chapter, as we are dealing primarily with the office and office holders rather than personalities, it is best to consistently refer to the position as speaker. For the most part there was no distinction within the house between speaker and lord chancellor except perhaps when there was interaction between the House of Lords and the presiding officer regarding his role as head of the Court of Chancery, such as when writs were to be sent out or when oaths administered or commissions for oaths were issued. When the head of Chancery was speaker he was never other than lord chancellor. Archbishop Boyle was initially appointed while lord keeper but by the time his first session as speaker had begun, he had been upgraded to lord chancellor.[13] Usually the records of the lords' house refer to 'lord chancellor' when he was such, but as 'speaker' when the presiding officer was not the head of Chancery. Indeed the issue came up in the late spring of 1644 when there was a question of how the speaker of the house should sign himself when signing a letter of both houses to military leaders in Ulster forbidding them to take the covenant.[14] When the letter, signed by the speaker of the Lords, was sent to the Commons, the Commons queried 'whether the lord chancellor ought not to write "speaker of the Lords' House of Parliament"? as well as their speaker writes, "Speaker of the House of Commons."'[15] The Lords replied in no uncertain terms that 'It was never a thing usual in that house, to sign *Canc* speaker of the house of the lords; for the chancellor for the time being is speaker (*natus*). And as in the case of Sir William Ryves, when he is chosen by the king, then to write speaker of the lords house.'[16]

In the normal course of events, there was no question of who would be speaker in the Lords. The lord chancellor received his writ to appear, drawn up by the clerk of the crown and hanaper and sealed, presumably by himself. This was then presented to the lord lieutenant, after the house was sitting, when the lord chancellor went below the bar, entered the house, and, kneeling, presented his writ to the lord lieutenant.[17] It is not abundantly clear from the available source material whether the writ commanded him to appear as a peer of parliament in his own right as Archbishops Jones, Bramhall and

Lord Ely might have done, or as lord chancellor in respect of his legal office and served with a writ to appear in the same way as the judges, masters of Chancery, the solicitor general, attorney general and prime serjeant at law. Bramhall, not a lord chancellor, presented himself at the beginning of the 1661–66 parliament with a commission for his appointment as speaker:

> Charles the second, by the grace of God, king of England, Scotland, France, and Ireland, defender of the faith, etc., to our right trusty and well beloved counselor, the most reverend father in God, John lord archbishop of Armagh, primate of All-Ireland, greeting: Whereas we have appointed our chancellor of our kingdom of Ireland to be one of our justices for the government of that our kingdom; whereupon we find it convenient for our service, that our said chancellor should, as hath in like occasion been usual for his predecessors, chancellors of that our kingdom, be engaged in the place and office of speaker of our house of peers, in our parliament to be held in that our kingdom, on the eight day of this instant May. Now know ye, that we, reposing special trust and confidence in your grace, diligence, and sincerity, of our especial grace, certain knowledge and mere motion, by and with the advice and consent of our right trusty and well beloved counselor Sir Maurice Eustace, knight, our said chancellor of our said kingdom of Ireland, and of our right trusty and right well-beloved cousins and counselors, Roger earl of Orrery, and Charles earl of Mountrath, our justices and governors of our said kingdom of Ireland, and according to the tenor and effect of our letter, dated at our court at Whitehall, the nineteenth day of April, in our thirteenth year of our reign, and now inrolled in the rolls of chancery of Ireland, have nominated, constituted and appointed, and by these presents do nominate, constitute and appoint you the said John lord archbishop of Armagh, to be speaker of our house of peers, in our parliament to be held in our kingdom of Ireland, on the eight day of this instant May, and we do hereby further authorise and impower you to use, exercise and enjoy the said office of speaker of our house of peers, in our said parliament to be held the said Eight day of May, during our will and pleasure, in as large and ample manner as any other person, formerly executing or enjoying the said office of our house of peers, in our parliament, held in our kingdom of Ireland, executed or enjoyed the same. In witness whereof we have caused there our letters to be made patents, witness the aforesaid Sir Maurice Eustace, knight; Roger earl of Orrery, and Charles earl of Mountrath; our justices of our said realm of Ireland, at Dublin, the seventh day of May, in the thirteenth year of our reign.
> Carlton & Exham.[18]

Ryves' appointment was different. Actions taken in concert with the House of Commons meant that the lord chancellor was deemed no longer fit to sit as speaker, although he was not relieved of his post as lord chancellor. There was no consensus as to his replacement either in the House itself or in the Privy Council.[19] The impeachment created some novelties in personnel also. Provisions had been made in Whitehall for the promotion of Sir William Ryves from the judges bench to the woolsack. He was provided with a commission and took his place, all of which appears to have been acceptable to the Lords.[20] Interestingly, early in the first session of the 1692 parliament, the House of Lords proclaimed their right to choose their own speaker should the lord chancellor be unavailable and if the king failed to make alternative arrangements.[21]

THE ROLE AND FUNCTION OF THE SPEAKER IN THE LORDS

The emergence of a distinct House of Lords and House of Commons and the retreat of the viceroy from regular attendance had taken place in Ireland by the early fifteenth century.[22] Later in the same century, there was growing awareness of the development of the peerage and all of their attendant privileges.[23] The net effect of this was that a unicameral assembly with the king's council and especially the legal community leading the assembly became a house of peers with the legal community reduced to the role of servants.[24] The lord chancellor, however, managed to survive this general reduction in status and influence. He was the one legal officer that managed to preserve his influential position by being retained as a conduit of communication between the House and the monarch.

So, over time, the office of the speaker was to emerge. One of his main functions was to address the king's representative in Ireland on behalf of his House, and indeed when the Commons were in attendance he spoke on behalf of parliament. All official and ceremonial interaction between the monarch's representative and the House of Lords was conducted through the lord chancellor and was done so in secret by whispering in the ear of the speaker. There is an example from the opening day of the 1634 session:

> The lord deputy being set, the lord chancellor and the lord treasurer take their places at each side of the cloth of estate; the lord chancellor having first spoken to the lord deputy, kneeling, the lord chancellor from that seat stands up, speaks aloud, viz... 'master of the rolls, it is the lord deputy's pleasure that you read his majesty's commission', which accordingly the master of the rolls did, standing by the woolsack among the judges; which being read, he delivered the same to the clerk; the judges sitting on the woolsacks on each side of the table, and the king's counsel on the back of the woolsacks, with their faces towards the lords temporal.
>
> The lord chancellor kneels again to the lord deputy, and then goes to his seat on the right hand of the state, and declares, that it is the lord deputy's pleasure to adjourn the court till tomorrow, ten of the clock; and then the house of commons to be called in, and none else, save those of the privy council and the king's learned counsel to be present.[25]

The lord chancellor also attended the lord lieutenant when the peers desired to send him a message. In 1634, the lord chancellor, along with two other senior members of the House, the lord treasurer (who by right sat as a senior officer of state but did little else) and the primate, attended the lord deputy with a message from the House of Lords regarding a petition and a remonstrance about tallow from the Commons.[26] The lord chancellor, when going to or coming from the House was always preceded by the serjeant at arms who carried the symbol of authority, the mace. He also wore distinctive clothes, a black velvet gown, probably lined with sable and with much gold embroidery, as was the style in England and is evident in later lord chancellors' portraits.

The speaker in the lords' house was also responsible for written communication with the lord lieutenant and, on occasion, with the king. On the appointment of the duke of Ormond as lord lieutenant in the closing months of 1661, the speaker was ordered to 'draw up a letter, containing the humble and thankful acknowledgement of this house unto his sacred majesty, for having been graciously pleased to appoint his grace the lord duke of Ormond, lord lieutenant of this his kingdom; and also a letter congratulatory to his grace the lord duke of Ormond'.[27] Speaker Bramhall was also instructed to write to 'Ormond and to Sir George Lane, knight, on the behalf of the said Lord Baron of Brittas, earnestly to request his majesty, that the said Lord Baron of Brittas may be provided for in the act of settlement'.[28] While what has been recounted above is an accurate representation of the official and ceremonial contact between the upper house and the head of the executive, it must be acknowledged that many within the House had regular and sometimes intimate contact with the lord lieutenant through governmental meetings in the Privy Council and through social occasions.

When the Commons arrived at the Lords with business to conduct, the lord chancellor took a lead role. The Commons would be permitted entrance after the gentleman usher of the black rod had informed the house of their attendance. At this point, the lord chancellor would walk to the bar and receive the message aurally. Once the Commons had departed, the speaker would walk back to the woolsack where he would, standing, relay the message to the peers present. Generally, the members of the Commons would be invited back into the House where they might be given an immediate answer by the lord chancellor or told that they would receive an answer in their own time, by the Lords' own messengers. There are several references in the Lords' journals to a procedure by which the lord chancellor was accompanied to the bar by other peers so that when he recounted the message to the house, they would 'help his memory, if any thing be mistaken'.[29] This is likely to have been a mechanism for keeping an eye on the speaker. It may be similar to the customary freedom of the speaker of the English Commons to correct any mistakes he may have made communicating on behalf of his house to the House of Lords or to the monarch.[30]

Indeed, there were occasions when the role of the speaker in this regard caused some umbrage between the Lords and the Commons. One incident was reported upon by an ad hoc committee of the Lords convened to discuss the issue:

> Some sent from the house of commons (who signified they had a message from that house to deliver) were admitted into the lower end of the lords' house, according to the usual manner: And the lord chancellor, accompanied with the lord primate, the lord treasurer, the earl of Ormond, the earl of Thomond, the earl of Castlehaven, the earl of Roscommon, the earl of Fingall, went down to the bar, and there stood covered, expecting the message, according as was used the last session; and those of the house of commons, who brought the message, approaching to the bar, the chief of them standing in the midst of the rest, having a parchment in his hand, offered himself to speak, but was kept back by one of those that accompanied him, who uttered these words, to this effect, 'we thought the house had been sitting, and we had a direction to deliver a message to the house sitting'. Whereunto the lord chancellor said, that his lordship conceived the house was sitting; whereunto answer was made, that 'some of the lords being out of their places covered' meaning (as we conceived) the lord chancellor and the aforesaid lords who accompanied him, 'that he took the house not to be sitting, and that they had no message to deliver, but to the house sitting'. The lord chancellor said, that he would communicate the matter to the rest of the lords; then those of the house of commons departed, without delivering their parchment, or using any more words; and went forthwith back to the house of commons, without making any stay in the out-room as was accustomed.[31]

A later ruling of the lords' house insisted that the lord chancellor and the accompanying peers should approach the bar uncovered.[32] Despite occasional difficulties, using the lord chancellor as a mouthpiece of the House worked very well.

The most important function of the speaker was to keep order in the House and organise the day-to-day agenda. It appears that order in the chamber was no great problem. There was no outbreak of violence or any other occasion when the speaker had to caution a peer about his behaviour or language in the House. This in itself is noteworthy since the Irish nobility expanded at an unprecedented rate over the seventeenth century. In 1613, just twenty-five temporal lords were eligible to sit, but by 1634 there were ninety-nine.[33] Visitors to the House, never, it appears, misbehaved to the extent that it was entered into the permanent record.[34] On the basis of punishment that was inflicted for opprobrious words or other offences against individual peers when outside of the House, chastisement for misconduct in or near the chamber is likely to have been heavy.

Where detailed debates are recorded, the presiding officer tended not to make any personal interventions but instead worked to push on to a conclusion.[35] This example, a fees bill, is from March 1640:

> The act concerning the establishing and reducing to certainty of all fees, etc., received a second reading.

Lord chancellor desires to know the lords' pleasure, whether a third reading shall be given; or the bill committed?

Lord Netterville desires a third reading.

Lord of Lowth, the same.

Lord of Derry conceives it is a publick act, not fit to be passed without committal and debate.

Two particular exceptions made by his lordship.

Lord of Lowth conceives, that in the committee, bishops, as well as others, are to be present, therefore fit be proceeded in.

Lord of Cloyne says, that this house ought to do justice to all, and conceives it fit that, as advocates, so lawyers and attornies ought to be included: Besides, in the act is expressed, 'taken by parsons and vicars;' whereas indeed they do not take any, neither can they sell, without it be simoneous. The act is so large, that if two of the lord Primate's chaplains being justices, may deprive the primate of his place.

Lord Kerry, fit to be committed as desired.

Lord Digby desires, that the lord chief justice Lowther may explain the act.

Lord chancellor desires to know, whether it be fit for the justices to deliver their opinion now, or at the committee, where it may be considered?

Thought best at committee, and so ordered.

Lord Clanmorish desires it may be passed, without any committal, being a good law.

Lord Ranelagh moves, that it being of consequence, and doubted of, ought to be committed, and the judge to declare his opinion then, and thanks the lord chancellor, by name, for the advice given to that purpose.[36]

The process of how the agenda for any particular day was decided is far less clear. As there is no evidence from Ireland, it is likely that English practice was followed. In England the speaker, along with the clerk, set the agenda, deciding which bills, petitions, and other issues should be brought into the House.[37] As a general rule, the lord chancellor had a good working relationship with the executive of the day (of which he was a senior member and an essential part), so it is a safe assumption that the agenda as set down in parliament was one ultimately controlled by the head of the executive. In short, the Castle guided the chamber. We know that Wentworth took a very close interest in certain aspects of both houses and his guiding hand can certainly be seen in the agenda of the overall sessions, in particular in 1634–35, when the supply bills were given absolute priority and the settling of grievances, in particular the graces, were put back to the second session so that the provision of subsidies would not be put in jeopardy.[38] The reason why it is obvious that the speaker worked alongside the clerk is simply that in terms of the processing of business, both the clerk and the speaker were absolutely essential, whereas the members were not. It made very little difference if there were many peers missing from the House, if anything it made the processing of bills and petitions easier. This is the reason why parliament could easily continue during the mid-1640s, even when attendance of peers dropped to as low as six.[39] However, if both the speaker and the clerk were to be missing, the session would founder. The clerk was essential for reading bills and petitions as well as keeping records and the speaker was essential for calling business and guiding it through the house.[40] The speaker's signature was necessary for most orders and warrants, and so if the house had proceeded on a number of matters other than legislation, these documents would have to be drawn up, signed (possibly, but probably not, sealed), and dispatched.

The lord chancellor's other legal functions occasionally crossed over into his activities in the upper house. The lord chancellor did much of the planning and preparation in advance of parliament. Permission to summon parliament and the prospective bills had to be sent to London for inspection and these documents had to be sealed by the lord chancellor. Once permission had been granted to the Irish executive to convene parliament, the Irish lord chancellor would then have to have writs drawn up in Chancery, usually by the clerk of the crown and hanaper. The peers were summoned by writ by right, as long as they were not indicted and outlawed for treason, as was the case in 1661 when a number of Catholic peers were excluded until their outlawries were eventually overturned.[41] Sealed writs were also sent out to the sheriffs and borough and civic authorities directing them to initiate elections for representatives to the Commons.[42]

Outside of the administrative functions of Chancery, the lord chancellor's work in the equity court and as head of the high court of parliament occasionally intersected. In the case of *Ranelagh & Keating v Molloy*, an initial petition of Viscount Ranelagh in March 1666 accused Connell Molloy of having forged a protection in the hand of the deputy clerk of parliament, John Keating, stating that Molloy was a servant of Ranelagh and therefore entitled to the benefits of his parliamentary privilege.[43] When Molloy was eventually hauled to the bar of the House, he entered a plea of not guilty, and informed the court, possibly hoping for delays to drag out proceedings until parliament was dissolved, that proceedings had already begun in the assizes of King's County and in the Court of Chief Place.[44] The House of Lords determined that the case was properly to be tried in the upper house, they being not only a senior court to King's Bench, but also the proper court to hear cases regarding the privileges of both their members and officers. Thus, the House ordered:

> that his grace the lord chancellor do issue out of his majesty's high court of chancery a writ of *supersedeas* for the superseding all such proceedings as have been had in the court of assizes, or any other of his majesty's courts of judicature, within this kingdom of Ireland, wherein the said Connel Molloy is concerned, touching the aforesaid forgeries; to the end the matter may come to a determination in this house.[45]

This is an interesting case for many reasons, but particularly as an example of the way in which the distinction between the role of speaker of the upper house and lord chancellor in the Court of Chancery could be blurred.

There were other occasions when writs from the Court of Chancery could cause upset in parliamentary circles both within and without the House of Lords, particularly in exposing the positions of many of the legal officers of the kingdom to the vagaries of justice in the House of Lords. In late 1665, attention was drawn to the presentments in the Court of King's Bench by the clerk of the crown against nuisances caused by several peers for their failure to mend the thoroughfares in the vicinity of their town houses in Dublin and also for their 'laying dung and filth in the streets'.[46] Valentine Savage, the aforementioned clerk, was brought to task and quickly submitted, admitted his guilt in making a presentment to an inferior court while parliament was sitting, and begged forgiveness from the House at the bar.[47] In the meantime, the peers had ordered the lord chancellor to issue a writ of *certiorari* from Chancery to the King's Bench in relation to the case. After a week of non-compliance, black rod was sent to Lord Chief Justice Santry, who appeared in the lords (as a member) some three weeks later.[48] Santry insisted that the writ of *certiorari* was insufficient. The lord chancellor answered him (not from the woolsack but from his own place on the bishops' bench) and would appear to have contradicted him, although his exact argument is not recorded. A grand committee was convened and judged that Santry was not guilty of contempt of the House. The matter was adjourned to a later date, when it was removed from the Court of King's Bench and the original presentments were vacated.[49]

Legal writs and warrants were not just directed to the inferior courts. In November 1644, the lord chancellor was instructed to direct a *Subpoena ad testificandum* to Philip Ferneley for his attendance in the Lords as a material witness in a case of *Lambert v Hatfield, et al.* (1644). This was surely of dubious legality as the issuing of a writ to a member of parliament or to one of its servants (Ferneley was clerk of the House of Commons) would appear to be an infringement of the privileges of the lower house.[50] If anything, the proper course would have been to send a message to the Commons, requesting his attendance. The issue disappears from the journals after this point and there is no mention of the subpoena after the order. It is likely that it was never delivered. Parliament was being regularly prorogued after just one day sitting throughout this period and so may not have made it to its destination.

Writs took a significantly more aggressive tone towards the end of the restoration parliament. According to the upper house, during the process of a dispute between Lord Kingsland and Colonel Willoughby (an MP), the Commons directed their serjeant at arms to arrest Robert and William Barnewall, both of whom were servants to Lord Kingsland. Upon report of this to the upper house, the lord chancellor was ordered to issue a writ of *Habeas*

Corpus, demanding that the serjeant at arms of the House of Commons attend the upper house to deliver the prisoners and show why he had taken them into custody.[51] This case then descended into what was probably the most serious division between the two houses in the period.[52]

Taking oaths and commissioning others to take oaths was another important function of the lord chancellor in parliament. It is not clear whether any of the other judges could provide this service since he was always the one to fulfil this role in the upper house. For example, in order to defend a suit in the House in *forma pauperis*, John Stanley had to swear an oath before the lord chancellor. The right to appoint other officials to examine others under oath could also be bestowed by the speaker when a commission was issued under the great seal to hear witnesses.[53] It did not seem out of the ordinary to have the clerk of the house to act as such a commissioner. In the 1640–48 parliament, the lord chancellor was ordered, at the beginning of each session, to issue a commission to the clerk of parliament to the end that he could swear and examine witnesses to give evidence to any of the committees appointed by the upper house.[54] The Commons were also inclined to use this facility. The clerk of the Commons in 1634 had to take his oath of office before the lord chancellor.[55] A committee was established at the beginning of the restoration parliament to ask the lords justices to instruct the lord chancellor to issue a commission to permit two or more persons (presumably members) 'to administer the oath of supremacy, which is established by act of parliament in this kingdom 2 Elizabethæ, and the oath of allegiance, which is established 3 Jacobi, in England, unto all and every of the members of this house that now are or hereafter shall be'.[56] However, it must be said that this was not always the case. There are examples in the Commons' journals where the oaths appear to have been taken in the lower house.[57]

There was no salary for the speaker of the upper house, though profit-taking was possible. The lord chancellor had a decent income from his judicial and governmental positions, which was added to by legislation in 1662.[58] Indeed, Michael Boyle amassed a considerable fortune due in no small part to his role as lord chancellor.[59] There is some sparse information about the speakers' entitlements. There were certainly some fees due to the speaker as they were discussed in the chamber and in committees, but it is not explicitly stated what they were.[60] In England, during the first half of the seventeenth century, the speaker could expect £10 from each beneficiary of a private bill.[61] There certainly seems to have been some reward for bills passed, as an order was made in 1662 that empowered the clerk 'to demand and receive all such fees and perquisites as shall grow due unto the speaker, and to the respective officers of this house, upon the passing of several bills that shall pass this house'.[62] The biggest private bill to pass through the Irish Parliament, the act of settlement of 1662, also provided income for the speaker.[63] Although not initially included in the proviso for fees, as the speaker of the Commons and the clerks of both houses were, the Lords' speaker was subsequently added to this group. Fees paid by restored innocents in 1663 'were to be divided amongst them proportionable'.[64] A general reward at the end of parliament was probably paid. At the end of the restoration parliament the House of Lords recommended to the lord lieutenant 'some mark of his royal favour and bounty' be given to the speaker.[65] A similar recommendation was made on behalf of Sir William Ryves at the end of his tenure.[66] In 1661, Dame Dorothy Ryves made a series of pleas in London and Dublin for payment of what was due to her in recompense of her late husband's services as speaker. She initially quoted £1,600 as due to her – comparable to the wage of Nathaniel Catelin in the Commons in 1634 in terms of length of service.[67] A few months later, in August 1661, she quoted a sum of £3,000 owing to her in addition to the £600 due for his services on the King's Bench.[68]

One point that does need to be remembered is the lord chancellor was ultimately a servant of the House. This was emphasised early in the 1634–35 parliament in standing orders which stipulated that the lord chancellor 'is not to adjourn the house, or do any thing else, as mouth of the house, without the consent of the lords first had', with the exception of rudimentary matters 'wherein the lords may likewise overrule, as for preferring of one bill before another, and such like. And in case of difference amongst the lords, it is put to the question'.[69]

THE SPEAKER OF THE COMMONS

The speaker of the Commons fulfilled a similar role as his upper house counterpart, but there were some important distinctions. The first mention of a speaker in the Irish House of Commons is that of Maurice Stafford, sometime around 1416.[70] In England, the first speaker, Sir Peter de la Mare, had occupied the chair in the Good Parliament (1376).[71] The speaker was invariably appointed for political reasons. He had to be reliable and able in the law. Generally, the executive exerted pressure and had their nomination carried. It was only on occasions when there was poor organisation in the preparation for parliament (1613 and 1661) that there was a contest. In only one instance was there a division. Mervin's election was unanimous when Domville's supporters saw themselves outnumbered roughly three to one.[72] The election in 1613 was conducted by a formal division. Although often emphasised as an episode of chaos, the scenes in 1613 were simply a dramatic deviation from the normal procedure. Probably originating in previous centuries, the speaker would normally be 'dragged' or led upon his election to the chair. The newly elected speaker would then usually make a speech declaring himself to be inadequate for the task, which the Commons would promptly reject.[73]

From there, the speaker was presented to the lord lieutenant for approval in the upper house. Although in theory, as insisted upon by Wentworth, the proposed speaker was only confirmed with the approbation of the viceroy, there was no case in the seventeenth century when the elected speaker was rejected.[74] When presented in the Lords, the speaker was accompanied by the privy councillors and any other MPs that cared to attend. Another speech was generally made in which the speaker again emphasised his reluctance and inability, and once approbation had been received, the speaker would depart, but this time proceeded by the serjeant at arms with the mace. Interestingly, there is also mention in the Irish Parliament of the traditional English supplication by the speaker for the free access to the monarch, freedom from arrest, freedom of speech, and advance forgiveness for unintended provocation.[75]

The position was one of real importance.[76] The fact that the vast majority of bills that passed through the Irish Parliament went first through the House of Commons and then up to the Lords made the role pivotal.[77] In keeping with this position of authority and importance, when going to and from the chamber, the speaker was accompanied by the serjeant at arms carrying the mace. The presence of the speaker was an absolute necessity for sitting. In 1666, upon the possibility of the commons' serjeant at arms being arrested by the gentleman usher of the black rod acting by direction of the House of Lords, the Commons, being a little overly-dramatic, replied that 'their lordships may discontinue the house of commons at their pleasure, because they cannot act without a speaker, the speaker cannot sit without a mace, nor a mace without a serjeant; and if he should be subject to their lordships summons, in his absence such discontinuance must of necessity happen'.[78] In 1634, when Speaker Catelin fell ill, the Commons could not sit.[79]

The primary movers of the day-to-day running of the House were the speaker and the clerk. As has been pointed out in relation to the lord chancellor, while there are few explicit references it is logical to conclude the speaker did set the agenda. In June 1640, the speaker directed the clerk to read some bills, and in October of the same year the journal states 'at the request of Mr Speaker, this house hath appointed to meet again in this house, at three of the clock this afternoon, to read over some bills'.[80] These are just two examples of something so regular that it was not worth recording. As part of his close work with the clerk, there is some mention of him being instructed to peruse the journals for precedents and also to have certain information entered at the behest of the executive.[81] For example, in January 1641 he was ordered by the king to insert an order concerning the levying of subsidies.[82]

In many other respects, the Commons' speaker was identical to his Lords counterpart. He always communicated with the lord lieutenant when he was sitting in the upper house and he usually spoke when the Commons wished to communicate with the viceroy outside of the house.[83] Mostly, such speeches were short, functional, and of no particular historical significance. The odd time the speaker could make highly charged speeches with real political consequences. In spring 1663, Speaker Mervin made a speech to the lord lieutenant in the presence chamber in Dublin Castle relating to the Court of Claims that was little short of inflammatory.[84] The prospect of a modest Catholic restoration in land proprietary had an already tense Protestant political nation on edge.[85] 'Hannibal is at the gates' Mervin claimed, adding that 'established religion, is in danger to be undermined, by casting the predominancy of temper upon a Popish interest'. The Commons ordered it printed later that day.[86] It is unlikely that the speech sparked Blood's plot, which was already advanced, but it certainly encouraged the conspirators.[87] When the plot was partially exposed in March 1663, Ormond wrote to the House of Commons detailing some of the interrogations, and added that: 'That they wanted an order of parliament, and that their pretence would be to have an order of parliament, which they expected, declaring against Popery, and for the English interest, and for the King and Parliament'.[88]

The speaker also spoke when there were strangers in the House. When judges came to the House on behalf of the lords, they were answered by the speaker. It is likely also, though there is no direct evidence for this, that when counsel came before the bar, it was the speaker who dealt with them. If prisoners were brought to the bar of the House it was usually the speaker who performed the interrogation. In June 1661, Speaker Mervin interrogated Nicholas Cahan for allegedly speaking the words 'that except such a man had his estate, King Charles should not wear his crown upon his head'.[89] Interestingly, in this case, when the original slander was reported to him, Mervin ordered the guard to take charge of Cahan until the House could be informed of the offence, effectively arresting an individual without the permission of the House. In late 1665, Mervin also performed his duty in declaring 'the judgement of the house concerning them [Blood's co-conspirators], with the grounds and reasons thereof, and so the said persons were dismissed'.[90] Another member received the 'sharp reprehension from Mr Speaker at the bar' when Dr Edward Lake, MP for the borough of Cavan, caused some unrecorded offence, worthy of imprisonment, to two other members, Jeffrey Browne and Sir Richard Osborne.[91] Lake, as advocate general for Ireland, in all causes ecclesiastical, civil, maritime, and foreign, was in all likelihood fighting a rear-guard action in the Commons on behalf of the government. He purged his contempt the following day, but felt the full force of the anger of the Commons later that year.[92] Having managed to have himself appointed chairman of a grand committee to debate the privileges of Michael Stanhope, register of the Court of High Commission, Lake 'did not perform the trust so reposed in him, but shifted, and put off the said committee, when by the committee he was required to put the question', and so before he was formally expelled he was to be 'called in, and upon his knees at the bar shall receive his doom and judgement by Mr Speaker'.[93]

The speaker issued the written messages of the House. The speakers of both houses signed a joint letter commending the lords justices' proclamation of 9 October 1643, condemning the covenant, and encouraging 'all the commanders, officers and soldiers of his majesty's army, and all other his majesty's subjects in this kingdom, whom it may concern, do render all due obedience and observation to the said proclamation'.[94] The speaker also wrote to government officials on behalf of the House, as in 1641, when he wrote to the commissioners of reducers informing them of the over-turning of a sentence against Zacharie Travers in the Court of High Commission and advising them to reduce the resultant fine against him to a nominal amount.[95] Incoming letters were also addressed to the speaker. An order concerning the agents in England insisted that 'the said committee shall direct their letters to Mr Speaker only, as to the whole house, concerning the affairs of their employments, subscribed with the hands of all and every of them, or the major part of them'.[96] In July 1641, Speaker Eustace wrote to the sheriff of Antrim for the staying of a writ of *Habere facias possessionem* against a petitioner of the Commons and also wrote to the judges of the assize that the claimant should forbear proceeding by *nisi prius* for the lands in question.[97]

The speaker was also responsible for signing, if not also writing up, warrants directing officers of state to perform certain functions. Among the most common of these was the signing of a warrant directing the clerk of the crown and hanaper in the Chancery Court to draw up a writ for election to replace a deceased, ejected, or absent member. There is firm evidence that by, at the very latest, the mid-seventeenth century, the Commons had control over their own membership.[98] Though this sole right was evidently disputed by the lord chancellor in 1640, when he failed to seal the writs for new elections for a number of boroughs and county seats, some of which had a disputed right to send members.[99] The Commons' speaker also issued warrants to MPs that were addressed to the clerk of the crown and hanaper in Chancery. These warrants directed the issuance of a writ for the MPs payment, graduated according to their status as a knight of the shire, citizen, or burgess.[100]

The speaker could also issue what were effectively bench warrants for arrest, such as one from Audley Mervin:[101]

> These are to require you, in pursuance of the order made this day by the house of commons, to apprehend and attach the bodies of William Den and John Den, and then so apprehend to bring unto this house, to answer unto such things, as shall be then and there objected against them, for violating the privileges of parliament, committed against Sir Paul Davys, knight, a member thereof: Given under my hand this twenty third day of July 1661.

| For Philip Carpenter, esq., Serjeant at Arms attending the house of commons. | Audley Mervin, Speaker. |

Similar warrants were also issued by the speaker for the discharge of prisoners of the House of Commons upon satisfaction and purgation.[102] In January 1641, Speaker Eustace was given permission by the House on an ongoing basis to issue warrants for post-horses in England and the pressing of ships into service for the dispatching of letters and agents from the Irish Parliament to the court in England.[103] In a similar manner, although not technically a warrant (termed a licence), the speaker was required to give formal written permission in advance for leave of absence for members.[104]

The speaker carried out other duties. As will be discussed later, the restoration parliament was the first to appoint a chaplain to the House of Commons. Up to this point, it would appear that it was always the speaker who opened the day's proceedings with prayers.[105] Interestingly, while Davies, Catelin, and Eustace were entrusted with leading prayers, Mervin was not.[106] If prayers were led by a member of the established church up until 1666, it would be very interesting to know who led prayers in 1689, for although the lower house was dominated thoroughly by Catholics and the speaker was obviously Catholic, the Church of Ireland was not disestablished at any stage. The lack of official journals leaves this a mystery.[107]

Supervising MPs' attendance fell, on occasion, to the speaker. Most of the time, the journals record that the House recommended that the House be called over, but on occasion they left the ongoing ordering of this to the speaker. In February 1641, the House gave the speaker direction that the House should be called 'at such time as the speaker see fit'.[108] Three months later the order was repeated with the further instruction that it should happen once a week.[109] When the speaker did order the House to be called, he kept a separate record of attendance from the clerk, which could then be compared if there were appeals by members fined for truancy.[110] The speaker was also given various ad hoc responsibilities. For example, although the collection and distribution of money was usually the responsibility of the clerk, in August 1641 the speaker along with John Bysse, MP and recorder for Dublin City, was ordered to 'dispose of the distributing of the monies, given by the knights and burgesses towards the prisoners and poor people'.[111] Speaker Eustace was also given responsibility for employing a goldsmith to create a silver basin and ewer with a suitable inscription for Captain Weldon, who had carried messages, documents and instructions from Dublin to the committee of the Commons in London.[112]

The Commons had a somewhat mixed attitude to the activities of the speaker outside the house, particularly when it came to the courts. While the speaker was expected to carry out his work faithfully in the Commons in the morning, he was to perform his other offices in the afternoon. Although most of the time there was no conflict between the Commons and the executive, there was the occasional tension which left the speaker, generally a loyal servant of government, in a difficult position. While sitting as speaker, Davies was attorney general of Ireland and a serjeant at law in England, Catelin was second serjeant, Eustace was both prime serjeant at law and later master of the rolls during his time as speaker, Mervin was prime serjeant at law, Temple was solicitor general, and Nagle the attorney general of Ireland. In June 1642, Eustace was formally given permission to attend the King's Bench and any other courts on royal service without any prejudice to him.[113] However, less than two years later, they asserted that they felt it not 'comely that the speaker of this house should be of council with any man, or promote any complaint in the Court of Castle Chamber against Sir Arthur Loftus, knight, being a member of this house, or any other the members of the said house, during the parliament'.[114] In 1647, the Commons also judged that it was not proper for the speaker to plead on behalf of litigants in the House.[115] In February 1663, the speaker was encouraged that 'from time to time, as his majesty's service shall require, and he see occasion, appear in causes and trials, which have been, or shall be, brought before the said claims'.[116] Indeed, probably the most dramatic appearance in any court involving the speaker must be when Mervin went against former Lords' speaker Bramhall over an estate in the Court of Claims, during which the bishop suffered a stroke and died some days later.[117]

Speakers in the Commons differed from their counterparts in the upper house in one vital respect – they were always members of the House in their own right. In the Lords, Ryves (1641–42) and Eustace (1662–63) were not peers and had no voice other than in their role as speaker. It is not immediately apparent whether the speaker could exercise more or less influence when he spoke in his own right, although it did happen on occasion. In July 1644, a grand committee was convened to discuss a number of issues such as the abatement of rents during wartime, parliamentary protections, and supplying Irish parliamentary agents then in England.[118] The speaker vacated the seat in favour of John Lewis and partook in the debate as a member. Of course, in their role as speaker they automatically had full privilege as an MP, but nothing more.[119]

Only once did a speaker participate in a delegation to London when Speaker Mervin was appointed to the committee that was sent to negotiate with the court on the all-important land legislation in 1661–62.[120] It is most likely that it was due to his intimate knowledge of the negotiations between parliament and the court that Mervin was drawn into the process. In July 1661, before his departure for London, he was desired to give his assistance to the committee drawing up clauses for the settlement bill.[121] Similar assistance was required for clauses for the heads of bill of an explanation act (which was returned to the House in a drastically different form and thrown out in spring 1663) in June 1662.[122] In the final session of the restoration parliament, Mervin was asked to peruse the oblivion bill and 'having thoroughly considered the purport and true meaning thereof, to inform the house what they judge necessary to be done concerning the same'.[123] The bill was eventually sent back to Ormond for amendment and re-transmission.[124]

Like the speakership in the Lords, the speakership in the Commons was not salaried, but again there was scope for profit. Despite the fact that the Commons' speakers in England around this time were paid £5 per beneficiary for private bills, there is no reference to such payments in Ireland.[125] Interestingly, an order of 1614 established it as a standing order of the House that £5 was to be provided for the poor on each private bill that passed.[126] There were, throughout the century, ad hoc miscellaneous payments. Catelin was, according to the petition of Dame Dorothy Ryves, paid a total of £1,600.[127] If this is true (and it does not appear to have been contradicted), it was £1,000 more than an order for him to be paid by the king in March 1635.[128] A later discussion of what Eustace should be paid confirmed the higher payment for Catelin.[129] Eustace appears to have got approval for a payment of £1,000 'as a first reward for his services as speaker in the Irish house, and as a compensation for his loss of practice'.[130] On three separate occasions in the years that followed, the House of Commons made recommendations that he be adequately recompensed for his efforts on behalf of the lower house.[131] At the end of his brief sojourn as speaker at the end of 1661 and the spring of 1662 (a total of 24 days sitting), Temple was given the gratitude of the House.[132] By the end of the parliament, the distribution of the money raised by the bill for £23,500 for defraying the costs of parliament included a payment of £500 for the speaker.[133] From that same fund, Mervin was awarded £1,000 for his work with the parliamentary agents in London in 1661–62 (two and a half times more than the other Commons' delegates). The Commons' speaker also received a set amount per acre from beneficiaries of the judgements of the Court of Claims, although exactly how much this was is difficult to gauge. The speaker received an additional £500 from the exchequer, most likely on a recommendation from the Commons in July 1666.[134] There was also a disagreement left unresolved before the end of the restoration parliament between Sir Audley Mervin and the yeoman of the wardrobe over the ownership of hangings in the House of Commons, Mervin claiming them for himself and some of the officers of the House.[135]

THE JUDGES AND LEGAL OFFICERS

Outside parliament, the judges of the three common law courts (Exchequer, King's Bench, and Common Pleas), the equity court (Chancery, not forgetting the Exchequer's partial equity jurisdiction also) along with king's counsel (prime serjeant at law, attorney general, and solicitor general) were of huge importance. For most of the seventeenth century, this legal community acted in parliament as servants, messengers, and advisers.[136] On rare occasions they could be the fulcrum of political events, but most of the time they abided by the rules of the upper house – that is, to sit quietly and not give their opinion unless they were consulted.[137]

It is safe to say that many of the judicial functions of the courts or their predecessors were emerging around the same time as the Irish Parliament; that is, in the middle of the thirteenth century.[138] In all likelihood, as was the case at the beginning of the English Parliament, the judges and king's counsel were likely to have had a prominent role. Their reduction to servants and legal advisers in parliament came when the peerage began to assert itself. The king's serjeant at law was a part of parliament throughout the middle ages and continued (in theory) as the most senior of the king's attorneys in precedence even after the point when strong figures such as Davies occupied the office of attorney general and began to exert more influence in government and law.[139]

Generally speaking, all judges in the seventeenth century were appointed 'during pleasure', and so as a rule they were dependent on the executive. In any case, appointments to the benches or to any of the three senior positions of serjeant at law, attorney general, and solicitor general were never made with a view to their possible influence in or involvement with parliament. From 1607 until the mid-1680s, the judiciary was entirely Protestant in its composition until soon after James II ascended the throne.

In advance of parliament convening, a writ of summons, similar to that sent to the peers, was forwarded to all senior judges and king's counsel.[140] These writs were evidently not taken too seriously, as many of that cohort went forward, probably with the encouragement of the executive, for election to the lower house.[141] There are instances when individuals were licensed to depart from the House of Lords. For example, the solicitor general in 1634 was licensed to be 'spared his attendance, by reason of an infirmity in his head, to which the lords were pleased to consent'.[142] In late May 1661, Sir William Aston, the second justice of the King's Bench, was granted leave 'to go into the country, to perform the funeral rites due to the body of his deceased wife'.[143] Cressy and Lowther were permitted to depart the summer session of 1634 to go on circuit.[144] Occasionally, the House of Lords might flex their muscles and demand the attendance of certain figures. In December 1634, the Lords sent their serjeant at arms to demand the attendance of the king's counsel and the masters of Chancery and then fined them for their non-attendance.[145] Manpower on the benches seems to have been in short supply at the beginning of the restoration parliament, as black rod was sent to the Four Courts to inform Sir Jerome Alexander and Sir Richard Kennedy that their attendance was necessary in parliament.¹⁴⁶ A general order was given that day 'that all that are or ought to be assistants in this house, do give their daily attendance in this house, except they be dispensed withal by leave of this house'. The same order was repeated twice in the following week.¹⁴⁷

At the same time, an event occurred which hints at how even the calling of legal officers to attend could become political. On the first day of sitting, Viscount Ranelagh, called for Mervin and Temple – prime serjeant at law and solicitor general respectively – to be sent for and answer their writ of summons, which was carried thirteen to seven. That same day word came from the Commons that Mervin was nominated as speaker.¹⁴⁸ The lords allowed it on the same day as the lords justices gave their approval to the Commons for Mervin to act as their speaker, and later took advice from the judges that it was not a matter of law, but of privilege.¹⁴⁹ What is striking about this episode is not the fact that Mervin was approved in his role in the Commons and given permission in the Lords, but that the attorney general, William Domville, was not summoned to the Lords at all, although presumably there was a writ of summons for him to appear also. This raises the question as to whether the Lords, generally a little more conservative and with strong ecclesiastical benches mostly nominated by Ormond, might have intended to thwart Mervin's campaign to become speaker but not Domville's. During the Jacobean parliament, judges' presence in the lower house was called into question as part of the general campaign by recusants to bring the overall balance of the house back into their favour by attacking any irregularities, particularly the elections of

> persons returned unto this house, some for non-residence, some for being judges of either of the benches, others of the king's learned counsel, some for not being estated in the places where they were returned, others outlawed or excommunicated; and, lastly, for that some were returned out of corporations, whose charters are said, in point of electing and returning burgesses to the parliament to be defective.¹⁵⁰

Once a peace of sorts had been effected, in part by the personal intervention of James I and in part by the temporary arrest and imprisonment of some of the Catholic MPs, an order was given in each remaining session for the temporary allowance of many of these MPs to continue sitting

> with caution, that the proceedings to the passing of any bill, or other affair of the house shall no ways be a precedent or conclusion whereby the benefit or advantage of those, and such like exceptions, may not at any time hereafter be taken and had, so far forth as the law, or allowable precedent before this parliament would warrant and approve.¹⁵¹

Interestingly, the example provided by the Elizabethan and Marian parliaments in Ireland is that the speaker could be a judge or one of the king's counsel. Nicholas Walsh (speaker in 1585–86) was second justice of the queen's bench, but James Stanihurst (speaker in 1557–58, 1560, 1569–71) was not a legal figure at all, although he was the clerk of parliament.[152] Aside from the high constitutional issues involved, there were sometimes practical implications to the judges' sitting in the lower house. In summer 1661, when many of the judges were away from the House, a message was sent to the Commons asking for Thomas Caulfield, to 'have leave to go up unto the house of lords, and to bring down a message from their lordships for this present time' and so a sitting MP had to temporarily play the role of messenger for the House of Lords and deliver a message on their behalf to his own house.[153]

The role of the judges and counsel as messengers was set out in the rules of the upper house in 1634:

> Here is to be noted, that the lords never send unto the house of commons any member of their own, but either by some of the learned counsel, masters of the chancery, or such like, which attend, and in weighty causes some of the judges; nor are the house of commons ever to employ unto the lords, any but their own body.[154]

For the most part this rule stood throughout the century; although in 1614, a committee of lords arrived to the House of Commons to make complaint against John Fishe, MP for County Cavan, on the grounds he had written some scandalous words about many of the aristocracy of the kingdom, claiming that 'they had no care of the commonwealth, or of their own consciences'.[155] It was usually two members of the corps of legal servants that took messages to the Commons.[156]

This part of the duty of judges and counsel was ceremonial as they had no role in drafting the message. The messengers usually departed the House of Lords, walked straight to the Commons, desired entry from the doorkeeper of the lower house, and once they were admitted below the bar, gave the message. This was always done orally – the one time it was delivered on paper caused a complaint from the Commons.[157] Occasionally they carried written documents for delivery, in particular bills (finance bills were always returned to the lower house when passed), declarations or joint letters of the upper and lower house.

Occasionally, but not often, the judges were used to send messages to others. For example, they were used to communicate with what is presumably but not explicitly stated to be the lower house of convocation. In both cases members of convocation were summoned to the upper house to answer for breaches of privilege.[158] This use is interesting in that it may tell us something about the relative place in the constitution that the Lords saw the lower house of convocation occupying. Judges were usually sent to the House of Commons, except for when the lord lieutenant was present, when the gentleman usher of the black rod was sent to request their attendance.[159] When sending for members of the public they always used their serjeant at arms, whether for an arrest or a summons. On one occasion during the restoration parliament, one of the masters in Chancery, John Westley, was advanced £20 to give letters of the House to the Lords' agents, then in London. He gave the letters, addressed to the duke of Ormond and the king, to Lord Kingston only and not to the agents as a group. For this misdemeanour, he was punished on his return by being forbidden to attend the House, which, considering the relative truancy of the other judges during this period, may not have been particularly disadvantageous to Westley.[160]

Besides providing a messenger service to the peers, the judges and king's counsel provided an important function when legal expertise was necessary. Their role was set out in the standing orders of July 1634:

> The judges sitting by, are not to be covered, until the lords give them leave, which they ordinarily signify, by the lord chancellor; and they being appointed to attend the house, are not to speak, or deliver any opinion, until it be required, and they be admitted so to do by the major part of the house; in case of difference, the learned counsel are likewise to attend on the woolsack, but are never covered.[161]

The nature of legal advice is probably best divided into two types: advice on forthcoming or prospective legislation and advice on legal questions that came before the Lords in their role as the highest court. Legislation was relatively terse. Many bills were less than one printed page long. The judges only attended committees when they were requested. In October 1640, the judges were commanded to attend a committee discussing the possible implications of the bill for the real union and division of parishes, and in particular what effect it would have on the estates of Lord Merryon in Symon's Town. The lord chief justice of the King's Bench gave his opinion, which was agreed to by the other judges present.[162] Usually the exact deliberations and advice of the judges is not reported in the journals. They were also employed in the preparation of bills. For example, in a burst of enthusiastic reform later to be quelled by Wentworth, the lords of the Committee of Acts were to be assisted by the judges and the attorney and solicitor general to prepare an act to prevent the stealing of hawks and another act for the preservation of game.[163]

The judges also provided advice on other issues of a legal nature that came before the lords. In September 1662, the judges were called to give advice to the Lords with regards to the raising of money for the duke of Ormond, and in particular on the question of the liability of the inferior clergy.[164] In May of the same year, the judges were ordered to assist viscounts Ranelagh and Massareene in composing an order to put into force the act for the repairing and upkeep of the highways.[165] In 1634, the judges and the attorney general were ordered to draw up an act (based on a petition to the king) requiring all of the Irish nobility to own land within the kingdom on pain of nullification of their Irish honours.[166]

There were other occasions when the judges were dragged into matters of real political significance. The most obvious example of this is the spring of 1641, when on a few occasions the judges had to run the gauntlet of a vociferous and vindictive parliament and satisfy the needs of their employers in Dublin Castle. The overall sense of crisis has left a more detailed account of judicial opinions. A number of issues had come before their judges for their deliberation in the first few months of 1641 that pushed them, largely unwillingly, into the fulcrum of the Irish component of the general crisis of the early 1640s. The judges were initially instructed to give their opinions on the legality of the continuance of parliament given the sudden death of the lord deputy, Sir Christopher Wandesford.[167] The lord chancellor noted that since the parliament had been prorogued, the lord deputy had died and the lord lieutenant, against whom impeachment proceedings had just begun, was lodged in the Tower of London. The judges were therefore asked to give advice on the status of the commission for holding parliament seeing as both the original lieutenant and his replacement were in no position to convene parliament as representative of the king. This was obviously an important question considering the role that the Irish MPs were playing in developments in both Westminster and Dublin.[168] The judges gave their answers orally and divided on the issue, four in favour of parliament dissolving and four in favour of continuance, but generally recommending an adjournment until the king's pleasure was known.[169] A new commission arrived within a fortnight.

In the following weeks, again as part of the parliamentary attack on Wentworth and parts of his administration, the 'queries' were sent from the Commons up to the peers asking 'the lords to order the judges to answer in writing, alledging they desire to look forward, to have everything in a due channel, not backward to hurt any'.[170] In fact, the queries were partially retrospective and targeted at individuals, particularly Wentworth and his circle, and their alleged innovations in government. They looked forward towards a new constitutional settlement which many in the Commons and the Lords were hoping would emerge. The queries were twenty-one questions, mostly of a governmental or constitutional nature, each for judicial resolution. The queries went from the general such as 'Whether the subjects of this kingdom be a free people, and to be governed only by the common laws of England and statutes of force in this kingdom' to specific matters such as the legality of monopolies, prerogative justice, martial law, and *quo warranto* proceedings.[171] This put the judges into a very difficult position, and although there were some in the Lords who wanted to prevent the issue moving forward, the majority were content to proceed.[172] The judges played for time, reasonable when one considers the delicate nature of the questions at hand.[173] On 23 February, a judge's petition was discussed in committee and it appears, although the petition itself is not extant, that the judges wished to avoid giving resolutions on the queries entirely. The committee took exception to the judges claiming that "'some of the questions concern matters that are now depending and in great agitation in the high court of parliament in England" as if this parliament were subordinate to the parliament in England'. The committee also ruled against the judges' own fourth query: 'Whether you hold it fit, without special directions from his majesty, to cause us, that are ministers of justice of and in the inferior courts, and to give any opinion concerning their proceedings.'[174] The committee was determined that the judges should answer, and upon their recommendation and further debate in the House proper, it was ordered that the judges should give their answers in writing.[175] On 1 March, lords Lambart and Slane, among others, wary of the impending prorogation, pressed for answers, but Lord Moore, the earl of Ormond and Lord Inchiquin successfully argued that the judges should not have to do so until Easter term and that, vitally, they need not answer on matters concerning the king's prerogative or such that might be against their oath.[176] In the meantime, the judges had become heavily involved in issues of *Lord Kerry v Fitzgerald*, the issue of bail, and the application of the 1352 treason act.[177] The Lords' journals for the session between May and August are not extant. However, we do know that the queries were eventually answered, though not to the Commons' satisfaction.[178]

THE CLERKS

The role that the clerks played in the day-to-day running of both houses should not be underestimated. The fact that the clerk of the upper house was officially called the clerk of parliament suggests that his office was in existence before the Irish Parliament divided into its constituent houses.[179] In all likelihood there were clerks working in parliament much earlier. In fact, there were probably clerks as long as there have been documents in use in parliament. There were, and in some cases still are, parliamentary records in a variety of collections and rolls stretching back to the thirteenth century, and it is obvious that these had to be drawn up by a clerk.[180]

Clerks were appointed by Dublin Castle through letters patent. As with many other non-elected positions, local influences and patronage counted. William Bradley, clerk of the Commons at the beginning of the century, was probably appointed on the basis of his links with Sir John Davies, as he was his agent in Ulster.[181] Bradley's permanent replacement in the post was Edmond Medhop, whose wife was a niece of Letitia Perrot, the wife of Sir Arthur Chichester, the lord deputy.[182] Formally, when the House was sitting, Matthew Davies and Edmond Medhop were appointed by the Commons, but Medhop's appointment is clearly linked to his relationship with the speaker.[183] Sir George Lane's appointment as clerk of the upper house in 1648 was no doubt, like all of his other appointments, traceable to his close connections with Ormond.[184] Secondary or under-clerks always seem to have been directly appointed by the clerk.[185] None of them are particularly noteworthy in the general history of the kingdom and disentangling the patronage network that resulted in their appointment is not within the remit of this book. There is only one known case of a clerk resigning, that of William Sandys, who maintained that his work in the office of the king's remembrancer took up too much of his time.[186]

Generally, it can be said that the clerk and his assistant clerks undertook all of the secretarial and clerical duties of their respective house. Among the most important of these was setting the agenda along with the speaker of the house. As has been noted above in the case of the speakers, there is little evidence for how this task was accomplished (in England, for example, it generally happened in the morning before the house sat).[187] Clearly, when the clerk held all of the supporting documents for the house, he would need knowledge of the agenda and, like the speaker, he was expected to have a very good working knowledge of parliamentary machinery and procedure. The clerk was required to announce what committees were due to sit that afternoon every day at the end of the morning session.[188] Indeed, it was also his responsibility to see that he or a member of his staff attended every committee.[189] The role of the speaker was frequently a politicised one but the clerk, on the other hand, was appointed by central government. Bradley and Medhop, and possibly Davies, clearly had close connections to Sir John Davies and are unlikely to have been at loggerheads. Ferneley was appointed in 1628 in preparation for Falkland's abortive parliament, when a relatively warm relationship could be said to have existed between the executive and the Catholic community, but he continued in the role until 1666, when the political mood of parliament and the personalities of the respective speakers had changed considerably. Although the speaker was a servant to the house, the clerk was, in many ways, a servant to the speaker.

There was only one serious clash between the clerk's office and the serjeant at arms, the other main supporting office in the Commons. In June 1666, the clerk petitioned the House of Commons that he and his clerks were in possession of the gate house and some other rooms in the parliament building at Chichester House, when the serjeant 'did, in a violent manner, with soldiers and others, dispossess the person in possession of the same, by and under the said Mr Ferneley, uttering many unbecoming and uncivil words against the said Mr Ferneley'.[190]

As shown in some detail in the chapters on bills and acts and on petitions (see pp. 21–24, 71–76, 83–84), the clerk of parliament was responsible for all of the paperwork that came before parliament. He held onto most bills until they were presented for the royal assent, with the exception of the money bills, which were always returned to the clerk of the lower house.[191] In the committee discussing the bill for tythings, oblations, and mortuaries in October 1640, the question was raised as to whether a bill read twice in the Lords but not passed could be returned to the Commons. Lord Lowther insisted that 'it cannot be done, it being a record of this house; and that the books of law are according: But saith, that this may be retained in this house, and the clerk of the house of commons may take a new copy out of the record'.[192] In March 1645, the Lords ordered that 'the clerk of this house do get such general acts of parliament as have been passed since this parliament began, inrolled, and do deliver the same to the clerk of the rolls, whereby they may be printed'.[193] This clearly indicates that it was the responsibility of the clerk of parliament to enrol acts, but not to have them printed.[194] It might also indicate the source for the printed *Statutes at large*, in that they too contained only the public acts in full and recorded just the title of the private acts.[195] Petitions of all sorts, along with supporting documents, were lodged with the clerk and it was his responsibility to have these to hand. Clerks in both houses were also responsible for all outgoing correspondence such as warrants, letters, commands, and declarations. One noteworthy exception to this rule is when the speaker had to write and send a warrant regarding the fees of Ferneley 'who cannot send forth warrants on his own behalf'.[196] The clerk was called upon to make occasional searches for precedents in the records.[197] In July 1634, the clerk was given a copy of 'orders and usages', which was presumably Hooker's *Orders and usage* to assist him in this task.[198] The length of Ferneley's tenure of office presumably made him particularly adept at this aspect of his work. The clerk was frequently called upon to undertake other types of investigation. Upon a complaint against one Dodson in 1661, the clerk was ordered to 'repair unto Mr Dodson's dwelling house, view what goods he hath in possession belonging to His Majesty, and a note of the said goods to bring into this house, and to take care that they be secured'.[199]

In the Commons, responsibility lay with the clerk himself to provide the materials and also coal for the House.[200] One of the other main functions of the clerk was to read aloud all documents that he was responsible for, primarily petitions and bills. In most instances this was not particularly taxing, since most bills were no more than a few pages long and most petitions ran to no more than a page. However, both the bill of explanation and the bill of settlement in the 1660s ran to several hundred handwritten pages, and were probably read by a team of clerks working in shifts. The reading of the explanatory bill in December 1665 extended from 8 in the morning until after dark on some days.[201] The clerks also had the job of registering and keeping record of protections and having this information to hand on request.[202]

Given the destruction of records in the early 1920s, it is difficult to gauge exactly how the clerks of both houses organised their parliamentary archive. In all likelihood, considering the time Bradley spent learning the craft of the clerk in London in advance of the 1613 parliament, it developed along similar lines to the English archives.[203] When clerical work was not being conducted at the table on the lower end of each house, it was conducted in the accommodation set aside for the clerks as described above. At the end of each parliament, if the clerk was diligent, papers were probably transferred to Bermingham's Tower in Dublin Castle for (not particularly) safe-keeping.

The clerk almost always undertook administration of accounts. The clerk of parliament was responsible for overseeing the accounts of Viscount Baltinglass in 1642 following the latter's agency on behalf of the Irish Lords in England.[204] In 1662, after an appeal on the basis of severity of fees by one Captain Coates, who had been arrested by the serjeant at arms for attacking and wounding a servant of the earl of Carlingford, the serjeant's fees were referred to the clerk 'to moderate the same'.[205] The clerk of the lower house seems to have been much busier in this aspect of his work. The clerk of the lower house was ordered to collect and pay out (sometimes on the fines of members for late- or non-attendance) monies to charitable institutions. Recipients included the poor prisoners of Newgate and the three Marshsalseas, for the release of small debtors and the relief of others; the poor people of Dublin; the organist, choristers, and six vicars of St Ann's guild, the relief and transport of Protestant refugees to England in 1643; poor ministers in Dublin (paid for by Catholics in the city in 1644); the dean of Christ-Church as recompense for the provision of chairs; and the poor of the hospital in Back Lane in Dublin.[206] Exactly where this money was stored is not clear. In most cases it was never much more than £50. In the restoration parliament, Philip Ferneley also undertook the considerable task of collecting and distributing the money raised from the act for defraying the costs of parliament, which amounted to £23,500.[207] Initially this had begun as a sum of £12,000 to pay for the expenses of the agents of Lords and Commons sent to London in summer 1661.[208] By the end of the restoration parliament, this cost had risen to the sum of £23,500 and included payments not just to the original agents, but also to a number of other figures.[209]

The clerks also took bails from prisoners during temporary releases. When Carpenter and Little were released on bail in February 1641, they were ordered to post £25,000.[210] No other bail came even close to this huge sum, but there were many other instances when the clerk held money for good behaviour by delinquents.[211] On one occasion he also held monies due by way of fees to the serjeant at arms, Peter Hill, with his approbation, to cover a debt owed by Hill to Nicholas Blake. The clerk also collected the fees of members of the House who had been fined for non-attendance or late arrival.[212] Of course, in both houses it was the responsibility of the clerks to take a record of attendance when directed to do so.[213]

In legal hearings in the Lords, the clerk of parliament was empowered and expected to administer the oath to witnesses as well as take depositions and affidavits of witnesses.[214] Before the clerk of parliament could take the oaths of others, he had to make his own oath on taking up office, as did the clerk in the Commons.[215] In the Lords it was as follows:

> Ye shall be true and faithful, and truth you shall bear to our sovereign lord the king, and his heirs and successors; you shall nothing know that shall be prejudicial to his highness, his crown, state, and dignity royal, but that you shall resist it to your power, and with all speed you shall advertise his grace thereof, or at the least, some of his counsel in such wise as the same may come to his knowledge. Ye shall also well and truly serve his highness, in the office of clerk of parliament, making true entries and records of parliament of the things done, and past in the same. Ye shall keep secret all such matters as shall be treated in his said parliament, and not disclose the same, before they shall be published, but to such as they ought to be disclosed unto. And generally, ye shall well and truly do and execute, all this belonging to you to be done, appertaining to the office of clerk of the parliament, to your power.

Naturally, once sworn in as clerk, he had the full protection and privileges of his house.[216]

Although usually messages for the executive and other branches of government were undertaken by members, the clerks were occasionally employed. On his return to Ireland in advance of the first sitting of parliament in 1613, the clerk was entrusted with bringing back all of the bills prepared for the second session.[217] In 1641, at a preliminary hearing regarding the question put to the judges in relation to fairs and markets, the clerk was instructed to acquaint the attorney general of the issue and to request his attendance.[218] In the same year, the clerk was sent to the clerk of the office of the master of the rolls and required to bring back the commission of the Court of High Commission for inspection.[219]

THE CLERKS' FEES

Because there were some differences in the way in which the clerks of the lower and upper house were paid for their services, they should be treated separately. The fees for the clerk of parliament were set down in an order in the Lords in November 1634.[220] For the introduction of every bishop or baron, at his first coming or by proxy, the clerk was to receive £2 10s; for every archbishop, earl, or viscount, £4 10s; for the entry every proxy, £1 10s; for every private bill £6 13s (per beneficiary, presumably); for every copy per sheet, 1s 4d. These fees were ordered to be paid in Irish pounds, with the exception of the fees for private bills and copies which were in sterling. This order was later confirmed by a warrant of Charles I.[221] In the restoration parliament, the same fees were confirmed, but with the stipulation that introductions were only to be paid on new creations and not those coming into the house by descent.[222]

Added to this were the fees for introducing new dukes and marquises, which were reckoned at £7 10s and £5 10s respectively. In 1640, Lord Ranelagh moved on behalf of the clerk that many of those called had not paid their fees or those for the proxies they held.[223] Payment of fees for proxies and introductions may have been difficult to collect due to the social standing of the peers. However, the fact that the clerk controlled the movement of private bills and the making of copies of any bills or orders gave him potential leverage.[224] Interestingly, no record appears of fees charged for the submission of protections or for the submission of petitions to the house, but they undoubtedly existed. There were occasional ad hoc payments to clerks for particular tasks. For example, John Keating (the effective clerk in the House due to Sir George Lane's presence in London in the first half of the restoration parliament) was awarded £300 for his 'great diligence and expedition'.[225] There was also a large payment that came from the restored innocents since the act of settlement was in many aspects a private bill.[226] In addition to this there was a request made by the House that 'John Keating and his clerks' be awarded a *concordatum* of £700 by the lord lieutenant for their work in parliament.[227] Finally, both the clerk and the assistant clerk were awarded £2,000 and £300 respectively in the act for £23,500.[228]

The position of the clerk of the lower house could also be quite lucrative, but in a different way. Obviously, there were no fees for introductions here and much of the clerks' income was derived from charging for services provided in clerical duties, plus there were the ad hoc payments from the members. In March 1634, the fees due to the clerk and his subordinates were laid down as follows:[229]

> For the copying, engrossing, passing, and enrolling of any private or particular bill, which shall pass for a law for the advantage, good, or benefit of any private persons, city, corporation, every such private person being thereby naturalised, or otherwise therein concerned, and every such city or corporation, shall pay to the clerk of this house five pounds, sterling.
>
> For the entry and copy of every order, both in the house, or before any grand committee, wherein any private persons is concerned, together with the names of the said committee, five shillings, sterling.
>
> For the reading and entering of every petition, answer, replication, or other pleadings, concerning the private good of any particular person, city, town, or corporation, five shillings, sterling.
>
> For the copying of any petition, articles, or other pleadings concerning any private person, by the sheet, twelve pence, sterling.
>
> For entry of every privilege [protection?] of parliament granted by the knights, citizens, and burgesses, five shillings, sterling.
>
> For the appearance of every delinquent, two shillings and six pence, sterling.
>
> For every bond to his majesty's use, to abide the censure of the house, etc., five shillings, sterling.

For cancelling the same, five shillings, sterling.
For every warrant from the house or grand committee for the bringing in of any delinquent, five shillings, sterling.
For every discharge, the like, five shillings, sterling.
For every summons, two shillings and six pence.

It is difficult to know what the fees were before this order, but in both houses, as well as in government and the courts in general, there was a movement against exorbitant fees in the seventeenth century, so they are likely to have been reduced. In 1634, the clerk was entitled to claim as much as 10 shillings from any member who desired a list of the members returned in the most recent elections.[230] In 1640, he was instructed to take 5 shillings for every copy of the declaration regarding the subsidies.[231] By June 1641, although it was confirmed that no petitions should be read or promoted until the clerk had received his fee, it was ordered that members petitioning were to pay no fees to the clerk.[232] The remaining ad hoc payments seem to have been voted by the House as recompense for services. For example, in 1615, Edmond Medhop was awarded £10 'as a gratuity from the said house, in part of the recompence and reward of his good and faithful service, done and performed this session'.[233] In December 1634, the knights were ordered to pay 10 shillings, and the burgesses and citizens 5 for the officers of the house. The clerks received two-thirds of the total, and the serjeant at arms and the rest of his 'department' the remainder.[234] There was no prompt payment, since two reminders had to be given to MPs early the following year.[235] A similar amount was voted for the officers (divided in the same ratio of 2:1) in April 1640, followed by a special payment to Ferneley alone of 20 shillings by the knights, 15 by the citizens, and 10 by every burgess.[236] Similar payments were expected of new MPs elected after 1642.[237] Highlighting the role that fees had in the regular income of a clerk, upon the petition of Ferneley 'that no considerable act did pass in the last parliament held for this kingdom, which might advance the benefit and profit of his place, and supply the great charge that he was at, in his service and attendance', an order was made for the Scots of Ulster to pay Ferneley £250 for the general act of naturalisation of the '*Antenati* of the Scottish nation' which had passed in 1635 'which, if it had been drawn out into several acts, to every person that reaped benefit and fruit of the same, would have been a very great reward unto him for his service'.[238] This order was made on the last day sitting before the outbreak of the 1641 rebellion and so the prospects of Ferneley recouping his fees from that part of the country were dealt a severe blow, but he successfully revisited the topic by petition to the Commons in July 1661.[239] In addition to his regular fees, the restoration saw Ferneley take in a considerable sum on two separate occasions. The first of these was the payment made, as described above in the clerk of parliament's fees, from the charges on restored innocents in 1663, based on a charge on the acreage they had been restored to. Although he was not a listed recipient in the act for £23,500, Ferneley was awarded the sizeable sum of 6 pence on each pound that he collected and disbursed.[240]

THE SERJEANT AT ARMS

The serjeant at arms is found in England as early as the crusades of Richard I and perhaps earlier, initially as a detachment of close cavalry that later become a bodyguard to the king. As part of this role, the serjeants at arms also undertook other roles such as arresting individuals suspected of treason, of debt, and impressing men and ships. In many ways his parliamentary functions appear to have been an extension of his medieval origins. It is likely that the English Parliament was given the services of a serjeant sometime in the first half of the fifteenth century. It is not clear when they were seconded to the houses of Lords and Commons in Ireland, but they were in place at the beginning of the seventeenth century and had probably been there before.[241] The lucrative nature of the post made it desirable, and there is evidence that the office could stay within families over generations. Like other officers, the serjeant at arms was responsible and answerable to parliament when it was sitting, but he was nonetheless appointed by the executive.[242]

The serjeants at arms fulfilled a role not too dissimilar to their medieval function in the king's household. Ostensibly they were there to keep order in the parliament chambers and within its confines, and also to execute warrants for summons and arrest of delinquents on the orders of either house. They also took responsibility for ongoing custody of delinquents and were occasionally used as messengers. It is in the area of summonses, arrests, and taking longer term custody of delinquents that they appear most frequently in the records, which does not necessarily mean that this was the aspect of their work most frequently performed. In as much as is obvious from the journals, the House of Commons could summon anyone to the bar of the House to answer for any misdemeanour they deemed opprobrious to their House, its dignity or for any number of offences conducted against any of its members, or indeed anyone that they wished to speak to or question regarding any grievances. No individuals (except peers) were particularly safe. Those arrested or summoned to the House included government officials, MPs, and sheriffs, as well as numerous others.[243]

For the breach of privilege in having a debtor arrested who happened to be his servant, Sir Francis Ruish had the offending creditor, one Carey, arrested by the serjeant at arms, who was also instructed to release the imprisoned servant and arrest the original arresting officer.[244] In this instance, when ordered, the serjeant at arms was instructed to apprehend 'with his mace', which is not usually the exact wording in how subsequent orders were made. In 1634, for irregularities in county elections in Kerry, John Blennerhasset was ordered to the bar by the serjeant at arms.[245] There were numerous cases when the serjeant was ordered to arrest individuals or groups of people for occupation of estates, particularly in the early years of the restoration. In 1662, Sir Oliver St George had, upon complaint made in the Commons, John Dawson and John Bourke of Ballynecourt, and Thomas Sampson of Moore in Tipperary arrested by the serjeant at arms and hauled to the bar of the House for dispossessing him of estates in Limerick.[246] Indeed, at times the serjeant at arms had so many summons and warrants for arrest to act upon that he had to report to a standing committee once a week to 'give an account of all such warrants and summons, as heretofore have issued'.[247] The serjeant was also given responsibility, as in a 1647 case, for attachments when the House of Commons ordered warrants to be issued upon the affidavit of a member before the lord chancellor that his privilege had been breached even after the ends of sessions.[248] Interestingly, there was no mention in the order of what was to become of the prisoner. It is not clear whether anyone was actually arrested for a breach of privilege in this time. In all likelihood, he would have been within his rights to take a bond from a prisoner for his return when parliament reassembled. This was what happened in the case of Sir Bryan O'Neill, who was arrested towards the end of the session that ended in December 1662, when the House of Commons neglected to make an order for O'Neill's release or continuing custody.[249] When the house was sitting, it was normal for the serjeant to be given permission to issue bail.[250]

Once the serjeant at arms, or his agents, had arrested someone, he was also responsible for their safe keeping until they were to be heard at the bar. Occasionally this meant lodging them in one of the city's prisons, usually either Newgate or in the Marshsalsea of the Four Courts, or even Dublin Castle. Often the serjeant at arms (and the gentleman usher too) kept custody of his prisoners in his own home, or indeed in rooms within the parliamentary complex. When Sir Bryan O'Neill was recaptured by the serjeant in February 1663, he was sent to the serjeant's house with two of his men.[251] It is important to keep in mind that whereas the limits of parliament's judicial responsibility might have been somewhat hazy, and particularly so for the Commons, competence over privilege of the house and the member was not in question. Therefore, the idea of arresting and keeping in custody a private individual or an office holder was not contentious. Both the Lords and the Commons could issue what in effect were bench warrants and custodial orders in much the same way as any of the other courts could.

In the same regard, when the serjeant at arms was sent out of Dublin city to execute a warrant, he could legitimately expect the assistance of local officials. Upon issuing an order for the arrest in 1662 of Peter Gerrard, John

Grogan, John Jones, Thomas Maglone, Matthew Barnewall, John Clarke, Patrick Kelly, Patrick Longe, and Thomas Hicky at the suit of Sir William Petty (MP for Inistioge in Kilkenny), the Commons insisted that 'for the effectual putting in execution of this order, all mayors, sheriffs, bailiffs, constables, and other officers or ministers for justice, are hereby required to give their utmost assistance, in the apprehending of the aforesaid persons'.[252] A similar order was made in 1645 requiring the assistance of the local military governors in apprehending Edward Brereton for stealing the corn of a member of parliament.[253]

The serjeant occasionally fulfilled minor functions within the House. In July 1634, he was instructed to inform several officers of state that their attendance was desired by the Committee of Grievances.[254] Again acting as messenger, the serjeant at arms was employed to deliver an order for the raising of funds for the agents in England in June 1641 to all members of the Commons.[255] A joint order of both houses a few days later was sent to the agents in England by the serjeant at arms, who was in any case going there on personal business.[256] In 1614, the serjeant at arms was commanded to investigate who wrote the petition of Ferrall O'Dally, obviously offensive in some manner.[257] Although there is mention of a doorkeeper in the restoration parliament, the serjeant at arms seemed to fulfil the role in earlier parliaments, and it would appear that he supervised the doorkeeper when that office appeared. In February 1641, probably aware of the tensions, the Commons ordered that the serjeant at arms 'from henceforth shall not permit or suffer any one, that is a stranger to the house, to listen or hearken within the two doors of the commons house, or in his inner room, or otherwise to understand the secrets of this house'.[258] Although it was usually the role of the clerk, the serjeant at arms occasionally collected fines and other monies raised on behalf of the Commons. On several occasions he was ordered to collect fines on MPs for absence and lateness.[259] He was also responsible for the collection and reporting upon of the monies raised by members of the Commons for the construction of a church for the expanding émigré French Huguenot population in Dublin.[260]

Like all other servants of parliament, the serjeant at arms was entitled to, and made frequent use of, parliamentary privilege. This was of particular use since the serjeant at arms was putting himself and his subordinates into the 'frontline' of enforcement of parliamentary justice. There are many references to the serjeant pleading privilege.[261] When recorded, the reasons vary. In one case debt was owed (and privilege not pleaded by the serjeant at arms) and in another, it was to have a billeted soldier and his wife removed from the serjeant's home.[262] A petition in the restoration parliament was lodged by Philip Carpenter, then serjeant at arms, complaining that he had been disturbed in his property in Knockloe in Wicklow.[263]

Like many other officers in parliament, the serjeant at arms was not paid a regular salary but extracted fees in the course of his work and occasional *ex gratia* payments. The fees due to the serjeant at arms are initially unclear, but they were discussed at a committee appointed for the settlement of fees of the officers of the Commons in 1641 and then confirmed:[264]

> For every bill that shall pass for a law, that concerns any man's private interest, or for several mens interest, the serjeant is to have twenty shillings, sterling, and to his men, in like cases, two shillings and six pence, sterling.
>
> That if any desire to have their councel, in opposition to any bill that is to pass for a law, they are to pay to the serjeant, for admittance for such party and his councel, ten shillings, sterling.
>
> That if any be naturalised, as born out of the king's dominions, he must put in a bill, and pay to the serjeant twenty shillings, sterling, and to his men five shillings, sterling.
>
> That upon a bill which is to pass for a law, and where it concerns more than one corporation, or such like, the serjeant is to have twenty shillings, sterling, and his men two shillings and six pence, sterling.
>
> For the arrest of a knight-bachelor, or baronet, the serjeant is to have twenty shillings, sterling.
>
> For every day that he is in keeping within the doors, besides his diet and lodging, six shillings and eight pence, sterling.
>
> And when he goes abroad with a keeper, *per diem*, ten shillings, sterling, for the arrest of an Esquire, thirteen shillings and four pence, sterling.
>
> For his keeping within doors, besides diet and lodging, *per diem*, six shillings and eight pence, sterling.
>
> For the arrest of a gentleman, or any other under the degree of an Esquire, ten shillings, sterling.
>
> For his keeping within doors, besides his diet and lodging, *per diem*, three shillings and four pence, sterling.
>
> When he shall go abroad with a keeper, *per diem*, five shillings, sterling.
>
> For every mile that the serjeant shall ride, from the place where the parliament is kept, unto the place where the party shall be arrested, for every mile's going twelve pence, and for every mile's coming twelve pence; twelve pence, sterling, a mile, going and coming.
>
> For every summons, the serjeant at arms is to have for every mile for his travelling charges, going and coming, six pence, sterling, viz., six pence for every mile going, and as much for every mile coming; six pence a mile, going and coming.
>
> No summons in any suit between party and party ought to be directed to the serjeant at arms, but only such summons as is granted at the suit of a member of the house, or where a summons is granted in some general grievance. Hugh Rochford, by direction of the house, explained it.
>
> If any knight or baronet be brought to the bar as a delinquent, thirteen shillings and four pence, sterling.
>
> If an Esquire be brought to the bar as a delinquent, thirteen shillings and four pence, sterling.

If any under that degree, ten shillings, sterling.

And if they be committed, he is to have, *per diem*, as aforesaid, *reddenda singula singulis*.

And if any one be brought in as a witness, the serjeant is to have of the party that produceth him two shillings, sterling.

Clearly all this depended upon the volume of business coming before the House and how much of it was referred to the serjeant. It is difficult to estimate what level of income this activity generated, but since the serjeant was regularly called upon it may have been quite substantial. Out of these fees, the serjeant at arms had to pay his own agents or deputies. In 1642, for unknown reasons, George Plunkett, deputy serjeant at arms, was awarded 12 pence out of every protection lodged 'to his own use, and not to the use of the Serjeant Hill'.[265] In November 1665, on the petition of serjeant at arms Philip Carpenter, the House reiterated the order of fees payable, in particular relating to the presence of counsel and witnesses at hearings before the House.[266] Later the same year, due to the problems of delinquents fleeing on appearance of the serjeant at arms, the fees were chargeable from the time that the serjeant demanded the wanted person at their usual residence rather than when they were actually apprehended.[267]

There were also less regular payments made to the serjeant at arms for his work on behalf of the Commons. In November 1614, they agreed that the serjeant at arms should have 2 shillings from every knight of the shire, and 2 shillings and 6 pence from every remaining MP.[268] The same figure was payable to the serjeant by MPs in the 1634–35 parliament by order of August 1634, followed by a further order in December for double the amount.[269] The existence of these orders in the earlier parliaments but not after 1645 indicates that fees for the serjeant at arms were to be generated by delinquents, pleaders, or beneficiaries of private legislation and as such to replace contributions of MPs. Ad hoc payments in later parliaments were not made by members of the Commons. At the end of the restoration parliament, the House voted to recommend to the lord lieutenant that their serjeant at arms be paid £600 for his work over the previous five years.[270] He was also awarded £150 from the act for £23,500 for defraying the costs of parliament and he also claimed and was awarded what were essentially fees for private beneficiaries of the act of settlement.[271] Occasionally, payment could be difficult to collect. There were times when a prisoner might plead poverty and the House would order his or her release without payment.[272] The fact that an order was passed in June 1641 emphasising that the serjeant had to be paid his fees before those summonsed or arrested could have their appearance accepted by the clerk shows that there were collection difficulties.[273] On the other hand, the serjeant at arms was able to increase the fees on occasion, as one order of the House recorded:

that John Agherin, Anstace his wife, and his servants, shall be forthwith discharged from the serjeant at arms attending this house, paying the fees of a summons only, since the time of issuing the said summons, until the said John Agherin was discharged by order of this house of the second of July last; and that the said serjeant at arms shall, upon sight hereof, restore unto the said Agherin the overplus of fees by him received over and above the fees of a summons.[274]

The Lords also had a serjeant at arms at their disposal, but he was not nearly as busy as his Commons counterpart. In the Lords, the gentleman usher of the black rod, along with his assistant the yeoman usher, fulfilled many of the functions of the serjeant at arms described above, and he appeared far less frequently in the Lords' journals. Essentially the role was very similar to that of the basic functions of the office of the serjeant at arms in the lower house. In the Lords, the serjeant was instructed to deliver summons to individuals and on occasion to arrest and keep in custody those who might have crossed the House. For example, in February 1635, the serjeant at arms was directed to serve a warrant by the House of Lords to William Farrer, sheriff of Donegal, for levying money for the payment of knights' wages from the estates of the bishop of Raphoe.[275] The journals show that execution of warrants and taking custody of prisoners was the responsibility of the serjeant when dealing with delinquents outside the general vicinity of the House. Obviously, the fact that black rod had to consistently attend within the House meant the possibility of travelling to arrest an individual was not an option, but so too did the serjeant at arms have to attend the lord chancellor when he entered and left the House with the mace. In all likelihood, both figures used agents in the course of their work, especially for arrests and committals. There were occasions where the lucrative business of taking prisoners led to disputes between the two offices. Upon the arrest of John Warren for speaking 'opprobrious words' against Viscount Dungannon, Robert Hall petitioned the House for custody, against the serjeant of arms who had already taken custody.[276] When the committee reported (nearly a month after Warren's release), it decided 'that for the time to come, the gentleman usher of the black rod do take into his custody all such persons that shall be committed from the bar, as aforesaid; and that, as to the time past, all fees which the serjeant at arms hath already received, are to be allowed the said serjeant, without rendering any account for the same'.[277]

THE GENTLEMAN USHER OF THE BLACK ROD

The gentleman usher of the black rod, along with his assistant, the yeoman usher, fulfilled a role that shared some characteristics with the serjeant at arms of both houses, but also had ceremonial functions that were peculiar to him alone. Although the English origins of the office are to be found in the creation of the order of the garter, where black rod had ceremonial and practical functions, in Ireland his role related solely to parliament.[278] His office was named after the ebony rod topped by a golden lion.[279] Appointment was decided upon by Dublin Castle, sometimes in consultation with Whitehall. They were normally appointed 'during good behaviour'.[280] Being a lucrative office, it was desirable. The position of yeoman usher was in the gift of black rod, although this was disputed in 1646 by Stephen Smith, keeper of the king's robes, cloth of state, and other goods in Dublin Castle, as a perquisite of his own office.[281]

Black rod fulfilled several roles. When the monarch was present in parliament or, as was usually the case in Ireland, his viceroy, black rod attended upon him. The royal presence usually necessitated the calling of the Commons up to the Lords. In such cases, black rod would go to the House of Commons and once he had been admitted to the lower house by the serjeant at arms of the Commons, who escorted him into the house on his right hand side, and after paying obeisance to the House, he would deliver his message that the viceroy required the Commons' attendance in the Lords.[282] When a writ of prorogation was read aloud in the Lords in October 1644, and the lord lieutenant was not present, the Commons' attendance was requested by two judges.[283] There is just a single example of black rod being sent to the Commons as an ordinary messenger when he was instructed to 'move the house of commons, to hasten what bills they had ready for this house'.[284] On only one occasion was there a moment when the gentleman usher of the black rod was shown less than perfect obedience in regard to a summons to the higher house. After waiting some time, the serjeant at arms of the Lords was sent down to know the cause of black rod's delay. He returned to the upper house and reported that 'the clerk of the house of commons came to him at the door, and told him, they were upon very urgent occasions; and that the kingdom would curse him if he did part them so suddenly'. His second attempt received no answer, and it was only his third attempt that elicited a positive response.[285]

The gentleman usher of the black rod also took responsibility for custody of delinquents that appeared before the bar of the upper house, usually for contempt or some breach of privilege.[286] When the serjeant at arms of the House of Lords queried this in 1666, the upper house confirmed that 'black rod do take into his custody all such persons that shall be committed from the bar'.[287] He was also sent to retrieve some prisoners from the grasp of other officers of parliament; for example, when, in July 1666, he was ordered to take custody of Robert and William Barnewall, servants of Lord Kingsland, who had been jailed by the Commons in the course of a dispute between the two houses.[288] Black rod was also, on rare occasions, expected to keep order of the Lords, which sometimes included taking peers into custody.[289] At the end of the spring session of 1641, the gentleman usher of the black rod was 'commanded to accommodate the Ld of Derry and Lord Louther as befitts them'.[290] Also, when Lord Santry was asked to attend the house to answer why presentments of nuisances were made in the King's Bench, black rod was sent to tell him.[291] Black rod also acted, in effect, as doorkeeper, in that he attended on the inside of the House (outside the bar) and admitted only members or permitted members of the public. It was also his responsibility to ensure that the House and its committee rooms were kept tidy and to make sure there was suitable seating for the peers but not for the commons, which caused difficulty on occasion.[292] A committee of the Lords in May 1646, found that

> upon consideration of the duty of the gentleman ushers office, which is to make ready the house of lords with seats and other necessaries, to take order for wood and coal to be brought thither, and to sit in the house in the lower end thereof, close, without the bar, to let in the lords when they come in.[293]

Black rod also had ceremonial functions from which much of his income derived. Along with the Ulster king of arms, black rod accompanied peers when they were being introduced. A committee of the Lords decided in 1634 that fees should be collected on the same basis as in England but in Irish money.[294] Black rod was entitled to, on the introduction of an archbishop or an earl, £4 10s; a viscount, £3 6s; a baron or a bishop, £2 10s; for each proxy introduced, £2 10s. For each attorney permitted to the bar to plead on behalf of a client, black rod was entitled to £1; for each person committed under the degree of baron, £3 6s 8d; and for each private bill passed, £5. The yeoman usher was paid exactly half that of a gentleman usher. In March 1666, the Lords confirmed the fees and gave an additional £7 10s and £5 10s to black rod for the introduction of a duke and marquis respectively, and £3 15s and £2 15s to the yeoman usher for the same ranks.[295]

OTHER OFFICERS

Of the other appointed officers of parliament, both the chaplain and the supervisor of the press were of much less political significance. However, in a study of the machinery of the parliament, they cannot be ignored. John Vesey, who was also an assistant clerk to the clerk of the Commons, was appointed chaplain to the lower house within four days of the opening of parliament.[296] What is interesting about the appointment of Vesey as chaplain was his background, given his father's 'flirtation with Presbyterianism'.[297] Kingston described how the speaker 'ordered [on behalf of the house of commons] an orthodox minister to reade ye Commons prayer every morning'.[298] He was later made bishop of Limerick.

The chaplain's job, to which there is no reference before 1661, was quite straightforward. He was to read prayers every morning to the Commons before any other business was done. On his appointment, he was instructed to 'observe the orders and discipline of the Church of Ireland'.[299] He does not appear much in the sources after this point except when there were discussions over whether to present him with some financial reward. In May 1662, the question was raised as to whether the chaplain should receive £100 for his services to the House. This was one of the rare occasions when the House divided and the motion was rejected by sixty-four to forty-two, probably on grounds of cost rather than issues with conformity.[300] By the end of the parliament, the clerk's report shows that he was listed in the accounts of the money, provided by the act for £23,500 for expenses of parliament, as having received £75.[301]

The Lords appointed John Sterne as a supervisor of the press in 1661. He was a great-nephew of Archbishop Ussher and seems to have been orthodox in both his politics and religion.[302] Educated in both Oxford and Cambridge, he had, however, been a fellow of Trinity College during the interregnum, establishing a separate medical faculty, and was one of the founders of the College of Physicians in 1667.[303] The supervisor of the press had two functions. The first was to print whatever material was requested. In the second week of the first session of the parliament, it was ordered that 'Doctor Sterne be supervisor of the press in all things that shall issue from this house to be printed'.[304] In July of the same session, it was ordered that 'Dr. Sterne [was] to receive £50 for his printing of Bills, Acts and Declarations and be recommended to oversee the printing of what this Parliament issues'.[305] In May 1661, the Lords instructed him to print 2,000 copies of the declaration concerning church government and the book of common prayer.[306] In the same month, he was ordered to print 1,500 copies of an order of both the Commons and the Lords for the burning of the covenant in every market town.[307]

Sterne was not only responsible for printing orders and declarations of the Lords and the parliament as a whole, but also took responsibility for searching out written material considered too dangerous to circulate. On the same day as he was ordered to print the declaration concerning the burning of the covenant, he was commanded to 'search booksellers of the city and bring copies of the Covenant into this House'.[308] He was also told to confiscate copies of the 'Letter Catechism of the Assembly at Westminster'.[309] On the motion of George Baker, the bishop of Waterford, the supervisor of the press was ordered to burn 'a primer, that hath a prayer in it for the Lord Protector' and that 'Dr. Sterne do make a search for it amongst the stationers of the city'.[310] Censorship continued two days later, when the Lords ordered that 'all Bibles printed by the late Usurper's Printer, calling himself "Printer to his highness the Lord Protector" shall have the title page removed ... and this order be directed to Dr. Sterne'.[311] Sterne seems to have continued in this role until the end of parliament, although he is referred to less frequently after the initial burst of activity. In the accounts for payments from the act for £23,500, John

Sterne is, by 31 July 1666, recorded as having been awarded £37, £20 of which was actually paid at that time and £17 in arrears.[312]

The existence and particularly the growth that the body of the nobility underwent in the seventeenth century meant that the work of the Ulster king of arms and his assistant, the Athlone pursuivant at arms, increased.[313] The office was concerned with heraldry and had been in existence in Ireland in various incarnations since the late fourteenth century. It is a direct equivalent of the Norray king of arms in England.[314] The office was important to the aristocracy and, as such, had little to do with sessions in themselves, so the appointments of both Thomas Preston (1633) and Sir Richard St George (1660) just a year before parliaments convened is nothing more than coincidental. In petitioning for the post, Sir Richard St George highlighted his loyalty to the Stuarts and the fact that his father was Sir Henry St George, formerly garter principal king of arms in England.[315]

Most of the time, the functions of the Ulster king of arms in parliament were ceremonial. He is mentioned when a new peer was introduced. Dressed in his ceremonial robes, the Ulster king of arms, along with the gentleman usher of the black rod, would escort a new peer, also in his robes, into the House, escorted by two peers of the same bench.[316] Other than this, the king of arms usually dispensed advice and information on heraldry or precedency when it was called for. For example, in the case of *Folliot, Digby, Blayney, and Esmond v Lord Castle-Stewart* (1634), where the four lords complained and took an action against the placing of Lord Castle-Stewart above them, Albion Leverett, Athlone pursuivant of arms (deputy to Ulster king of arms), was ordered 'to deliver his knowledge in writing, concerning the lord of Castle-Stewart's cause, and that by seven of the clock to-morrow morning'.[317]

The Ulster king of arms received a salary from the state for his general work but was also paid directly through fees in parliament.[318] All of the fees came from introducing peers. The pursuivant at arms was usually paid directly by the king of arms. In Irish money, the Ulster king of arms was awarded the following: on the 'first introduction of a baron into parliament, as well coming by descent as by writ and new creation, in person or by proxy', £2 10s; the same for a bishop that never sat; for a viscount, £3 10s; and for an earl or an archbishop that never sat as an archbishop, £4 10s.[319] A later investigation into the fees for introductions by the Lords confirmed what they had been previously, and recommended they stay the same but with some important changes. Obviously, since 1634, there had been the introduction of a marquis (Ormond in the 1640s and Antrim in the 1660s) and a duke (Ormond again, but only by proxy, he was in London until July 1662) and Tyrconnel in 1689. In March 1666, a committee in the Lords recommended that the king of arms be paid £5 10s for every marquis and £7 10s for a duke (both sterling).[320] Although this addition was no doubt welcomed by the Ulster king of arms, he surely cursed the committee when it ruled that these introductions were henceforth to be paid only on newly created peerages and not by peers who appear by descent. This would obviously have put a severe dent in the income of the king of arms and his subordinate. New creations had slowed down considerably in the second half of the seventeenth century from its heyday between the first two parliaments. Privilege of association was also allowed to the Ulster king of arms and the Athlone pursuivant, as it was to all other servants of the upper and lower houses. When John Bee presented a petition to the House of Commons against Leverett (the Athlone pursuivant of arms) in June 1641, they ordered the actions 'shall be absolutely dismissed this house, notwithstanding any former order made to the contrary, in regard the said Albon [sic] Leverett is an officer attending the lords house'.[321] The case was later, on application to the Lords by the plaintiff, left to the regular courts notwithstanding Leverett's privilege.[322] Sir Richard St George made use of the legal force of the house when he petitioned for the 'books, papers and other ornaments and records ... that concern the office of the house' from Sir Richard Carney, the previous Cromwellian incumbent.[323]

There were also some very junior servants of either house who, although playing only a minor role in the events of parliament in seventeenth century Ireland, deserve some mention. In 1677, a keeper of the parliament house was established in Dublin. For an undefined rent, William Robinson, who was also superintendent general of fortifications and buildings, took possession of the complex of buildings at Chichester House during the intervals when parliament was not sitting. In return, he was obliged to keep the house in a state of repair at his own cost.[324] William Craig, keeper of the speaker's chambers, and Highgate Lone, doorkeeper to the House of Commons, usually show up in the records when petitioning for payment, which seems to indicate that they were not paid as a subordinate of any other officers nor directly through fees. In July 1661, the first time their offices are mentioned in the journals, an order was passed to try and secure them £20 for their service to the House.[325] Three months later, they petitioned the House again, asserting that their warrant for £50 was being ignored by Alderman Bellingham (deputy treasurer of the kingdom): 'he pretending there is no money in the treasury'.[326] Lone and Craige, along with Samuel Price, described as a messenger of the house, petitioned for payment and were successful – Lone to the tune of £30 and £25 for Craige and Price (or more accurately for his wife and children, he having died a few days before the order).[327] Highgate Lone put his payment in jeopardy when Colonel Dillon, an MP, complained that the former had been 'giving notice of attachments or proceedings of this house against some persons, whereby they have kept out the way, and avoided the punishment due to such offenders'.[328] In late July 1666, although the House knew of his indiscretions, the original order for his payment was allowed to stand.[329] The Lords also received several petitions from their doorkeeper and messenger, always desiring payment for their services.[330]

The clerk of the crown and hanaper was a clerk of Chancery, even though parliament occasionally ordered him to draw up writs for elections.[331] However, the journals of the upper house show that the clerk of the crown occasionally appeared in the House and fulfilled certain functions. When the royal assent was being given to bills, the clerk of the crown was sometimes recorded as the individual who, 'rising from the woolsack, goeth to the left side of the house', and who read out the titles of the bills.[332] At the end of the first session of the 1640–48 parliament, the clerk of the crown brought in the engrossed writ for prorogation, and this was sealed by the lord chancellor in the house, and the writ was then read by the clerk of the crown's deputy.[333] In 1662, it was the clerk of the crown who read the writ for Lord Ossory's translation from the Commons to the Lords.[334] Short of reading titles of bills during the assent, and occasionally being involved in some other procedural aspects of parliament's work, he is a shadowy figure. His English counterpart had a similar role in reading the titles of bills at the assent stage. It may be a step too far to include him in a study of the officers of parliament.[335] However, the fact that a petition of the deputy clerk of the crown was read in the House of Lords and referred to the committee considering the 'fees of the officers of the house' might suggest that they had some role worthy of payment at least.[336]

NOTES

1 The only possible exception to this rule is the serious breakdown in the relationship between Wentworth and his lord chancellor, Lord Loftus of Ely, although this was to happen several years after the dissolution of parliament and did not have any negative implications in parliament. Kearney, *Strafford in Ireland*, p. 72.
2 Archbishop Bramhall was selected, although the choice would seem to be very much in keeping with the prevailing opinion in Whitehall and reflective of the wishes of Ormond and Clarendon. Lords justices to Vane, 18 May 1641, *CSPI*; Orrery and Mountrath to Ormond, 30 April 1661, Bodl., Carte MS 31, f. 159; Orrery to Clarendon, 8 May 1661, Bodl., Clarendon MS 74, ff.383–86; *Morrice's memoirs of Roger, first earl of Orrery*, 15 November 1711, National Archives of Ireland, Dublin (hereafter NAI), MS M.2449, f. 234.
3 *The earl of Strafforde's letters and dispatches with an essay towards his life by Sir George Radcliffe*, ed. by W. Knowler (2 vols, London, 1739), vol. 1, pp. 276–92.
4 Smith, *The Stuart parliaments*, p. 79.
5 Jackson, 'A document on the parliament of 1613', pp. 47–58; McCavitt, *Sir Arthur Chichester*; Ó hAnnracháin, 'Imagining political representation'.
6 O'Donoghue, 'Parliament in Ireland under Charles II', p. 256.
7 The criticism of Mervin seems a little unfair, for although it must be acknowledged that his printed speeches of spring 1663 caused discomfort for Ormond

and the government, and possibly danger to the kingdom, he did preside over the provision of a very generous financial settlement. The early biographers of Ormond seem to have pushed a strong anti-Mervin line that has been followed by most subsequent historians. Dennehy, 'The restoration Irish parliament, 1661–6', pp. 56–57, 65–66.

8 Barry was raised to the peerage as baron of Santry in 1661, but for the sake of consistency, throughout this chapter he is referred to as Lord Santry.
9 Orrery to Clarendon, 8 May 1661, Bodl., Clarendon MS 74, ff. 383–86.
10 *LJ Eng.*, 2 May 1621; Foster, *The House of Lords*, p. 28.
11 Orrery and Mountrath to Ormond, 30 April 1661, Bodl., Carte MS 31, f. 159; Orrery to Clarendon, 8 May 1661, Bodl., Clarendon MS 74, ff.383–86; Morrice's memoirs of Roger, first earl of Orrery, 15 November 1711, NAI, MS M.2449, f. 234.
12 Dennehy, 'Speakers in the 17th century Irish parliament'.
13 C.J. Smyth, *Chronicle of the law officers of Ireland* (London, 1839); The king to the lord lieutenant and lord deputy, 7 July 1665, *CSPI*.
14 *LJ*, 15 April 1644.
15 *LJ*, 18 April 1644.
16 *CJ*, 18 April 1644.
17 *LJ*, 14 July 1634.
18 *LJ*, 8 May 1661.
19 *LJ*, 27 February 1641. The lords justices and council to Secretary Vane, 8 March 1641, *CSPI*.
20 The lords justices and council to Secretary Vane, 18 May 1641, *CSPI*. The Lords' journals for the summer 1641 session are missing (possibly purposely) and so we rely on the opinions of the privy councillors.
21 Rule 39. *LJ*, 2 November 1692; NLI, MS 2091. It would probably be more than a stretch of the imagination to link this to the attempt to impeach the lord chancellor, Sir Charles Porter, in 1695. This arrangement had already been provided for in England as early as 1641. Foster, *The House of Lords*, p. 28.
22 Richardson and Sayles, *The Irish Parliament in the middle ages*, pp. 119–36.
23 *Ibid.*, p. 145.
24 Dennehy, 'Privilege, organisation and aristocratic identity', pp. 117–30.
25 *LJ*, 14 July 1634.
26 *LJ*, 2 August 1634. In general, the lord chancellor was part of such committees that attended the lord deputy, but occasionally he was not. For examples, see *LJ*, 30, 31 July 1634.
27 *LJ*, 5 December 1661.
28 *LJ*, 21 March 1662.
29 Rule XIII, 23 July 1634, 30 July 1634.
30 Elton, *The Parliament of England, 1559–1581*, p. 330.
31 *LJ*, 11 November 1634.
32 *LJ*, 28 March 1640. They also confirmed that he should bring his purse carrying the seal of the kingdom with him when he went down to the bar, further emphasising his importance within the constitution. This of course would only work when the lord chancellor was speaker.

33 Kearney, *Strafford in Ireland*, p. 49.
34 In all likelihood, as was the case in England, the throne at the top of the house behind the woolsack was also outside the House of Lords. J. Wells, *The House of Lords: from Saxon wargods to a modern senate* (London, 1997), p. 4.
35 The few occasions when he might speak on a matter were when asked to explain the implications of prospective bills or give some other legal advice in the context of being a senior legal officer of the kingdom.
36 *LJ*, 31 March 1640.
37 For example, see Foster, *The House of Lords*, pp. 32–33.
38 In particular, see Strafford's dispatches in the first volume of *The earl of Strafforde's letters*.
39 *LJ*, 6, 12 April 1644.
40 For example, it would be difficult for business to be dispatched if the speaker suggested the reading of a bill and the clerk did not have the bill to hand to be read aloud. In the same way, a petition was unlikely to be considered if the clerk did not notify the speaker in advance of its existence. In the same regard, these two central figures must also have worked together after each sitting.
41 Particular sent to the king, with his answers thereon, 22 December 1660, *CSPI*.
42 For copy of the writ and instructions to the local officers, see *CJ*, 18 May 1613. Indeed, during the sitting of parliament, the House of Commons frequently ordered that the speaker of the lower house issue a warrant to be sent to the clerk of the crown in Chancery, instructing him to issue writs (which must have been sealed by the lord chancellor) for new elections to replace members or for new members to be voted in the case of double returns. *CJ*, 4 November 1665, 20 March 1640. The same issue does not appear as frequently in the Lords, as writs tended to be issued as a matter of course for the heirs of the deceased. There was one instance where the House decided that the lord chancellor should not issue to the lord bishop of Killala a writ of summons to parliament, the bishop 'being a favourer of the covenant of Scotland, and like … [and] fit to be thrown into the sea in a sack not to see sun, nor enjoy the air'. NLI MS 9607, p. 24.
43 *LJ*, 19 March 1666. He was sometimes referred to as Connell O'Molloy.
44 *LJ*, 25 May 1666.
45 *LJ*, 25 May 1666.
46 *LJ*, 22 January 1666.
47 *LJ*, 16 December 1665.
48 *LJ*, 23 December 1666, 15 January 1666. Although in normal circumstances the lord chief justice would have attended the House as a legal assistant and messenger, Santry had been ennobled at the beginning of the restoration and so sat in his own right as a peer. He appears frequently on committees in the sessions up until the end of 1662, but appears on none after that point with the exception of his appointment to the Committee of Privileges in relation to this case in early 1666.
49 *LJ*, 15, 22, 29 January 1666.
50 *LJ*, 30 November 1644.
51 *CJ*, 24 July 1666.

> *Carolus secudnus dei gratia, Angliae, Scotiae, Franciae, et Hiberniae Rex, fidei defensor, etc. Philippo Carpenter Armigero, servienti ad arma, salutem. Praecipimus tibi, quod habeas coram nobis in presenti parliamento nostro apud Dublin, immediate post visum presentium, corpora Roberti Barnewall et Willielmi Barnewall, servorum praedilecti consanguinei nostri Henrici, vice-comitis Kingsland, unius dominorum praediciti Parliamenti nostri, sub custodia tua, ut dicitur, detenta, quibuscumque nominibus vel additionibus nominum iidem Robertus et Willielmus censeantur: una cum die vel diebus, causa vel causis captionis et detentionis eorundem Roberti et Willielmi, ad faciendum quod per nos in parliamento nostro praedicto consideratum et ordinatum suerit; et hoc nullatenus omittas, et habeas ibi hoc breve. Teste praedilecto et perquam fideli consanguineo et consiliario nostro Jacobo Duce Promodn, Locumtenente nostro Generali et Generali Gubernatore Regni nostri Hiberniae, apud Dublin, decimo septimo die Julii, anno regni nostri decimo octavo.*

52 This is explained in greater detail later in the chapter, when describing the role of the serjeant at arms in the House of Commons – See pp. 140–45.
53 *LJ*, 22 December 1665.
54 *LJ*, 3 March 1641.
55 *CJ*, 16 July 1634.
56 *CJ*, 15 May 1661.
57 Although this may have been organised outside the confines of parliament with no record appearing in the official journals. *CJ*, 25 November 1614, 18 April 1615, 12 May 1615, 21 June 1642.
58 14 & 15 Charles II, Sess. IV, c. XXI. An act for increasing the fee of the seal due to the lord chancellor of Ireland.
59 Barnard, 'Boyle, Michael (1609/10–1702)'.
60 *LJ*, 24 May 1662.
61 Foster, *The House of Lords*, p. 30. For example, in the 1634–35 parliament, no private bills were passed.
62 *LJ*, 24 May 1662.
63 That is, if we take Sheila Lambert's or John Neale's definition that a private bill was one where the clerks could extract fees from a beneficiary. J. Neale, *The Elizabethan House of Commons* (Oxford, 1963), pp. 336–37; S. Lambert, *Bills and acts: legislative procedure in eighteenth century England* (Cambridge, 1971), p. 29.
64 *LJ*, 25 September 1662. The fees were to be paid on the lands of restored innocents and raised upon such lands as were liable to the new quit rents in the following proportion: Leinster, 2 ¾ pence per acre; Munster, 2 pence per acre; Ulster, 1 ¾ pence per acre; Connaught, 1 ¼ pence per acre.
65 *LJ*, 6 August 1666.
66 *LJ*, 1 August 1642.
67 Petition of Dame Dorothy Ryves to the king, 29 March 1661, *CSPI*.
68 She does not seem to have been particularly successful, as she petitioned the House of Lords in Ireland in spring 1663 for their assistance. *LJ*, 26 March 1663.
69 *LJ*, 23 July 1634.

70 There may have been a speaker before this date. Richardson and Sayles, *The Irish Parliament in the middle ages*, pp. 159–60, n. 100.
71 A. Curry, 'Speakers at war in the late 14th and 15th centuries' in P. Seaward (ed.), *Speakers and the speakership: presiding officers and the management of business from the middle ages to the 21st century* (Oxford, 2010), p. 8.
72 Orrery to Ormond, 8 May 1661, BL Add. MS 37,206, f. 20.
73 Davies highlighted all the qualities necessary in the speakership, and insisted that he had none of them, while Eustace 'humbly prayed them to excuse him, and to free him of so great a burthen, alledging his own imperfection for so great an imployment, and humbly prayed the house to make a choice of a more able man for that great service; which his request was not agreed unto, but he was again, by a new and free consent of the house, chosen and called to the chair; but he again, as before, with much modesty and gravity, endeavoured to excuse his weakness for the service, and prayed the house to make choice of another', *CJ*, 16 March 1640; Speech of Davies on becoming Speaker, BL, Lansdowne MS 1208, p. 6.
74 *The earl of Strafforde's letters*, vol. 1, pp. 276–92.
75 A. Hawkyard, 'The Tudor speakers, 1485–1601: Choosing, status, work' in Seaward (ed.), *Speakers and the speakership*, p. 34; NLI, MS 836, f. 38.
76 It is probably no real surprise that the men who became speakers usually were knights of the shire, as this was of greater prestige and more financially lucrative. Davies sat for Fermanagh, Eustace for Kildare, Mervin for Tyrone, and Nagle for Cork. Catelin, the only one not to represent a county, sat for Dublin City, by far the most prominent of the non-shire seats, being a county-borough. For the purposes of elections, this essentially means that Dublin, along with Carrickfergus, Drogheda, Waterford, Galway, Cork, Kilkenny, Limerick, was a small county with a sheriff as returning officer.
77 Mervin, in particular, seemed to enjoy the importance of his role. In 1663 Lord Aungier advised Sir Henry Bennet, the secretary of state for the South, to ingratiate himself with Mevin 'whose humour it is to love courtship especially from men in your place; and I am sure three kind words from you will make him watch the most seasonable opportunities of offering the bill [for Clanmalier's estate, which Bennet coveted] to the house, wherein lies no small art, especially in so populous and factious an assembly'. Aungier to Bennet, 6 May 1663, *CSPI*. For Bennet's work in getting an estate in the midlands, see V. Barbour, *Henry Bennet, earl of Arlington, secretary of state to Charles II* (Washington, 1914); Dennehy, 'Sir Winston Churchill and restoration Ireland' in R. McNamara (ed.), *The Churchills and Ireland: connections and controversies from the 1660s to the 1960s* (Dublin, 2012).
78 *CJ*, 27 July 1666.
79 *CJ*, 18 March 1635.
80 *CJ*, 1 June, 22 October 1640.
81 *CJ*, 12 June 1662.
82 The king to the lords justices, 4 January 1641, *CSPI*.
83 There are a handful of isolated incidents where the speaker was not the individual who addressed the king's representative in Ireland. For example, a committee

of the Commons, led by Sir Thomas Worsopp (MP for Belturbett in Cavan) addressed the duke of Ormond suggesting a one-off payment for Richard Warburton, assistant clerk in the Commons, as compensation for his time and effort in the role.

84 J. Velona, '"The speech of Sir Audley Mervyn", speaker of the Irish House of Commons, demanding reforms in the Court of Claims: a reinterpretation through the lens of legal history' in Dennehy (ed.), *Law and revolution in seventeenth-century Ireland*.
85 Dennehy, 'The restoration Irish parliament, 1661–6', p. 60.
86 *CJ*, 13 February 1663.
87 Greaves, *Deliver us from evil*, p. 146
88 *CJ*, 10 March 1663.
89 *CJ*, 26 June 1661.
90 *CJ*, 17 November 1665.
91 *CJ*, 16 June 1640.
92 *CJ*, 17 June 1640.
93 *CJ*, 9 November 1640.
94 *CJ*, 15 April 1644.
95 *CJ*, 4 August 1641.
96 *CJ*, 20 February 1641.
97 *CJ*, 28 July 1641.
98 By way of example, see *CJ*, 4 November 1634, 20 March 1640, 4 November 1665.
99 *CJ*, 6, 9, 10, 21 October 1640. The boroughs were Newcastle in Dublin, Naas in Kildare, Ardee in Louth, Fore in Westmeath, and Bannow, Taghmon and Clonmines in Wexford.
100 *CJ*, 8 July 1662.
101 *CJ*, 23 July 1661.
102 *CJ*, 5 March 1661. Purging their contempt usually involved kneeling at the bar of the House, acknowledging their crime, and begging the forgiveness of the House and the particular member offended against.
103 *CJ*, 30 January 1641.
104 *CJ*, 22 July 1634.
105 *CJ*, 18 April 1614, 21 March 1640, 17 November 1642.
106 In this case, it seems unlikely. For an explanation of Mervin's involvement with the Covenanters and his subsequent work on behalf of the established church, see Dennehy, 'The restoration Irish parliament, 1661–6'; A. Hart, 'Audley Mervyn: lawyer or politician?' in W.N. Osborough (ed.), *Explorations in law and history* (Dublin, 1995).
107 Indeed, the same question posed of the House of Lords in 1689 is at least as interesting. Again, dominated by the Catholics, the Church of Ireland bishops were summoned, and although most evaded attending, some did, in particular the bishop of Meath, Anthony Dopping, who came closest to being an opposition leader or spokesman. In all other parliaments, prayers in the Lords were led by the most junior bishop attending.
108 *CJ*, 18 February 1641.

109 *CJ*, 15 May 1641.
110 *CJ*, 20 May 1641.
111 *CJ*, 5 August 1641.
112 *CJ*, 25 May, 25 June 1641.
113 *CJ*, 22 June 1642.
114 *CJ*, 17 February 1644.
115 *CJ*, 10 June 1647.
116 *CJ*, 21 February 1663.
117 'Hee was the day before at the Court of Claims and while a difference between him and Sr Audley Mervyn was in hearing before the Com^{rs} his Grace fell in a trance and continued in it never speaking one word till hee dyed'. Lane to Manchester, 27 June 1663, Bodl., Carte MS 49, f. 211.
118 *CJ*, 11 July 1644.
119 For William Gawran's abuse committed against Richard Coman, a servant of Nathaniel Catelin, he was whipped on Fishamble Street. *CJ*, 2 August 1634. On behalf of his servant Anthony Flood, Speaker Eustace had John Sterne (probably the censor for the Lords in the restoration parliament) arrested and jailed for a time for what seems to have been a dispute over probate of a will on the goods of one John Joyce. *CJ*, 24 February 1646. Eustace also claimed parliamentary privilege on his own behalf when one Lieutenant Harman had cattle in Clontarf commandeered for military purposes. *CJ*, 26 May 1647. Mervin, like so many of the members of the Commons in the early 1660s, petitioned the House for his privilege in a dispute over land with John Talbot of Malahide. *CJ*, 20 December 1662.
120 Mervin always had to be one of the quorum of members that attended the king. He was congratulated by the House upon his return for 'his service thereof, and their high esteem of his actings in England in the affairs of this house'. *CJ*, 31 July 1666; 1 May 1662. The MPs that went to London in 1613–14 did not contain the speaker, in the first place because it was not an official agency of the House of Commons and second because the speaker was the effective architect of the situation they were appealing to the king to overturn. McCavitt, *Sir Arthur Chichester*, ch. 10, 11. The second instance of agents being dispatched was formally assented to by the House of Commons, but as Eustace was to be identified with the executive in Dublin Castle, although never in the sights of the parliamentary opposition as others were, this would have made him an unlikely candidate.
121 *CJ*, 11 June 1661.
122 *CJ*, 5 June 1662.
123 *CJ*, 19 February 1666.
124 *CJ*, 3 August 1666.
125 Neale, *The Elizabethan House of Commons*, p. 336.
126 *CJ*, 24 October 1614. Interestingly, in England, the fees were to be paid on the first reading, so if a sessional break was to kill a bill, the beneficiary would have to pay a second time if the bill were to be recommenced in the following session.
127 Petition of Dame Dorothy Ryves to the king, 29 March 1641, *CSPI*.
128 The king to the lord deputy, 7 March 1635, *CSPI*.

129 Lords justices and council to Sir Henry Vane, 23 February 1641, *CSPI*.
130 The king to the lords justices, 30 March 1641, *CSPI*.
131 *CJ*, 11 January 1642, 15 August 1642, 14 June 1647.
132 *CJ*, 1 May 1662.
133 *CJ*, 31 July 1666.
134 Copy of a warrant from Ormond to Anglesey, NAI, Wyche MS 126; *CJ*, 28, 30, 31 July 1666.
135 *CJ*, 30 July 1666.
136 To emphasise the point that judges were servants of parliament, the rules of 1692 stated that 'The Committees are to be attended by such Judges as shall be appointed, who are not to sit there; nor be covered, unless it be out of Favour. For Infirmity, some Judge sometimes has a Stool set behind him, but never covers; the rest never sit or cover.' *LJ*, 2 November 1692.
137 *LJ*, 23 July 1666.
138 P. Brand, 'The birth and early development of a colonial judiciary: the judges of the lordship of Ireland, 1210–1377' in Osborough (ed.), *Explorations in law and history*; G.J. Hand, *English law in Ireland, 1290–1324* (Cambridge, 1967); J. Otway-Ruthven, *A history of medieval Ireland* (London, 1980); Richardson and Sayles, *The administration of Ireland*.
139 Hart, 'The king's serjeants at law in Ireland: a short history' in Osborough (ed.), *Explorations in law and history*, p. 52; *A history of the king's serjeants at law* (Dublin, 2000); 'The king's serjeants at law in Tudor Ireland, 1485–1603' in D. Hogan and W.N. Osborough (eds), *Brehons, serjeants and attorneys: studies in the Irish legal profession* (Dublin, 1990); Richardson and Sayles, *The Irish Parliament in the middle ages*, pp. 164–65.
140 *LJ*, 14 July 1634. Second and third serjeants were appointed in 1627 and 1682 respectively, but these office holders do not appear to have been summoned.
141 As has been mentioned already, the judges had a history in parliament stretching back to its origins, but it was formally verified by an act of 1460. 38 Henry VI, c. XLVII, An act that John Cornewalsh, chief baron of the Exchequer to appear and answer for not attending in parliament is one of the council.
142 *LJ*, 8 December 1634.
143 *LJ*, 25 May 1661.
144 *LJ*, 29 July 1634.
145 *LJ*, 6 December 1634.
146 *LJ*, 16 May 1661.
147 *LJ*, 20, 22 May 1661.
148 *LJ*, 8 May 1661.
149 *LJ*, 11, 14, 30 May 1661. Temple was also released for service in the Commons on the same order. The three masters of Chancery sitting in the commons were permitted to continue by an order of the upper house at the end of May 1661.
150 *CJ*, 9 November 1614.
151 *CJ*, 9 November, 1614, 24 April 1615.
152 *Patentee officers in Ireland*, ed. by Hughes, pp. 122, 135.
153 *CJ*, 30 July 1661.

154 *LJ*, 23 July 1634.
155 *CJ*, 4 November 1614.
156 On only one occasion (in 1644) did a single member of the judiciary undertake the sole responsibility of passing a message to the lower house. Justice Mayart had helped Baron Hilton to deliver messages earlier in the day. There is no reason given as to why to just one judge delivered some messages that day, but the author of the Commons' journal thought it sufficiently important to note that the message was delivered by 'Mr Baron Hilton alone'. *CJ*, 18 April 1644; *LJ*, 18 April 1644.
157 *LJ*, 15 April 1635.
158 14 October 1640. The fact that in both instances it is non-bishops that are summoned, and in the second instance there is mention of the proluctor, the lower house's presiding officer, means the communication must have been with the lower house. 'It is this day ordered, by the lords spiritual and temporal in this present parliament assembled, that Doctor Rives shall attend the house of convocation at their next sitting, and there signify the desire of this house to be, that Mr William Burley and Mr Samuel Clark, both members of that house, who have invaded the priviliges of this house, as is alleged, may attend in this place on Friday morning, to the end the matter may here receive examination.' *LJ*, 8 April 1635. 'Doctor Rives reports, that he delivered his message, according to the lords' directions, to the prolocutor of the convocation house, and that the answer was, that Doctor Coote should have notice to appear at the time and place appointed, whereof if he failed, it should be at his own peril.' *LJ*, 14 October 1640.
159 The only time judges were used in such a situation was in July 1634, when Justice Cressy and Justice Philpot were sent to request the Commons attendance at the bar of the upper house. *LJ*, 28 July 1634.
160 *LJ*, 9 December 1661, 22 January 1662.
161 *LJ*, 23 July 1634.
162 *LJ*, 20 October 1640.
163 *LJ*, 30 July 1634.
164 *LJ*, 15 September 1662.
165 *LJ*, 24 May 1662. On several occasions the restoration parliament made a number of orders of an executive nature, such as ordering the streets of Dublin to be kept clean and the pulling down of the Blind Gate on Dame Street, deemed to be a public nuisance.
166 *LJ*, 1 August 1634.
167 *LJ*, 26 January 1641.
168 A full explanation of the parliamentary and political events of the early 1640s is not within the remit of a book such as this. Excellent accounts can be found in Clarke, *The Old English in Ireland*; McCafferty, 'To follow the late precedents in England'; Ohlmeyer, 'The Irish peers, political power and parliament'.
169 *LJ*, 26 January 1641.
170 *LJ*, 18 February 1641. The phrase 'not backward to hurt any' is not in the printed journals, but is found in NLI MS 9607, p. 81.
171 The full list of the queries can be found in *CJ*, 16 February 1641.

172 *LJ*, 18 February 1641.
173 *LJ*, 22 February 1641.
174 *LJ*, 23 February 1641.
175 *LJ*, 24 February 1641.
176 *LJ*, 1 March 1641.
177 Dennehy, 'Surviving sources for Irish parliamentary history'.
178 *CJ*, 28 May 1641.
179 Although, as in England, the clerk in the upper house was usually called the clerk of parliament, there are several instances when Philip Feneley and Edmond Medhop signed themselves off as 'Cler Parlm', despite being clerks of the lower house. Copy of parliamentary order, 12 February 1641, BL, Egerton, MS 2541, ff. 212, 214; *CJ*, 29 November 1614, 12 December 1662.
180 It is not necessarily the case that there was a clerk of parliament *per se*, but more likely a Chancery clerk who followed the chancellor into parliament. Initially, the clerks were, in all likelihood, clergy – indeed the etymology of both words come from the Greek κληρικός. Clergy employed in Chancery were literate in what was a generally illiterate world, and interestingly the non-clergy *clericus oxoratus* did not emerge until the end of the fourteenth century in England, possibly later in Ireland, and was forbidden up to this point. A.F. Pollard, 'The clerk of the crown', *EHR*, 57 (1942), p. 314; Williams, *The clerical organisation of the House of Commons*, p. 4.
181 Bagwell, *Ireland under the Stuarts*, vol. 1, p. 108.
182 Gilliespie, 'Arthur Chichester', *Dictionary of Irish biography* (hereafter *DIB*). It may be just a coincidence, but the temporary stand-in clerk between Bradley and Medhop, was Matthew Davies, who obviously shared a surname with the speaker and attorney general in 1613. There was also one 'Edward Davis to be one of the Serjeants at Arms to attend the speaker and the services of the House of Commons'. The king to Chichester, 26 September 1612, *CSPI*.
183 *CJ*, 25 November 1614, 18 April 1615.
184 Charles I to chief governor or lords justices, NLI MS 8642:1 [n.p.]; Cronin and Clavin, 'Lane, George', *DIB*.
185 *CJ*, 7 November 1634, 27 May 1661, 31 March 1666.
186 *CJ*, 7 November 1634. Interestingly, his superior in the Commons, Philip Feneley, was to become his superior at the remembrancer office in the Exchequer within two years. *Patentee officers in Ireland*, ed. by Hughes, p. 49.
187 Foster, *The House of Lords*, p. 47.
188 *CJ*, 18 November 1634.
189 *CJ*, 21 July 1634.
190 *CJ*, 19 June 1666.
191 *CJ*, 30 July 1662.
192 *LJ*, 19 October 1640.
193 *LJ*, 17 March 1645.
194 An order of September 1662 would seem to indicate that the printing of all acts and declarations was the responsibility of the king's printer in Dublin. *CJ*, 18 November 1662. These suppositions appear to be confirmed in NLI MS 8008.

195 *The statutes at large.*
196 *CJ*, 7 August 1641.
197 *CJ*, 10 July 1641, 21 June 1641, 2 September 1662; *LJ*, 10 April 1644, 2 June 1662, 17 November 1662, 23 November 1665. In this last instance noted, Sir George Lane was ordered to communicate with the clerk of the upper house in England asking him for information on the fees of officers in the English House of Lords.
198 *CJ*, 18 July 1634; Snow, *Parliament in Elizabethan England.*
199 *LJ*, 22 May 1661.
200 *CJ*, 15 May 1615, 7 December 1661.
201 Churchill to Arlington, 27 December 1665, *CSPI.*
202 *CJ*, 14 December 1642, 28 May 1661, 6 December 1661.
203 Englefield, *The printed records of the parliament of Ireland, 1613–1800*; Foster, *The House of Lords*, pp. 44–63; Williams, *The clerical organisation of the House of Commons*, pp. 190–213.
204 *LJ*, 1 August 1642.
205 *LJ*, 19 December 1662.
206 *CJ*, 15 May 1615, 1 April 1640, 11 January 1642, 20 April 1643, 18 April 1644, 19 June 1661, 2 August 1662.
207 14 & 15 Charles II, Sess. IV, c. XXII.
208 *CJ*, 29 July 1661.
209 *CJ*, 9 April 1663, 31 July 1666. Because this work was paying out to members of the Lords also, his work was audited by the House of Lords towards the end of the final session. *LJ*, 9 November 1665, 13 February 1666, 6 August 1666.
210 Copies of parliamentary order, 12, 14 February 1641, BL, Egerton MS 2541, ff. 212, 214.
211 *CJ*, 13 February 1641, 23 February 1641, 7 August 1641.
212 *CJ*, 28 May 1662.
213 *LJ*, 29 October 1640.
214 *LJ*, 3 March 1641, 21 March 1662, 16 July 1662.
215 *LJ*, 18 July 1634; *CJ*, 17, 18 July 1634.
216 The journals of the Commons in particular have several references to petitions being preferred to the House by the clerk. The lords' house was rarely petitioned by their clerks, and on the rare occasions when it was, the details tend to be sparse. *LJ*, 26 March 1666. When detail is recorded in the Commons' journals regarding the clerks' petitions, it tends to throw up a similar complaint as the most popular among the members: disturbance in his estates. *CJ*, 14 May 1662, 26 May 1662, 19 March 1663, 3 July 1666.
217 English Privy Council to Mr Attorney General, Mr Solicitor General, the chief justice of Ireland, and Sir James Ley, *Acts of the English Privy Council*, 30 September 1613; Lords of the council to Lord Chichester, 13 April 1613, *CSPI.*
218 *CJ*, 14 July 1641.
219 *CJ*, 21 July 1641.
220 *LJ*, 28 November 1634.
221 *LJ*, 10 April, 1635.
222 *LJ*, 15 March 1666.

223 *LJ*, 17 June 1640.
224 *LJ*, 24 May 1662.
225 *LJ*, 22 January 1662.
226 *LJ*, 20, 25 September 1662. The fees were to be paid on the lands of restored innocents and raised upon such lands as were liable to the new quit rents in the following proportion: Leinster, 2 ¾ pence per acre; Munster, 2 pence per acre; Ulster, 1 ¾ pence per acre; Connaught, 1 ¼ pence per acre. This was to be presented to the clerks of both houses, and divided proportionally amongst the other officers and speakers of both houses.
227 *LJ*, 27 July 1666.
228 Although the award to Sir George Lane was for his assistance in London in the negotiations for the Bill of Settlement rather than for any work he might have undertaken (probably none) in the chamber. *LJ*, 18 December 1662. The £300 for Keating is likely to be the same £300 voted to him in January 1662.
229 *CJ*, 3 March 1641.
230 *CJ*, 17 July 1634.
231 *CJ*, 15 June 1640.
232 *CJ*, 5 June 1641.
233 *CJ*, 15 May 1615.
234 *CJ*, 14 December 1634.
235 *CJ*, 26 March 1635, 7 April 1635. The second reminder came with an order for fining those who continued to refuse payment an extra five shillings.
236 *CJ*, 1 April 1640, 25 February 1641. The April 1640 order was followed up by a committee of two MPs to give an account to the House of those who had not yet paid their 'voluntary contribution'. *CJ*, 25 May 1641.
237 *CJ*, 31 March 1647.
238 *CJ*, 7 August 1641. For a very interesting discussion of one of the unforeseen implications of 10 Charles, Sess. III, c. IV, see J.H. Baker, '"United and knit to the imperial crown": an English view of the Anglo-Hibernian constitution in 1670' in D. Greer and N. Dawson (eds), *Mysteries and solutions in Irish legal history* (Dublin, 2001).
239 *CJ*, 17 July 1661.
240 *CJ*, 9 April 1663.
241 In the English Parliament, the serjeant-at-arms in the Commons is usually spelled with hyphens between the words, as distinguished from the House of Lords' serjeant at arms, which is spelled without. This system does not appear to have been used in the Irish Parliament.
242 Docquet of grant of the office of serjeant at arms, 27 June 1660, *CSPI*; Documents relating to the case of Captain Philip Carpenter, 19 November 1660, *CSPI*.
243 E.L. Wolfe, '"Into the custody of the serjeant at arms": inducing parliamentary attendance in Dublin and Westminster, 1690–1859', *Parliaments, estates and representation*, 38 (2018), pp. 205–26.
244 *CJ*, 29 October 1614.
245 *CJ*, 12 November 1634. County Kerry was also the location of a second false election when the same happened in 1661, except this time Blennerhasset was the

eventual beneficiary of the dispute, being declared lawfully elected two months after the first sitting of parliament. *CJ*, 8 July 1661. McGrath, 'Sex, lies, and rigged returns'.
246 *CJ*, 22 August 1662.
247 *CJ*, 19 May 1641.
248 *CJ*, 18 June 1647.
249 *CJ*, 29 November 1662, 5 February 1663. In this instant, the serjeant reported that upon challenging O'Neill to return to custody, he responded that 'I had his bonds, and wished me to sue them if I pleased ... calling me a drunken fellow, knave, and other base language: at last he began to ruffle me, and take hold of my belt near my throat'.
250 *CJ*, 6 December 1634.
251 *CJ*, 5 February 1663.
252 *CJ*, 16 May 1662.
253 *CJ*, 18 November 1645.
254 The occasion was for the inspection of their fees. *CJ*, 28 July 1634.
255 *CJ*, 4 June 1641.
256 This in itself is very interesting, that the serjeant at arms could be spared from his duties in June 1641 at quite possibly the most dramatic time in the history of the Irish Parliament in the early modern period. *CJ*, 10 June 1641.
257 Interestingly, it would appear that the petitioner did not know how the material was offensive when presented – perhaps he was illiterate and the draftsman who drew up the document included manner or meaning that was not intended by the petitioner. *CJ*, 26 November 1614.
258 *CJ*, 15 February 1641.
259 *CJ*, 3 March 1645, 21 May 1647, 22 June 1661, 21, 26 July 1662, 2 August 1662.
260 *CJ*, 1 February 1666. See R.P. Hylton, 'The less favoured refuge: Ireland's non-conformist Huguenots at the turn of the eighteenth century' in K. Herlihy (ed.), *The religion of Irish dissent* (Dublin, 1996), pp. 83–86; C.E.J. Caldicott, H. Gough, and J.P. Pittion (eds), *The Huguenots and Ireland: anatomy of an emigration* (Dublin, 1987); G. Lawless Lee, T*he Huguenot settlements in Ireland* (London, 1936).
261 *CJ*, 10 November 1640, 19 May 1641, 29 July 1641, 7 August 1641, 19 November 1642.
262 *CJ*, 11 June 1641, 5 April 1647.
263 *CJ*, 30 May 1666.
264 *CJ*, 3 March 1641.
265 *CJ*, 14 December 1642.
266 *CJ*, 15 November 1665.
267 *CJ*, 13 December 1665.
268 *CJ*, 19 November 1614.
269 *CJ*, 1 August 1634, 14 December 1634.
270 *CJ*, 2 August 1666.
271 *CJ*, 12 December 1662, 9 April 1663.
272 *CJ*, 20 May 1641. Rice Davis was described as 'a very poor man' and so did not

have to pay the fees for his summons. John Gibson also had a similar description in the journals and received the same treatment. *CJ*, 28 June 1641.
273 *CJ*, 7 June 1641.
274 *CJ*, 7 August 1641. It is not abundantly clear exactly what the nature of the disagreement was, but a committee on 17 July had been asked to look into the 'abuses done by Thomas Dee, deputy serjeant at arms attending this house, for restraining the body of John MacTirlagh Agherin, when the order of this house was shewn by the said Agherin to him, the said Dee, and to make report thereof, with all convenience, what they conceive fit to be done therein'. *CJ*, 17 July 1641. This was not the only occasion that Dee appears to have been over charging, as in June of the same year another order of the house instructed 'that Garrett Birne shall be forthwith discharged from the serjeant attending this house, without paying any fees; and that the three pounds received by Thomas Dee, deputy to the said serjeant, shall be forthwith paid back to the said Garrett Birne by the said serjeant, or his deputy Thomaas Dee'. *CJ*, 22 June 1641. It is also quite possible that the same problem existed in the Lords, as on one occasion, the fees being claimed by George Piggot, serjeant at arms in the Lords, were referred to the clerk of the lords 'to moderate the same'. *CJ*, 19 December 1662.
275 *LJ*, 4 February 1635.
276 *LJ*, 23 May 1666.
277 *LJ*, 14 June 1666, 6 July 1666.
278 Walter Whitehorse was the first gentleman usher of the black rod in England, appointed in 1361, although it is not clear if the office had parliamentary functions this early.
279 Currently on display in the House of Lords chamber in the Bank of Ireland at College Green, along with the lord chancellor's purse.
280 The king to the lords justices for Robert Hall, 7 March 1661, *CSPI*.
281 *LJ*, 2 May 1646. Interestingly, this issue was raised with the lord lieutenant rather than with the House of Lords. Appointments were in the gift of the crown, but once parliament was sitting, it would usually take control of such disputes. Ormond passed it to the lord chancellor and the earl of Roscommon, who investigated the issue, heard witnesses, and read documents pertaining to the case. They found that although the previous two holders of the junior office (Robert Cottrell and James Horncastle) were also keepers of the king's robes, that it was merely coincidental. The House of Lords accepted the report.
282 *CJ*, 31 July 1661, 6 March 1662, 18 June 1666.
283 *CJ*, 31 October 1644.
284 *LJ*, 9 September 1661.
285 *LJ*, 4 June 1644. The Commons' journals recorded the event simply as 'Memorandum. That the gentleman of the black rod came into the house, and desired Mr Speaker and this house to come and attend the lord's house'. *CJ*, 4 June 1644. Robert Hall, in fulfilling his role inside the House but outside the bar as a doorkeeper, did something similar when 'Mr Weaver reported, that he, with divers of the members of this house, repaired to the door of the house of lords, and acquainted the gentleman of the black rod, that they were come to deliver a

message to their lordships from the house of commons, that having staid there near an hour, the black-rod at length came, and called for the lord chancellor's purse-bearer, saying, the house of lords were adjourned; whereupon the said Mr Weaver and the rest of the members thought it their duty to return to this house.' CJ, 26 March 1666.
286 LJ, 25 February 1635, 16 April 1635, 14 June 1640.
287 LJ, 6 July 1666.
288 LJ, 30 July 1666.
289 NLI, MS 2091.
290 NLI MS 9607, p. 128.
291 LJ, 23 December 1665.
292 CJ, 17 June 1666. The gentleman usher of the black rod refused to provide seating for the Commons; traditionally the Lords always sat while the Commons stood. In England, it was normal that black rod also ordered and billed for writing materials and other necessaries for the clerks, although this is not confirmed by any sources as to how the Irish Parliaments' procurements were organised. Foster, *The House of Lords*, pp. 64–65.
293 LJ, 2 May 1646.
294 LJ, 20 November 1634.
295 LJ, 15 March 1666.
296 CJ, 11 May 1663.
297 J. Bergin, 'Vesey, John', *Oxford dictionary of national biography* (hereafter *ODNB*).
298 Kingston to Ormond, 15 May 1661, Bodl., Carte MS 31, f. 183.
299 CJ, 11 May 1663.
300 CJ, 23 May 1662.
301 CJ, 31 July 1666.
302 T.C. Barnard, *Cromwellian Ireland English government and reform in Ireland, 1649–1660* (2nd edn, Oxford, 2000), p. 242.
303 Ibid., p. 242; LJ, 31 May 1661.
304 LJ, 17 May 1661.
305 LJ, 27 July 1661.
306 LJ, 17 May 1661.
307 LJ, 28 May 1661.
308 LJ, 28 May 1661.
309 LJ, 28 May 1661.
310 LJ, 27 July 1661.
311 LJ, 29 July 1661.
312 CJ, 31 July 1666. There is a warrant in the British Library that awards John Stearne £600, but it is not clear whether this is for his work in parliament. BL Add. MS, 11,312, f. 63.'
313 My understanding of the role of the Ulster king of arms and the Athlone pursuivant was greatly increased by discussions with Dr Stuart Kinsella of ChristChurch Cathedral.
314 T.B. Butler, 'The officers of arms in Ireland', *The Irish genealogist*, 2 (1943), pp.

2–12; S. Hood, *Royal roots, republican inheritance: the survival of the office of arms* (Dublin, 2002); M. Noble, *A history of the college of arms and the lives of all the kings, heralds, and pursuivants* (London, 1804); A. Wagner, *Heralds of England: a history of the college of arms* (London, 1967).

315 Petition of Richard St George to the king, 27 June 1660, *CSPI*.
316 Occasionally, if the house was not full, there may not be enough of one bench; such as in February 1645, when Viscount Ranelagh had to be accompanied by Viscount Moore and Lord Lambart. *LJ*, 3 February 1645.
317 *LJ*, 1 August 1634.
318 There were a number of petitions and representations made in the Commons regarding fees of the office, but this is almost certainly a reference to fees collected through his work outside of parliament, because, as the Ulster king of arms was a servant of the House of Lords, it would be a high breach of privilege to have the lower house concerning themselves with his fees for work in the Lords. *CJ*, 21 January 1641, 10 April 1644, 26, 30 March 1647, 5 April 1647.
319 *LJ*, 28 November 1634. The king of arms had been hoping to rate the archbishops as dukes, as they were in England at that time. *LJ*, 20 November 1634.
320 *LJ*, 15 March 1666. In this committee report, as printed in the journals, there is surely an error as it lists a baron's introduction costing £5, which is obviously ridiculously high.
321 *CJ*, 10 June 1641.
322 *LJ*, 3 June 1645.
323 *LJ*, 24 April 1661, 14 May 1661, 30 June 1662. It is quite interesting to see such an office so concerned with rank in society in a republican regime. While we know that the interregnum was not entirely republican, in the sense that the aristocracy still existed throughout the period, it is far more significant that the office, although renamed and modified to some degree, largely continued on in the Irish Free State and Irish republic as the office of the chief herald of Ireland. The first holder of the office was a noted republican, Edward MacLysaght, also a genealogist, who was keeper of manuscripts at the National Library of Ireland and inspector for the Irish Manuscripts Commission.
324 J.T. Gilbert, *An account of the parliament house, Dublin, with notices of parliaments held there* (Dublin, 1896), p. 7.
325 *CJ*, 31 July 1661.
326 *CJ*, 6 November 1661. Bellingham, who later became the first lord mayor of Dublin, was reputed for his meanness with state money. Edward Smythe wrote to Ormond in anticipation of his return to Dublin as a commissioner of the Court of Claims asking that 'some more hospitable person towards strangers than Sr Daniell Bellingham may be appointed to feede & keep us alive ... wee are to live in Ireland without eateing, at all considering, that all the pleasures of this kingdome consists in eateing and drinkeing, and then your grace will conclude it to be the woorst country in Christondome to starve in'. Smythe to Ormond, 14 January 1665, Bodl., Carte MS 34, f. 22.
327 *CJ*, 26 July 1666.
328 *LJ*, 6 April 1666. Carey Dillon must be the 'Dillon' was being referred to. Although

Carey Dillon represented Banahger in King's County and Arthur Dillon sat for Trim in Meath, both are referred to as knights in the list of members. However, early reference to Carey Dillon in the journals always mention him as Colonel Carey Dillon.

329 *CJ*, 28 July 1661.
330 *LJ*, 7 December 1661, 8 December 1662, 11 April 1663, 8 December 1665, 14 April 1666. It could be possible, though unlikely, that the same messenger and doorkeeper served both houses – the names are never mentioned in the record of the Lords.
331 *LJ*, 20 March, 21 October 1640.
332 *LJ*, 12 June 1661, 29 January, 7 August 1666.
333 *LJ*, 18 March 1640.
334 *LJ*, 8 August 1662.
335 Pollard, 'The clerk of the crown', p. 319.
336 *LJ*, 12, 15 March 1666.

5

Privilege, precedent, and self-regulation

THE THEORY AND PRACTICE OF PRIVILEGE

Parliamentary privilege as practised today both in Ireland and elsewhere is based on medieval precedent. In the medieval period, parliament was a representative body of both church and state, attended by all the senior officers of the state. It was the apex of the judicial arm and had all the senior members of the judiciary in attendance. Parliament was an effective conduit of communication between the monarch and his subjects for the presentation and resolution of grievances in return for the provision of financial assistance. If Helli Koenigsberger was correct to state that the emergence of feudalism highlighted the fact that mutual 'loyalty between lord and vassal was the psychological cement of early medieval society', it must be tempered with the advice that the medieval monarch was 'a leader, not a master ... [and] relied on the conscious and willing collaboration of his subjects as the most effective and easiest instrument of success'.[1] Parliaments over the centuries were, for the most part, collaborative and consensual in nature.

Occasionally this theory was actually played out in reality, although the various competing interests of those with a stake in parliament naturally pushed for their own needs to be met first and were sometimes a little more reluctant in giving. Whatever their perspective, all could see the fact that in theory, parliaments were of supreme importance to the state and community. It was with this theory in mind, and being cognisant of the practical benefits that could accrue from successful parliamentary meetings, that parliamentary privilege emerged in the medieval period. While such an important meeting was occurring, no other issues could be allowed to obstruct this work. The idea that individual peers or MPs could have their attention diverted from the important business in parliament because of a civil action for debt or some other minor, local, or personal disagreement was not to be countenanced. As John Selden opined in the later 1620s: 'Priviledge of parliament is to keepe a parliament man free from any disturbance, that he may freely attend the busines of parliament and the kingdom.'[2] This is the basic premise behind parliamentary privilege as it developed and evolved. But what was termed 'privilege' extended far beyond protection from prosecution during parliament time. Generally any breach of the privilege of a member was treated with the same severity as if it had been an attack on the whole house. In the seventeenth century there was no discernible difference in the attitude of a house in dealing with the privileges of one of its members, regardless of the religious, political, ethnic or regional background of that member.

Because the individual houses had by the first half of the seventeenth century (and probably, for the most part, much earlier) assumed full and sole control of assessing exactly what privilege was and how breaches of it were to be judged and punished, privilege could be and was extended to many more areas. Although during the period these were referred to as matters of 'privileges of the house', they are probably better understood as being areas where a house might have a particular and usually sole competence. For the purposes of this chapter, it makes sense to continue that broad use of the word 'privilege'. In reality, these were not privileges *per se*, but particular procedures and processes, based on precedence, and jealously guarded by each house. For example, the House of Commons successfully emphasised their preeminent role in raising finance as a privilege peculiar to them alone within parliament, at least until 1692; whereas the House of Lords consistently insisted that it was their privilege to set the time and location and size of conferences between both houses.[3] Privileges of the constituent houses were not solely seen as a set of procedures to define the relationship between the two, but also to define the relationship between the house and its individual members and finally the relationship between the houses and the wider community, in particular the executive.

In the seventeenth century, there were a number of treatises available about the English parliament as an institution and about its workings, defining at length what privileges were.[4] These accounts are very useful but must be used with caution. First, we do not know to what extent they were circulated in Ireland. There were copies of the *Modus tenendi parliamentum* in Ireland in the medieval and early modern period.[5] Despite the uncertainty over where exactly Hooker's *Orders and usage* were published, his connections with Ireland, the probability that it was written in Ireland, and the fact that the so-called Fitzwilliam edition was dedicated to a sitting lord deputy, can leave us in little doubt that it was available in Dublin throughout the seventeenth century.[6] Elsynge's work, which gets so much attention from historians of the English Parliament, was not published until the restoration despite having being written some forty years earlier.[7] Reference in the usual sources to any of these treatises is scant. There may be an oblique reference to Hooker's *Orders and usage* in the Commons of July 1634 when it was ordered that

> for avoiding of disorder in the proceedings of the house, that the orders and usages of the house be entered with the clerk; and that he shall give copies thereof unto such as desire them, to the end, those, that have not been formerly acquainted with the orders of parliaments, may the better inform themselves, how to demean themselves in the house.[8]

There are no other references to other treatises. Even in the case of the creation of standing orders in the Lords in the opening days of the 1634 parliament, which look as if they were based on the work of Selden, adopted by the English upper house in 1621, no particular mention is made of Selden's work.[9]

This is not to suggest that the peers and commoners that sat in the Irish Parliament in the seventeenth century were not cognisant of how the English parliament worked. In 1634, when staving off the attempt by the Commons to claim some right to try Vincent Gookin, Lord Mountnorris told the Commons that they had no right to judicature or to administer an oath based on 'such scraps as he had gotten from the parliaments of England'.[10] When the baron of Howth had business in the House of Commons in 1615, the Commons discussed whether he should have a stool, a chair, or be made to stand. The example of the earl of Hertford being offered a chair in England was cited.[11] Once lines of communication had opened between the Westminster and Dublin parliaments in 1640, there was information sharing. These are just a few of the many citations of English precedence in Ireland.[12] Indeed in 1662, the speaker of the Commons was ordered to peruse the records of

> the precedents of former parliaments, held either in this kingdom or in England, which concern and relate unto the continuance, orders, or privileges of parliament, and thereout to make a collection of such particulars, and at his conveniency to report the same to the house, which service will be esteemed and accepted of by this house, as of great use and advantage both to them and succeeding parliaments.[13]

Irish precedent was the clear guiding light for Irish MPs and peers in judging breaches. As mentioned elsewhere, both houses created committees of members to supervise entries into the journals and this was used regularly as a source of precedent for privilege cases. Although there were statutes regulating parliamentary privilege, and also theoretical treatises and what could be described as 'English case law', the Irish parliamentarians tended to follow each case, and judge each one on its relative merits. Therefore, it really is only by working across all of the available parliamentary journals and building up a corpus of judgements and statements of privilege, that we can really understand its nature in seventeenth-century Ireland.

One major respect in which Irish parliamentary privilege was quite different from England was that it had a statutory basis from 1463/4 which confirmed common-law provisions:

> At the request of the commons, where the privilege of every parliament, and great council of this land of Ireland, is, That no minister of the said parliament, coming or going to the said parliament, during forty days before, and forty days after the said parliament finished, should not be empleaded, vexed, nor troubled by no mean ... And further, it be also enacted and established, that every minister, as well lords, proctors, as commons, be discharged and quitted of all manner actions had or moved against them, or any of them, during the time aforesaid, and this to endure for ever.[14]

The implications of this act are immediately apparent. First of all, in its very first proviso the act confirms that the tradition of parliamentary privilege providing for the protection of members of parliament from any sort of molestation, legal or otherwise, was in existence before 1463/4. The first section of the act simply confirms the forty-day rule before the beginning and after the end of parliament. The second section extends privilege by allowing for any legal actions taken against an MP or peer during parliament-time to be killed off permanently, although this aspect of privilege was legislated against in 1635.[15] Therefore, if an action were brought against an MP for payment of debt during a parliament, for example, not only would the action not be allowed while parliament was sitting, but it would effectively obliterate the debt altogether. It is unsurprising, therefore, that such privilege became so unpopular in later years. Eight years later an act of parliament further explained the original act, including servants of MPs and peers within the remit of parliamentary privilege.[16]

Many early modern Irish members seem to have been aware of the provisions of these fifteenth-century acts. The Lords did not discuss the acts by name but were certainly cognisant of them. The Commons did make several references to the acts by name. In 1614, the House resolved that the forty-day rule extended to not only before parliament sat and after its conclusion, but also included the full period of time of its prorogations and adjournments.[17] Interestingly, the same issue was discussed in the Lords in the following parliament. Lord Lowther, one of the judges, 'by direction of the house, declares the law to be, that the privilege is to continue forty days before and after the parliament begun and ended, if it be continued by adjournments; but, in case of prorogation, it continues only forty days before and after each session'.[18] Both of these judgements are based on the same statute; but because each house had control of adjudging the limitations (if any) of their privileges, they could directly contradict each other and yet both variations could stand as good law. The forty-day provision was a statement of when parliament time began and ended and did not originate in Ireland when 3 Edward IV, c. I was promulgated. As was traditional, the writs of summons to peers and the writs for election sent to the sheriffs and urban officers should have been sent out at least forty days in advance of the parliament convening.[19] Although it was somewhat archaic by the seventeenth century, the period of forty days was to account for travel from all corners of the island to the place of sitting. There are several other occasions when the specific statute was mentioned, such as in 1640 when the forty-day rule was again discussed in relation to the case of the arrest of John Johnson outside of the sitting days, and also when considering the election of John Fitzgerald while there was a judgement against him in the Castle Chamber.[20] Again, the Commons referred, later in the same parliament, to 'tertio Edwardi Quarti, capite primo' and reiterated that privilege stood 'as well during the time of every adjournment and prorogation, as during the time of every session of parliament ... [and confirmed] that they are the sole judges of their privileges.'[21]

The issue of being sole judge of privilege crops up regularly in the journals of both houses. The Commons generally held firm to it throughout the seventeenth century. They also made a convincing argument at a conference between both houses regarding the issue of sole jurisdiction over cases of privileges of the Commons in March 1645.[22] Aside from this, there are really only a handful of specific incidents where the right to parliamentary privilege was questioned or the method of dealing with breaches was irregular. In the first instance, the special case of the Court of Claims in its second (1662–63) and its third (1666–69) incarnations allowed for successful claims against MPs' and peers' estates as part of the overall restoration settlement, where an 'innocent' claimant could have a warrant issued by the Court to the sheriff for possession of an estate, which would in normal circumstances have been deemed a breach of parliamentary privilege.[23] The issues of a sole right to judicature of parliamentary privileges were not pushed to their full extent in times of war; for example, when there were questions over the cessing of MPs and the billeting of soldiers in their homes. During peace time in the 1660s, the Commons moved swiftly against any who attempted to billet soldiers on members.[24] During the later 1640s, the Commons made an application to the lord lieutenant to show restraint rather than making an order against billeting.[25] It must be stated that this was not a formal abdication of the privilege of MPs but instead a recognition of circumstances and the murky middle ground between the rights of parliament and martial law. Perhaps in the same regard, the Commons appear to have done nothing about the complaint by one of their members, William Plunkett, 'that musquetiers are now in his house, and laid on by the command of the right honourable the lord Lambert', the military governor of Dublin.[26] And finally, the other instance when the Commons held back on occasion from demanding sole judicature was when there were breaches of privilege by a member of one house against a member of the other. Naturally, these disagreements could be highly problematic as, in theory, both houses had equal privileges and both could legitimately claim to exercise the sole right to manage these. Breakdowns in relationships could have a detrimental effect on the business, and so only occasionally would the Commons be insistent and force an issue.[27]

The Lords were not as emphatic or loud on their right to sole judicature of their privileges, but held it as a principle none the less. One of the reasons why this may be so is that privilege may have sat more comfortably with the peers.[28] With regards to a formal proclamation shunning the interference of any body or persons other than the House of Lords itself, the peers inserted a rule in their 1692 codex (outside the time of this book, but almost certainly a codification of previous customs and rules) explicitly stating that:

> Lords *not to answer* Accusations *in the* House of Commons
> No Lord shall either go down to the House of Commons, or send his Answer by Writing, nor appear by counsel to answer any Accusation there, upon penalty of being committed to the Black-Rod, or the Castle of *Dublin*, during the Pleasure of the House; it being the Privilege of the Lords, to answer Accusations in their own House.[29]

There were several exceptions to this general rule in the 1613–15 parliament, where several peers attended the House of Commons on matters of privilege. In October 1614, the bishop of Waterford and Lismore successfully petitioned the Commons to have counsel address the House on his behalf in regard to a bill then before them for restoration of the temporalities of the diocese to the bishop.[30] The following month, the bishop of Dromore had a petition entered into the House of Commons, probably relating to the drafting and presentation of a new bill (a previous one having failed earlier in the month), for the restitution of the possessions of the bishopric.[31] Neither of these two cases could be deemed to be privilege cases, as both were concerned with legislation and prospective legislation before or to be put before the House, but the idea that a member of the upper house would petition the lower house while sitting in the upper house was irregular and was not repeated later in the century. Indeed, it may not be an exaggeration to suggest that it would have been deemed a breach of privilege against the House of Lords in general to have the lower house even accept a petition of members of the upper house.

The following year, members of the Lords directly appealed to the lower house on matters of individual privilege on three occasions. In April 1615, Thomas Jones, archbishop of Dublin and lord chancellor, submitted a petition to the Commons complaining against Paul Sherlock MP for the city of Waterford.[32] In the petition, the lord chancellor accused Sherlock of attempting to corrupt the lord chancellor with 40 angels in overturning an earlier judgement regarding ownership of 50 acres in Waterford.[33]

He also 'scandalously' accused him, in a complaint to the privy council of England, of failing to allow his counsel in Chancery to be fully heard at the initial hearing.[34] The petition asked for some unspecified satisfaction. The Commons agreed to hear the case, and a committee (to whom Jones appears to have submitted both oral and written evidence) reported some days later in his favour.[35] The Commons agreed entirely with their committee, and had Sherlock suspended from the House, confined to Dublin Castle, and fined 40 gold angels.[36] Finally, the House insisted that Sherlock go to Chancery and acknowledge his crime on his knees and beg the lord chancellor's pardon, upon which being done 'his lordship, being sorry, that he should plunge himself into a world of troubles, with tears in his eyes, freely forgave him, and returned many thanks to the house, but desired the house to set down such order, that the lords in England be certfyed thereof'.[37] Most interestingly in this case, in the original petition presented to the Commons by the lord chancellor, he refers to the House of Commons as 'this high and honourable court of justice': standard words for any normal petitioner to the Commons, and while just the usual courtesy, it had added resonance coming from the then speaker of the Lords.[38]

Two other cases in the same session saw complaints of members of the upper house presented in the Commons. In April 1615, the baron of Howth preferred a petition to the commons against Thomas Lutterell, MP for the shire of Dublin, claiming that the latter had proceeded against him before the lord deputy in a disagreement over a portion of marriage goods, but at the hearing had stated that 'your petitioner was so insolent, that he cared not what to affirm to say'.[39] Howth gave evidence orally in a meeting of a grand committee of the house (being seated in 'the chief place', presumably the speaker's chair, it being held in the commons' chamber), but his case foundered for lack of evidence, the witnesses he called (all members of the Commons) failed to acknowledge hearing the statement.[40] And finally, the very elderly Miler Magrath (c. 93 years old), archbishop of Cashel, petitioned directly to the Commons, complaining against Gerald Nugent, knight of the shire for Leitrim. Nugent had apparently openly accused Magrath's son, James, as being a 'base priests chit, and a scald priests son'. Nugent rejected the claim, insisting that he had called him 'a paltry fryar's son' before collapsing in the chamber and falling 'down into a trance, his senses being for a season taken away, being troubled with the falling-sickness'.[41] The Commons found in favour of the archbishop of Cashel, but the censorship recommended against Nugent was put off as 'being now come to this sense again, might fall into the same sickness, whereby his life might be endangered'.[42]

As there are no extant Lords' journals for 1613–15 we are left with a one-sided story, making it difficult to ascertain exactly what was going on. The Commons had no difficulty in having the petitions read in the lower house and there is no mention of the situation being extraordinary. As there are no journals for the preceding parliaments either, it is impossible to say whether this happened in the sixteenth century. The types of petitions do not inform us any better. The petitions of the bishops of Waterford and Lismore and of Dromore dealt with church lands, but the situation does beg the question as to why they could not have dealt with this in the upper house. In the case of the three petitions of the lord chancellor, Howth and Cashel, they dealt with an action and with opprobrious words; to move unilaterally against a member of the Commons would indeed have been a breach of the privileges of the MP and indeed of the Commons in general, but for the member of the upper house to beg for justice from the lower house and to put the Commons in total control of the process seems to be an affront against the collective privilege of the Lords.[43] Certainly this is how it would have been seen later in the century. It can be argued that the Lords involved in these instances were asserting their dominance by insisting the Commons take collective responsibility for errant members. As mentioned above, a later rule of the Lords explicitly forbade the behaviour that seemed unexceptionable in 1614 and 1615.[44] It was not all one-way traffic: in 1661, Archibald Stewart, MP for Tallow in Waterford, got an order from the House of Lords to suppress the collection of rents in Carey and Rathlin Island in Antrim, against Dr Ralph Kinge, MP for Rathoath in Meath.[45] To this, the Commons insisted that Stewart 'being a member of this house, ought not to have made application to the house of lords in a case, wherein another member of this house was concerned, but should, if there had been any cause or reason for the same, have acquainted this house with his complaint, and have abided their order and pleasure'. They also sent a message to the Lords 'desiring' that they rescind any orders they had made relating to Kinge and his business in Antrim 'that so the privileges of this house in general, and of their said member in particular, may be preserved free and inviolable'.[46] Interestingly, the message by the Commons is not recorded but the Lords renewed their original order in favour of Stewart later in the month.[47]

The fact that four of these five 1613–15 petitions were made by spiritual lords is probably coincidence. Admittedly, the occupants of the spiritual benches were not aristocrats and did not have the same access to aristocratic privilege outside of parliament, but when parliament was sitting they were almost indistinguishable from the temporal lords as far as claiming and having their privileged status as being lords of parliament confirmed was concerned. This matter came up in the Lords as a question raised by the archbishop of Tuam in November 1634, when the house confirmed that the bishops had the same privileges as temporal lords.[48] The only caveat to this was the right of the bishops to abstain from 'trials concerning matter of blood' – capital trials.[49] This was confirmed by the judges during the preliminary hearings of the impeachment trial in 1641, but they also allowed for spiritual lords to waive their privilege if they so wished.

Indeed, this brings us onto the case of Bishop Atherton of Waterford in 1640.[50] An important cog in Wentworth's 'thorough machine', Atherton had, by his own admission, spent far more time in his law business than conducting his spiritual responsibilities.[51] In particular he had gained the enmity of the earl of Cork by vigorously pursuing the interests of the state church at the expense of Cork. He had been arrested for allegedly having sodomised John Child, one of his servants.[52] He was tried by jury in King's Bench in November 1640 and executed on 5 December in Dublin.[53] The trial, if not inherently political, must have been touched by political developments. It always seems strange that Atherton accepted a jury trial in King's Bench. Parliamentary privilege did not extend to treasons and felonies, and despite the fact that there was not much in the way of precedent for a bishop to be tried for sodomy, the trial took place in a jury court. It is likely that Atherton could have demanded the right to be tried by his peers (if this was a right of bishops) or in the Court of High Commission or other of the ecclesiastical courts, where he most probably would have gotten a more sympathetic hearing, or at least the rules on evidence and procedures could have been used to his advantage – unlike the Court of King's Bench, where he was denied legal aid.[54] Having said that, Castlehaven, tried and convicted on the same charge, although convicted by his peers, was not afforded much in the way of access to legal counsel either.[55] In any case, Atherton was never going to be acquitted once his friends in both church and state had abandoned him, and his failure to take the charges seriously in the summer and autumn of 1640 sealed his fate. Again, even with the manner of his execution, one would imagine that beheading would have be preferable to hanging, for although certainly not an aristocrat, the fact that he was never degraded from his episcopal appointment meant Atherton was a lord of parliament at the time of his execution.[56] Despite some commonly held beliefs, Atherton was not a lord of parliament at the time the buggery act was passed in the Dublin parliament and so was not the first victim of his own legislation.[57]

INDIVIDUAL PRIVILEGE

So what exactly was privilege as it developed in the seventeenth century? It makes sense to look at privilege in two segments: privilege of the individual and collective privilege. This is only for ease of understanding, as there is nothing to suggest that those who sat in parliament saw the issue in such compartmentalised ways.[58]

The privilege and protection acts of 1463 and 1471 respectively do not clearly identify what exactly parliamentary privilege should be. In short, MPs and peers of parliament should 'not be empleaded, vexed, nor troubled by no mean' and a similar privilege was extended to their servants, based on the same principle that any trouble to one attending parliament would in effect retard its business – a disservice to the kingdom.[59] This privilege was to extend forty days either side of parliament. Considering the deficiencies in both the statements by the houses themselves and also in the parliamentary manuals mentioned above, it is best to look at how parliament conducted its system of privilege to fully understand what it meant.

We may start with the example provided in the two fifteenth-century acts; that is, an action being brought against a member during parliament-time. In November 1614, Robert Blennerhasset (MP for Tralee) complained to the Commons that he had a subpoena issued against him in the 'star chamber' and the House ruled it a breach of privilege.[60] The issue was revived ten days later and the House ordered that the attorney, Samuel Raymont, and one Gray be arrested and brought before the House.[61] The following day the case came before the Commons. A learned argument ensued as to whether an attorney, acting on a client's behalf in breaching parliamentary privilege should be punishable, and a precedent emerged that both the attorney and the principal should be punished, but not the counsel.[62] Therefore, Raymont, despite his protestations of ignorance as to Blennerhasset's membership of the Commons, was punished by having to stay in prison until 2 that afternoon. In November 1614, the House of Commons ruled that it was a breach of privileges to have an MP impanelled on a jury, if, in advance of being sworn, he made his membership known to the sheriff.[63]

Breach of privilege in relation to property both real and personal was the most frequent type to come before either house. In the restoration parliament these complaints were heard almost daily. The case of Sir Paul Davys, secretary of state for Ireland, makes a good example. He complained in the Commons that his privilege had been disturbed in his property in Saggart, West Dublin. On 8 May 1661 (the first day of parliament), William Den had warned his tenants not to pay their rents to Davys, despite the fact that he had been in possession since before the restoration. In mid-July, he forcibly entered and mowed several acres of hay on the property and threatened to kill anyone that opposed him. A week later, John Den harassed the tenants and demanded eight sheaves of corn. All of this was verified by one John Birne.[64] An order for attachment was issued to the serjeant at arms to bring both culprits before the bar. Within a week, John Den was brought in and

> being upon his knees, the serjeant standing by him within the bar, with the mace upon his shoulder, had his accusations read unto him; whereupon he submitted himself to the mercy of the house, expressing sorrow for his fault, and that it was committed through ignorance, and, after a reproof was given him by the speaker for his said crime, he was appointed to withdraw.[65]

Afterwards, both he and William Den were ordered released on payment of their fees.

Similar breaches could and regularly did occur against the privilege of individual peers and bishops. In April 1635, James Ussher, archbishop of Armagh, complained in the Lords that entry to a house named the White Hart on Merchant's Quay in Dublin, which he had leased for the previous nineteen years, had been blocked by the owner, John Morton. Morton was brought to the bar of the House, where he blamed the erection of a door in the passageway leading to the house on his wife. He also maintained he was owed rent on the property and had petitioned the archbishop for it.[66] The House dismissed the excuse, ordered the obstruction dismantled, and jailed Morton with the serjeant until the following day when he petitioned for release and submitted his apology.[67] In 1665, Valentine Savage, deputy clerk of the crown in the King's Bench, drew the wrath of the peers for issuing writs against a number of them on presentments made in a case of nuisance.[68] The House found

> the said presentments and process are adjudged to be erroneous, and contrary to the right of the peers, and that privilege due to them, whilst they attend the great affairs of the kingdom: To the end therefore that no memory of the same may remain, but the just judgment of this house, in dislike and censure thereof.[69]

It is obvious that it was difficult to extract payment or debt from a member or a peer of parliament if they were reluctant to engage. Tackling them inevitably drew cries of 'privilege', and because the two houses were judges of their own privilege, unilateral attempts inevitably ended in failure. The most successful way to deal with such a problem was to apply directly to the house in question and present, usually by petition, a case for rescinding a member's privilege. When one Francis Morton (possibly a relation of John above) 'petitioned ag[t] the Earle of Thomond for distraining of his goods desireing Liberty to Sue a replevin on security which was thought fitt' it worked.[70] As each parliament wore on, especially longer ones, the houses tended to be more sympathetic to such applications.

As emphasised by the explanatory act of 1471, servants of the members were also protected by parliamentary privilege. Although again the wording of this act, like the earlier one, is a little vague, it effectively gave servants of members of both houses more or less the same rights as their masters.[71] In October 1614, Sir Francis Ruish, MP for King's County, reported to the house that Thomas Gibbes, his servant, had been arrested on what appears to have been a debt recovery action by John Carey. The Commons immediately issued a warrant 'for the privilege of Thomas Gibbes' and instructed the serjeant at arms to arrest the serjeant or officer that had acted on the creditor's behalf and have him incarcerated in the castle until he petitioned the Commons for his release.[72] Carey 'and his man' were brought to the bar of the House four days later where they acknowledged their error and Gibbes was awarded £10 in damages.[73] In November 1634, James Rome and his assistant, John Rourke, were sent for by the Commons 'for their contempt, in serving a subpoena upon William Kelly, servant to a member [unknown] of this house'.[74] A week later, 'Teige O Higgins, esq., now or late high sheriff of the county of Sligo, shall be sent for by the serjeant at arms of this house, to make answer for his contempts, in arresting and imprisoning a servant to a member of this house'.[75] William Crips, owner of the Three Tuns tavern in Dublin, his wife and servants were sent for by the serjeant at arms to answer for their 'contempt done to the a servant of one of the members of this house'.[76]

The Lords were equally vigorous in defence of their servants. In February 1635, Richard Thorpe, clerk and chaplain to the earl of Meath, complained that he was arrested at the suit of Bernard Stratford on execution of an action of debt.[77] Upon examination, the Lords accepted that Thorpe had identified himself as protected and had since paid the debt, so they committed Stratford and also William Thimbleby and Marcus Clarke, respectively sub-sheriff of Dublin City and bailiff, to custody.[78] Stratford and Thimbleby were released on apology, but Clarke had to pay costs of 13 shillings and 4 pence to Thorpe.[79] On petition by the earl of Clanrickard, John Cooper, William Hobbs, Thomas Daniel, and George Davys were called before the Committee of Privileges for disturbing the earl in his possession of the ferry at Portumna and for beating his servant.[80]

Just as the Commons and Lords regularly asserted their personal parliamentary privileges and their right to protect servants, the crown also exercised parliamentary privilege. In England, protection was given to the servants of the king during parliament-time. This had been accepted practice since at least Henry VIII's reign, and was confirmed on several occasions under Elizabeth and James I. Even after fighting in the English civil wars had begun, several royal servants and the families of such servants had parliamentary privilege extended to them up until 1644.[81] It is difficult to ascertain to what extent this operated in Ireland. In England it was usually just personal and household servants, including chaplains, who were included. All state, judicial, and military officers were obviously servants of the king in the broad sense, but not in any way that they could claim a protection. However, the person of the monarch was rarely in Ireland during parliament time, and so a lord lieutenant, lord deputy or lords justices fulfilled his role. For example, when giving the royal assent, Chichester, Ormond, and Wentworth sat on the throne. The tantalising question is whether such individuals were entitled to parliamentary privilege. The answer is difficult to ascertain, as all of these figures, with the exception of Wentworth, were either members of the Commons or the Lords, although their membership appears to have been, in effect, suspended while they were viceroys. Orrery and Mountrath, for example, did not appoint proxies while they were lord justices in the early 1660s. There is one hint in the Lords' journals where Borlase appears to have used parliamentary privilege in his capacity as a lord justice:

> Upon reading of the petition of William, earl of Meath, desiring liberty to proceed in a real action against Robert Dixon, clerk, for the right of presentation of St Catherine's church, Dublin: Forasmuch as it appears, that the said Dixon is chaplain to the lord justice Borlace, and therefore privileged: It is ordered by the lords, that the lord viscount Baltinglass and the lord Lambart shall forthwith repair to the said lord justice, and acquaint his lordship that this house thought fit to give way to the petitioner's request, without acquainting his lordship therewith, who (they doubt not) will think it reasonable that the said action do proceed, the said Dixon's person thereby not being touched.[82]

Despite there being no specific mention of Borlase's privilege as the representative of the monarch, neither is there any mention of him being an MP (although he had not sat as one for the previous eighteen months) or application or reference to applying through the Commons as would normally be the case when the Lords approached an MP about waiving his privilege. Borlase reacted to the request suggesting that as Dixon was in England, it would be wrong to remove his protection, but at a later meeting of the Lords Committee of Privileges, the Committee recommended that if Dixon did not attend a hearing that his protection should be considered void.[83]

Officers and servants of both houses were also privileged. Speakers of the lower house were always members in their own right. In the Lords there was a mix of speakers who were members on the basis of being peers (Viscount Loftus of Ely) and archbishops (Jones, Bramhall, and Boyle), but Bolton, Ryves, and Eustace were not, the latter having been offered his family's ancient title of Portlester but after excessive dithering turned it down.[84] In any matter, no distinction was made as all officers of the House were privileged and protected. In many cases, their privilege was more justified as their work was essential to the running of the House. In May 1645, the House of Lords continued to uphold the protection made by the lord chief justice of the King's Bench to a butcher, one Richard Styles. It had been questioned by Henry and Frances Vynch [sic] and also by Frances Parker. Upon an affidavit by the chief justice's clerk saying that he was too infirm to attend the House to answer the petitions, the Lords upheld the protection until at least the first day of the next session.[85] In midsummer 1662, black rod successfully petitioned the upper house to have the soldiers he had billeted on him taken out of his home.[86] The Commons produced similar protections for their officers and servants. Philip Ferneley, clerk in three separate parliaments (1634–35, 1640–48, 1661–66) presented a petition to complain of the 'breaking the privileges of parliament' in being dispossessed of lands in Ballybane, Angerstowne in Dublin, and a house and lands in Milltown, also in Dublin by Nicholas Pasmore.[87] Without delay or committal, the Commons immediately ordered the sheriff of Dublin to restore Ferneley to all lands and also to summon Pasmore to answer for his transgressions.[88]

Obviously, this system for privilege and protections was open to abuse both by members and those associated with them. 'An act for new executions to be sued against any which hereafter shall be delivered out of execution, by privilidge of parliament' did not reduce parliamentary privilege during parliament-time *per se*, it simply allowed for resumption or initiation of an execution after the conclusion of parliament, in a case where privilege had been successfully claimed by the defendant either as a member or as a protected individual associated with a member.[89] Interestingly, this first dent in the system came during the shorter parliaments, and certainly in the years before this they had usually lasted just a few months.[90] An altercation between Laurence Lambert and Thomas Johnson MP shows how sittings might seem long to those outside the houses. Lambert was accused of pulling Johnson's hair and declaring his Welsh nationality to be of less worth than some men he had hanged, but he was also indicted for asking aloud 'Would this parliament never be at an end?'[91] Clearly having so many privileged and protected persons in a relatively small city must have caused friction over a long parliament. Why did the Irish Parliament legislate to remove some of these privileges if there appeared to be no great outcry against them before 1635? It is likely is that this act was brought in as part of Wentworth's programme of reform in the 1635 parliament. It may have been part of a thrust to make parliament a more pliable institution, but it is more likely that extensive and creeping privilege was to the detriment of commerce and trade. It is also likely that it was an effort to bring Irish privileges into line with practice in England where there had been an identical act since 1604.[92] It is difficult to gauge to what extent this made any real difference to privileges.[93] The bill certainly passed through both houses with remarkable ease.[94]

Although there may not be much evidence for discontent with privilege and protection in the two earlier parliaments in seventeenth-century Ireland, it certainly seems to have emerged in the 1640s and 1660s. The first order against protections was made in April 1643. A series of messages between Lords and Commons produced orders made in both houses concurrently, which if not identical in word were in substance.[95] The initial order made by both houses highlighted the damage done to the subjects of the kingdom by the multiplicity of protections issued by members of both houses, to the effect that individuals well able to pay debts were avoiding their responsibilities. All protections granted by members who had been out of the kingdom for the previous six months were immediately cancelled.[96] All protections granted to any persons 'other than waged, menial, or necessary attending servants, really employed' were to be made void in cases where they were outside the remit of what was thought appropriate following the order. The protector also had to pay costs and damages to the injured party. Finally, all future protections had to be registered with the respective clerks within ten days of being given. This order was to last for the lifetime of the 1640s parliament, but it did not solve the problem. Within a year, both houses were again communicating on the issue of the damage that protections were doing.[97] This was followed eight months later by what was in its context an extraordinary meeting of the speaker of the lower house along with the lord chancellor and lord lieutenant, at which all agreed that the numbers of protections were harmful.[98] In February 1646, again the Lords and the Commons tackled the issue together, declaring that any persons entitled to protection but who failed to plead it until after a judgement was given, or indeed anyone who procured one after a judgement was given, was not to have benefit.[99] There is no evidence as to how many persons were protected either in general or protected by a specific member, but an example of a peer being censured in the eighteenth century highlighted that the earl of Roscommon had protected as many as eighty-four unqualified individuals at a given time (and the rules were tighter in 1721) and had 'obstructed the cause of Justice, prostituted the Honour of the House and deserves the Censure of the House'.[100]

Within a few months of the opening of parliament in 1661, the Commons voted to make all protections void except those that were made to 'menial servants and necessary attendants'.[101] The upper house did not go quite as far as the Commons would have liked, but insisted that as the 'abuse of protections is a great hindrance to trade', all protections must be first registered with the clerk before they had any legal force.[102] Within just a month, though, both houses had to revisit the issue.[103] The Lords moved in autumn of 1662 that no protections were to be allowed that hindered members of either house from distraining for their rents. They also declared that no privilege whatsoever was to be allowed that would hinder or disrupt the king from recovering rents or debts from MPs or peers.[104] In spring 1663, both houses repeated the earlier orders, defining servants further as 'a menial servant ... who serves his lord in his family, or receives yearly wages from him for service abroad'.[105] What is glaringly obvious from this series of almost identical orders is that peers and MPs were breaking their own rules. In early 1666, the Commons unilaterally moved to restrict each MP to three protectees, all menial servants, and promised the 'displeasure and heavy censure of the house' for those who flouted the directive. Significantly, the order was to be publicly advertised.[106] On 12 April 1666, after negotiations between both houses, they jointly agreed to suspend all personal privileges (including protections) for a total of two years from 17 May 1666.[107] As parliament dissolved on 7 August 1666, privilege expired entirely on 16 September 1666 anyway, but this was quite a move and must surely indicate the extent to which privilege, and protections in particular, had become odious. A request for a bill to confirm this order was sent to the Castle, in accordance with Poynings' Law. When it returned, although the Commons passed it without any difficulty, the Lords threw it out after its third reading.[108] It is not clear what the issue was, and it is a little strange for the Lords to have given it three readings, a hearing at a grand committee, and then to vote it down. It may have been rejected because there had been a serious disagreement between both houses and the Lords felt that they had been slighted. As the general order made by both houses in April still stood until the end of the parliament, it was perhaps a way for the Lords to register their displeasure without any material changes to the situation regarding privilege and protections.

No evidence has surfaced to show that individual MPs or lords were selling protections, but considering what seems to have been a plague of protections and the number of peers and MPs entitled to issue them, it would be naïve to not consider the possibility. There certainly was a counterfeiting trade in Dublin as there was in England. Elizabeth Read Foster asserts that it was both lucrative and thriving, taking in anything between 40s and £6 a protection.[109] In the case of *Ranelagh & Keating v Molloy* (1666), Connel Molloy was found to have forged a protection of John Keating, deputy clerk of the upper house, and also a letter purporting to be that of Lord Ranelagh.[110] Molloy then absconded (possibly with the loss of his considerable recognisance of £1,000).[111] Thus, judgement and sentence could not be formally read to him, but a committee recommended that

> the said Connel Molloy shall be made exemplary, by being put to stand in the pillory, in Corn-Market, Dublin, from the hour of ten in the morning till the hour of twelve, for three market-days, and there to have his ears nailed to the said pillory, and his crime to be written in paper, to be fixed upon his breast, and to be imprisoned during the pleasure of the house.[112]

Indeed, Rule 27 of the standing orders of the House of Lords in 1692 insisted that 'Of all Encroachments and Breaches of Privileges, some strict Examples should be made at first, and Records kept exactly both of all things to be observed, and of all Punishments to be inflicted upon the Breakers, to deter others, be it out of Malice or Negligence.'[113]

Members of parliament had other privileges. Chief among these was freedom from arrest for MPs on all matters arising from civil cases, the peers having this as a matter of course whether parliament was sitting or not. When both houses ruled that privilege might be laid aside for a time at the end of the restoration parliament, in the summer of 1666, the privilege of freedom from arrest was still preserved. In 1614, George Bagnall, MP for the county of Carlow, was arrested by John Johnson, on an execution for debt. Johnson was immediately hauled before the bar, found in contempt of the privileges of the House and incarcerated in Dublin Castle for a few days. Other than this case, the privilege of members to be free from arrest on civil matters remained intact and unchallenged.[114] There are many other examples of both MPs and peers being arrested and incarcerated during or near parliament-time, but none of them were reckoned to be within the remit privilege as it did not extend to cases of treason, felony, or breaches of the peace. Several leaders of the Catholic party that appealed directly to James I were jailed in prisons across London in May 1614.[115] Lord Dunsany was arrested, held, and tortured in the aftermath of the 1641 rebellion, and although the Lords did not make an attempt to have him freed, they did accept many petitions from him and continued to refer to him as 'the right honourable the lord Baron of Dunsany'.[116] In the summer of 1663, eight members of the lower house were arrested, tried, and one was executed for involvement in Blood's Plot.[117] In what is an interesting aspect of the historiography of parliamentary privilege, the freedom from arrest is what tends garner most attention from historians of the English parliament, Elizabeth Read Foster being a notable exception.[118]

Members of both houses of parliament were of course also to be free from physical harm. In the summer of 1642, Laurence Lambert was accused of having pulled the MP Thomas Johnson's hair, 'pull him by his belt, and hawl him through the streets'.[119] The following year, Terence Magrath (who himself later became an MP in the same parliament) went to the home of Charles Foster to recover a debt and 'called me a Raschall … stepped three or four steps into the entry of my house, and the said Magrath drew out his sword, and I verily believe, and think, that if Captain Burroughs had not been present, the said Mr Magrath had killed me'.[120] In December 1665, William Howse appears to have done injury to Humphry Abdy MP for Tuam. According to Abdy's petitions, Howse struck him 'with a cudgel to the ground, and, lighting from his horse, did wound and beat the petitioner, treading upon his breast and belly, calling him a rogue, said, he would kill the petitioner'.[121] Assaults on MPs were not frequent, and they certainly were not clever, as parliament always found in favour of the member.[122] Although such events could hardly be described as common, many who attended parliament saw it as an essential privilege to bear arms. Ormond, in youthful exuberance in 1634, insisted on taking his sword into the chamber, and when challenged to surrender it, he told the gentleman usher of the black rod that 'if he had his sword it should be in his guts'. When questioned, Ormond pointed to his writ of summons, which indicated that the king had instructed him to attend the Lords '*cum gladio cinctus*' (girth with a sword).[123] Indeed, Wentworth may have had a practical reason to disarm members as they entered parliament as there had been violence in the chamber at the opening in 1613. During debates at the end of 1665, swords were half drawn 'with words sometimes sharper than they'.[124] In November 1642, several members of the upper house complained that their servants had been disarmed by the mayor of the city under a general order for the disarming of Catholics, and although there is no mention of the word privilege, they did assert that they 'are less able to attend the service of this house' as a result.[125] There is no mention of any difficulty in this regard when some prominent Catholic peers attended later sessions of the same parliament.[126]

One privilege which sits comfortably both within the collective and the personal privileges of parliament is that of offensive words been spoken against a peer or a member of the commons. Although only mentioned in Irish sources once as *scandalum magnatum*, the offence has its origins in English law as far back as the thirteenth century.[127] It was legislated for in 1378, just a few years before the peasant's revolt, and is likely to have been to reduce antagonism between the classes in the aftermath of the black death and its knock-on effects on societal relations.[128] This, like all English public legislation before 1494 (or perhaps 1468), was applied to Ireland (see p. 99, n. 41). The statute, as enforced in Ireland and generally taken by the Commons to apply to them also, was to punish defamation whether by libel or slander, although the latter was by far the most common. Both houses were generally vociferous in their defence of offended colleagues. Most of the complaints of having offensive words spoken to an MP or peer occurred outside the house either by direct speech or by report. The vehicle for satisfaction was to make a complaint, almost always by petition, which would be heard by the house, sometimes referred to the Committee of Privileges, and from there the slanderer would generally be brought before the bar, where he would purge his contempt of the house by apologising to the individual. He was sometimes kept in confinement for a few days, although occasionally corporal punishment was meted out. Of course, one of the difficulties with bringing a prosecution against the individual who utters the scandalous words is that they need to be repeated to the house, causing further embarrassment to the plaintiff. In the Lords, in addition to the accusations mentioned with regard to the archbishop of Cashel and the lord chancellor in 1614, some of the offensive terms referred to included the calling of the earl of Tyrconnel a rogue and the earl of Clanrickard a knave.[129] Members of the lower house were also victims of verbal abuse on occasion. In 1661, Colonel Carey Dillon complained to the house that Major John Desborow had accused him of lying to the sheriff of King's County and disrupting the election held two months previous.[130] The following year, Daniel Hutchinson, MP for Queen's County, complained that on delivering a message from the Commons to the lord lieutenant, he was 'opprobriously, scandalously, and menaciously abused by the lord Viscount Dungan'.[131] A year later, in the Court of Claims, Sir William Petty, was accused of trying to suborn a witness 'for lucre' to swear against a Catholic claimant, Lord

Barnewall.[132] Finally, William Connell was attached by the serjeant at arms on the petition of Thomas Evans, MP for Kilkenny City, for giving the petitioner 'several provoking and opprobrious words, calling him a base stinking fellow, in contempt of the privileges of parliament'.[133] Perhaps the most interesting case is one where two members of the Commons traded insults in the chamber itself in 1634. During a debate on the purging of the house, Sir John Dungan called Captain Charles Price a liar after he had first called him 'a sawcy fellow'.[134] This argument apparently erupted again after the end of the first session and Wentworth had Dungan taken into custody, questioned at the council board, and ordered him to submit an apology to Price in person. He then presented Dungan, as a prisoner, to the House of Commons for appropriate punishment and reserved the right to further punish him on behalf of the king. Clearly, Wentworth could never be described as a governor sensitive to the rights and privileges of the House of Commons, but to arrest, question, judge, and incarcerate an MP days after a session for firm words spoken to another MP within the chamber was a clear breach of the privilege of the House in judgement of its own members between sessions.[135]

LIBERTIES OF PARLIAMENT

The collective rights of the two houses of parliament, while usually known as 'privileges' by contemporaries, are probably better described as 'liberties of parliament'. These are a set of rights assumed by both houses as a way of guaranteeing them freedom of action in performance of their duties. As with the individual privileges of members, both houses could be over-zealous, petty, or pedantic in the advertising and enforcement of their collective privileges, but they originally came about as a practical way of dealing with the business of counsel, legislation, and representation that parliament was expected to provide to their monarch.

In seventeenth-century England, the speaker of the lower house traditionally asked the monarch for four privileges upon election: freedom from arrest for all members of the commons, free access to the monarch, advance permission to correct errors he may make in speaking on behalf of the Commons, and freedom of speech.[136] Unsurprisingly, considering how often the Irish Parliament looked to England for example, this formulaic request was usually mirrored in the western kingdom. It really did not matter either way, as it was merely a tradition by the early seventeenth century, the monarch (through the lord chancellor) never denied the speakers' request, and did, on occasion, breach these privileges.

How might these privileges have fared had they been desired at the beginning of parliament in Dublin? The issue of the right to correct errors in speaking on behalf of the Commons is not something that was necessary in that it never really came up as an issue in seventeenth-century Ireland. As has been commented upon above at some length, freedom from arrest was, by the seventeenth century, a largely self-regulatory affair and one that was breached at great risk to the transgressor. Obviously, occasionally members were arrested for treason or felony, but almost always the courts and officers of the state were wary of the Commons and stayed within the parameters of parliamentary privilege in this regard. Freedom of speech was never really an issue for the Commons or indeed for the Lords either. The Irish Parliament in this regard tended to betray its position of being at best a junior to the assembly in Westminster, or perhaps more accurately as a colonial assembly. They always stayed within the confines of what was considered reasonable for parliament to discuss. Apart from sending a congratulatory address to Charles II on his marriage to Catherine of Braganza, the Irish Parliament never discussed dynastic marriages. Foreign policy was largely kept out of the Irish Parliament. Sir George Lane, a privy councillor, introduced some evidence from the earl of Arlington about preparations apparently being then made on the Normandy coast for an invasion of Ireland that elicited nothing more than a loyal declaration and a valuable subsidy.[137] Certainly the actions of the English Parliament in relation to foreign policy and its attempts to steer policy on war and peace and dynastic marriages in the 1620s and the restoration is not seen in Ireland.[138] Largely because the Irish Parliament never really wandered into areas considered to be outside its accepted competency the issue of free speech never came up as a cause of conflict.

Access to the king is a little more complex and it does not exactly translate over to the Irish system of representative and executive government. In the first instance, we need to differentiate between the person of the king and the king's deputy in Ireland. Communications between the two houses and the king's deputy do not appear to have been problematic. The usual method was for the house to collectively nominate a committee or occasionally an individual to go to the presence chamber in Dublin Castle and address the lord deputy there. Sometimes the houses would communicate in writing with the lord deputy (and vice-versa). It would appear that the lord deputy was always available to receive the representatives in person, and, on one occasion, the duke of Ormond even put his dinner off to receive the messengers from the Commons.[139] There were also several unofficial conduits of interaction between the two houses and the lord deputy. The presence of privy councillors in both houses allowed for regular updates of activity in the house to be available to Dublin Castle. In similar fashion, these same privy councillors were usually available in the house to give some indication as to the executive's attitude to any business then before the house. Indeed, these men-of-business frequently led their respective houses.

Obviously, we must acknowledge that direct access to the king would generally take at least a week and, weather depending, sometimes several weeks' travel. While direct interaction between the Irish Parliament and the Whitehall administration could, carefully managed, be mutually beneficial in providing solutions to problems faced, in Ireland in the restoration period it was not always seen as such.[140] Too many lords deputy had seen their administration perish on the rock of direct communication between the Anglo-Irish community and Whitehall and so it became clear in the early seventeenth century that, ideally, this was to be avoided if possible. Chichester was not in a position to prevent the recusant delegation going to London following the mass walkout after the opening of parliament in 1613, and although the delegation was not officially representing parliament, it was clear that they represented 'the Papist party' in parliament. None of the competing interests in Ireland could claim an outright victory in the exchanges in London, but the Catholic party had more than a modest success. Despite being referred to as 'half-subjects' and occasional incarceration at various locations, they managed to undermine, at least in part, the administration of the lord deputy, had some illegally elected MPs removed from parliament, and had the proposed anti-Catholic bills removed from the legislative agenda.[141] Wentworth clearly learned from the mistakes of Chichester and others, and forbade official travel between the two kingdoms in advance of and during the early sessions of the 1640–48 parliament. It was not until John Bellew and Oliver Cashel (knight of the shire of Louth and MP for Dundalk, respectively) effectively ran the gauntlet and broke the embargo in November 1640 (some eight months after parliament had begun) that the Irish Parliament could link up with Westminster and have direct contact with English politicians.[142] The official representative committee of the Commons followed on some weeks later, and although their immediate task was to work hand-in-hand with the English Commons in impeaching Wentworth they did also conduct a protracted negotiation with the king.

If those liberties of the English Parliament only exercised the minds of Irish members on relatively rare occasions, there were others that were rigorously defended and used in the Irish Parliament. As such, it might be most accurate to suggest that the liberties or privileges of the house, or indeed of parliament altogether, was more about self-regulation and most of the matters described affected the way that the houses organised themselves. In addition to the election of their own speaker, the Irish House of Commons had, by the seventeenth century, taken full control of elections once it was sitting. This is likely to have been a relatively recent event, as it was still an issue of uncertainty in England under Elizabeth.[143] Obviously the organisation and execution of a general election could not be conducted by a House of Commons that had not yet formed. After 1613, once it was sitting, the House of Commons assumed full control of all things electoral.[144] Normal procedures at the beginning of parliament demanded that a Committee of Privileges (sometimes referred to as the Committee of Privileges and Elections) would be composed in the opening days.[145] Once formed, the Committee would then go about its business. This was never explicitly stipulated (though usually it was whatever the House thought fit to refer to it), but both elections and privileges created a significant workload. In these early days of the first session, elections took precedence, and the Committee got down to work on what could be politically charged issues. In 1640, probably due to mischief-making, a question was raised as to whether the House should first examine the election returns and the House be purged before the speaker was elected, but this was rejected after Sir George Radcliffe argued in favour of the election, stating that 'no act or order could be made or entered, till the speaker were first agreed on'.[146] Upon the examination of the returns brought to the House by the clerk of the crown and hanaper in Chancery, the House would usually insist all doubly elected members choose which borough or county they wished to represent. This came about because some individuals hedged their bets by running and being elected in several constituencies. Victory in more than one contest allowed MPs to sit for their preferred constituency, and they usually chose the more prestigious or better paid seats. Knights of the shire got a better daily rate of pay than the borough seats. If anything else out of the ordinary in the returns was noticed, this was dealt with in the opening days; such as the double return for the borough of Tuam in 1661, when four members were returned.[147] In the weeks following the opening of parliament, the Commons regularly considered petitions concerning false returns. In 1661, the Commons issued a cut-off point of two weeks for submission of complaints about undue elections.[148] However, it was a full two months after the opening of parliament before they pronounced judgement against the return of Richard Chute as a knight of the shire for Kerry.[149] Thomas Crosby, the sheriff of Kerry who made the return, asserted that the irregularity came about 'not from any wilful acting in him, but merely upon the advice of others, who pretended to know the statutes for the ordering of elections, he having never before seen an election of that kind, your petitioner being of no capacity, when the last parliament was held in this kingdom'.[150] However, the House was adamant in its belief that the sheriff was thoroughly corrupt as he had returned his brother-in-law, Chute. They judged that he had purposefully reduced the number of voters for John Blennerhasset Senior, and even when the poll showed Blennerhasset's majority being two-to-one, Crosby still returned in favour of his relation.

The year 1613 was quite different. It was, in effect, a rigged general election, planned and executed by the highest levels of the executive in Dublin Castle.[151] After the walk out of the recusant 'party', it was obvious to all that the problems brought about in no small part by recent constituency innovations could not be solved in the lower chamber. The decision to seclude the

MPs from many of the recently created boroughs was taken in London and was not likely to be queried by any of the Catholic MPs nor any government supporters. All that remained to be done once parliament had resumed was to order fresh polls for the boroughs of Cavan and Kildare.[152] Usually after the preliminaries of election returns had been dealt with, the House of Commons, as a matter of course, made orders for elections to be held to replace members who had been expelled, died, or retired due to illness. Self-regulation in regard to admission to the House was further extended when the Committee of Privileges considered in 1641 the issue of minimum age for members. The Commons deemed 21 to be suitable.[153]

Although the Lords were returned by right rather than by election, they also governed their own affairs. By the beginning of the seventeenth century, and probably much earlier, it was an uncontested and well-established fact that all peers, bishops, and archbishops were entitled to a writ of summons to parliament. As was the case with the Commons, the Lords obviously could not organise themselves before parliament convened. Writs were sent out by Chancery. There were certain occasions when questions were raised by the authorities as to how appropriate it was to send certain individual writs. For example, in 1613, questions were raised concerning Lord Barry 'as he had an elder brother, deaf and dumb living'.[154] In 1634, questions were raised about the baron of Slane who had the king recommend he receive a writ, but his elder brother had, in the lifetime of his father, departed the kingdom for Paris to become a friar (and was officially 'presumed dead').[155] As soon as parliament did convene, the issue of Slane's writ was discussed in the house with Patrick Darcy appearing as counsel for 'William, lord baron of Slane', and the writ was ordered to be issued in favour of William but with a *salvo jure* for Thomas (the elder brother) that if he were living and returned, he would re-assume the title.[156] In 1661, both the English and the Irish council boards exercised their minds on the question of whether outlawed or indicted peers should be sent a writ of summons before their outlawries were overturned in the Court of King's Bench, but once parliament had convened, the Lords assumed that responsibility for themselves.[157] On the second day of sitting, the restoration parliament ordered a list of the outlawed peers of the kingdom to be brought into the house and then ordered 'that the lords at the door, demanding introduction, be admonished, if either they or their predecessors stand outlawed for high-treason, that they forbear coming into this house; and if they come in, that it be at their peril'.[158] In the following months, they considered several cases of lords desiring admission to the House, despite their indictment or outlawry for treason.[159] In 1689, most Protestant peers were attainted during the course of the short single-session parliament, although most had already either gone over to William III or were assiduously avoiding taking sides.[160]

Both houses continued to exert influence on their membership and attendance throughout the course of the century. In the Lords, a series of rules were issued stipulating the attendance responsibilities of peers. In 1634, the House ordered that 'it is to be observed, that on the first or second day, the house be called, and notice taken of such lords as either have not sent their proxies, or are not excused by His Majesty for some time, and the house to be called as oft as cause requires.' They followed this by a rule regarding attendance at prayer time:

> Every lord that comes not within a quarter of an hour after prayers, if he be a bishop or baron, is to pay one shilling, and if he be any degree above, two shillings to the poor man's box; for absence he is to pay nothing, but to make excuse by any member of the house, which if it be done and allowed as just, he is to be excused; if not he is to be blamed as the fault requires.[161]

This rule was re-confirmed at the end of the century and again in the early eighteenth century.[162] Interestingly, in the Lords in the early days of the restoration parliament, it was ordered that peers should be fined if they were absent for prayers, but any that were not of the Church of Ireland continued to be permitted to arrive within fifteen minutes of the start of proceedings without censure. Before parliament, with licence from the king (or the lord deputy) peers and bishops could absent themselves from the House on condition that they left a proxy. The upper house occasionally gave permission for peers to be absent, such as when 'upon consideration of the age and weakness of the right hon. Randall, earl of Antrim, that his lordships shall be licensed to depart for this present session of parliament, leaving his lordships proxy, directed to the right hon. earl of Westmeath, in the hands of the clerk of parliament'.[163] However, the Lords sometimes accepted interference from outside. On several occasions, the attorney general (who was a member of the Commons) entered the House and on behalf of the king, asked the House to call itself over and to amerce the absent lords, thus confirming the theory that parliament was called to perform a duty to the monarch.[164]

In the same manner, the Commons also self-regulated for attendance. If a member expected to be away from the House, either elsewhere in Dublin, the country, or outside of the kingdom, it was standard practice to get a licence to depart, usually for a specified length of time, and to have it entered into the journal.[165] In October 1614, on information that James Montgomery (MP for Strabane) was ill, the House gave him permission to depart.[166] At the end of the same parliament, on taking a roll call in the House, seventeen members were punished for the lack of proper attendance. In most cases, the fine was 20 Irish pounds and loss of wages for that session.[167] Similar fines were levied in April 1635, although the MP for Bandon, William Wiseman, had his remitted on grounds that on arrival in Dublin he had received news of the death of his wife and returned home.[168] In May 1662, the Commons gave their speaker permission to call the House over any time he saw fit, and all members who failed to answer were to be fined and excluded from the House until they paid.[169]

In other areas, the peers were less able to have sole control of the processes within their own house. The lords in the first half of the century did not have control over the sometimes vexed issue of non-resident peers. The peerage of Ireland mushroomed in the early seventeenth century at least three-fold.[170] Although many of these new peers had little genuine vested or even residual interest in Ireland, their membership of an ever-increasing caste inevitably caused problems. Wentworth saw the value of such peers, who were disinclined to spend several months in Ireland where they had neither residence nor estate. Royal permission to absent themselves from parliament was made conditional on their leaving their proxies blank so that when they arrived in Dublin, the name of the recipient could be inserted by the executive and thereby gave them massive influence in the upper house. During the first session of the first Caroline parliament, Wentworth was able to distribute as many as thirty-five proxies among a small number of government-inclined peers, these votes along with those of the usually compliant episcopal benches gave the government a solid working majority in the House.[171] Whether for distinctly political reasons or more a general dissatisfaction at having landless (and therefore untaxable) peers voting in a tax-raising parliament, the issue of non-resident peers caused discontent. The Lords attempted to have an act passed forcing non-resident peers to purchase estates in Ireland and making them liable to all taxes and public costs, but it came to nothing.[172] Spring 1641 saw a renewed attack on non-residency, when the Lords attacked the loose system of proxies, insisting that all proxies must have advance permission of the executive, allowed by the House, and the clerk must be paid his fee in advance. A second order the same day provided for a petition to the king, arguing against the right of peers with no estates in the kingdom to sit in parliament.[173] In May of the same year, the Lords voted the use of proxies by non-resident peers a grievance.[174] Obviously the outbreak of the rebellion shelved the issue, but by 1661 it was yet again on the table.[175] The House formally adopted (some thirty-five years after the English upper house had done the same) that no single peer could hold more than two proxies, on recommendation from the Committee of Privileges which quoted the king's commission from May 1641.[176] However, the same Committee reported a month later that they recommended that non-resident lords who did not hold estates in Ireland should be entitled to representation in the house by proxy.[177] By 1692, the Lords appear to have brought that number up to three, and stipulated that episcopal proxies must go to other bishops, and temporal go to temporal lords, although this was generally the way proxies were disposed of anyway.[178]

In the Lords, there was a facility for noting a protestation by a particular lord or group of lords, a privilege that was not shared by members of the lower house. Highlighting what was likely to be the heightened privileges of individual lords, a peer or a group of peers was entitled to proclaim a protest against a particular order or action of the house or parliament. The first recorded protestation in the seventeenth century was in fact the entire House of Lords making reference to a Commons failure to come to a conference at a pre-arranged time, which they 'conceive to be so great an indignity offered to this house, and we conclude and protest not to give any meeting to the house of commons, until we have reparation of our honours, by their acknowledge of our undoubted right'.[179] In September 1662, John Clotworthy, Viscount Massareene, entered a protest against the assessment for his home county of Antrim and County Down on the basis that it did not bear an equal proportion to other counties and 'are exceedingly overcharged, to the great detriment of these two counties'.[180] To the same assessment, the episcopal bench en masse entered a very detailed protest, basically suggesting that they should not be taxed on this occasion (according to the act for £30,000 for the duke of Ormond) as it was not of 'invincible necessity', and therefore they should have been taxed in convocation instead.[181] The bishop of Cork also entered a personal protestation against a judgement by the Committee of Privileges, confirmed by the House against the bishop and in favour of the earl of Inchiquin's right to collect impropriate tythes in parishes in County Cork.[182]

Although not formally registered in their journals as a protest, the House of Lords entered a complaint with the lord deputy in May 1615 against the House of Commons for proceeding first in matters concerning the restitution in blood, which they conceived to be a privilege particularly reserved to themselves:

> Where all honour is derived from the king, and matters concerning point of honour should properly descend from the higher house to the house of commons, they assumed the same to themselves, as appeareth by the act of restitution of John Heydon to his blood.[183]

This point was emphasised again in the general rules of the upper house, where they pointed out that all bills concerning restitution in blood should first be assented to by the monarch and then proceeded upon in the upper house.[184] Indeed, it is surprising that the Lords did not make reference in the same complaint in 1615 as to the case of the four daughters of the earl of Desmond, who had petitioned the king for their restitution in blood and subsequently presented this to the Commons, who took it upon themselves to draw up a bill and present it to the lord deputy in accordance with Poynings' Law.[185] Aside from these two cases it appears to have been normal practice for all blood and attainder cases to proceed through the upper house first.[186]

While the Lords may have had certain superior privileges, either in theory or in practice, the Commons did have the privilege of being the originating house for all money bills.[187] Besides the odd occasion when the Lords first read a bill for poundage and then passed it down to the Commons in 1614, this protocol was never breached. Obviously, once the Irish Parliament began to produce their own heads of bills with gusto from the restoration onwards, the importance that this particular privilege took on cannot be overstated.[188]

By the very fact that privileges of the House of Commons and of the House of Lords were mutually exclusive and largely self-regulated, it is not surprising that there were breakdowns in relations between houses. An example of one such breakdown occurred in spring 1641.[189] In late 1640, John FitzGerald was brought before the Court of Castle Chamber in Dublin for publicly questioning the paternity of Lord Kerry's children.[190] Kerry won the case and FitzGerald was fined £5,000 to be paid to the complainant and a further £10,000 to the king. While the case was proceeding, a writ was issued for an election for the borough of Inistiogue in Kilkenny to replace Sir Robert Loftus who had died. FitzGerald, probably with the assistance of his numerous connections both in the Commons and the Lords, was elected MP.[191] Before judgement and censure could be given on 2 December 1640, FitzGerald produced his certificate of election and formally claimed parliamentary privilege as an MP. This was denied by Castle Chamber which proceeded to the substantial fine and custody. At the beginning of the next session in late January 1641, FitzGerald petitioned the Commons for his release from prison citing his membership of the House and therefore his privilege.[192] The Lords, upon prompting by Lord Kerry, sent messengers and later a committee to meet with the Commons, citing the 'disrespect done to this house by the house of commons, in admitting the gentleman into that house, before a resolution in this house'.[193] Chief Justice Lowther recommended to the House on 26 February 1641 'that FitzGerald was not well delivered out of prison by the house of commons, without application therein to this house, where the sole power of judicature in this case remains, as they [the judges] conceive'.[194] This was surely an overestimation by the judges, as the case had proceeded in the inferior Court of Castle Chamber. Had they wished to up the ante, they could have issued a writ of *supersedeas*, as they were to do later in 1666 from King's Bench, to extract the case from Castle Chamber up to the Lords.[195] It is quite likely, considering the size of the award in Kerry's favour, that his reasons may have been financial. The Lords were clearly within their rights to be affronted, but the case was that of the Court of Castle Chamber, and as the executive in general had been tamed by Wentworth's arrest and Wandesford's death, the government was not prepared to dig their heels in and the Commons asserted their superiority in this case; although, in a matter of privilege, it was questionable whether it ever could have been in doubt.[196] The Commons heard argument by the attorney general on behalf of the king, Richard Martin for Lord Kerry, and Patrick Kirwan for FitzGerald. Numerous questions were asked and apparently convincing answers given as to the legality of the election itself, applicability of privilege to a member who had yet to take his seat, and the damage to the king's interest by the loss of the fine. The Commons found in favour of FitzGerald's claim to privilege and he was formally admitted as a full member, his censure and fine quashed.[197] Still smarting on the issue, there was little more the Lords could do in this case other than draw up a 'state of the case', as the Commons did, to be presented to the king, along with a similar representation from Dublin Castle, for his decision.[198]

Several other cases emerged during the course of the century of a similar hue, generally involving an initial breach of privilege, followed by a counter claim of privilege by the other house. In 1662, the earl of Carlingford complained that his servant, Patrick Bellew had been arrested by the serjeant at arms of the Commons at the complaint of Sir Henry Ingoldsby.[199] Carlingford again complained in the Lords about the arrest in spring 1662 on behalf of another servant, George Warren, who upon discovering the arrest 'rescued' the same Warren from the custody of the serjeant at arms, which was deemed by the Commons to be a breach of privilege.[200] In many cases, conferences and messages between the houses could help to resolve such situations without any major fall out between the houses. However, this was not the case in 1666, when nothing short of paralysis in relations between the houses was created by the arrest by the serjeant at arms of the Commons of two servants of Lord Kingsland: Robert and William Barnewall.[201] The lords moved a writ of *habeas corpus* and when Thomas Sanderson refused to bring the prisoners before the upper house, they ordered black rod to take him into custody, and following a similar refusal by Robert Dolphin, one of Sanderson's colleagues, they fined him £100.[202] The Commons pointed out that the Barnewall brothers had been arrested due to a breach of privilege, but failed to understand that their own original arresting action was a breach of the Lords' privilege, who in turn violated the Commons' privilege by summoning the serjeant at arms to the upper house, arresting Sanderson and fining Dolphin.

Considering the respective violations and escalation of animosity between the houses on the basis of breaches of privilege, in this instance it is of little surprise that Ormond elected to dissolve parliament soon after. Although this surely was not the sole reason, it may well have been the straw that broke the camel's back, and informed his conclusion in general that 'parliaments here are uselesse & ridiculous assemblies'.[203] It is perhaps an indictment against the general reputation of parliament in Ireland that many of the times the houses became most animated and passionate was in defence of their privileges, both collective and of their individual members.

NOTES

1. H.G. Koenigsberger, *Medieval Europe, 400–1500* (London, 1987), p. 100; Marongiu, *Medieval parliaments*, pp. 33–34.
2. Quoted in W. Notestein and F.H. Relf, *Commons debates for 1629* (Minneapolis, 1929), p. 165.
3. C.I. McGrath, 'English Ministers, Irish politicians and the making of a parliamentary settlement in Ireland, 1692–5', *EHR*, 119 (2004), pp. 585–613; J.I. McGuire, 'The Irish parliament of 1692' in T. Bartlett and D.W. Hayton (eds), *Penal era and golden age: essays in Irish history, 1690–1800* (Belfast, 1979).
4. H. Elsynge, *The manner of holding parliaments in England* (London, 1768); *Judicature in parlement by Henry Elsyng*, ed. by E.R. Foster (London, 1991); Snow, *Parliament in Elizabethan England*.
5. O. Armstrong, 'Manuscripts of the *Modus tenendi parliamentum* in the library of Trinity College, Dublin', *PRIA* 36, C (1921–24), pp. 256–64; M.V. Clarke, *Medieval representation and consent: a study of early parliaments in England and Ireland, with special reference to the* Modus tenendi parliamentum (London, 1936).
6. Snow, *Parliament in Elizabethan England*, pp. 29–39.
7. *Judicature in parlement by Henry Elsyng*, p. xi.
8. *CJ*, 18 July 1634.
9. John Selden was a clerk in the peers' house in England at the end of James I's reign. His research into the precedents and privileges of the upper house was adopted as a set of standing orders on privilege. *LJ Eng.*, 8 February 1621, 15 December 1621; Foster, *The House of Lords*, pp. 137–38.
10. Wentworth to Coke, 18 August 1634, *The earl of Strafforde's letters*, vol. 2, pp. 276–92.
11. *CJ*, 2 May 1615.
12. McCafferty, 'To follow the late precedents in England'. See also the petition of the Lords and Commons to the king, *CJ*, 24 May 1641.
13. *CJ*, 30 May 1662.
14. 3 Edward IV, c. I. An act whereby the lords and commons of the parliament hath privilege for certain days before and after the said parliament. The English parliament did pass a law confirming and regulating freedom from arrest, but much later than the Irish Parliament did. 1 James I, c. XIII [Eng.].
15. 10 & 11 Charles I, c. XII. This act closely resembles the parliamentary privilege act of 1604 (1 James I, c. XIII [Eng.], legally cited as 1603) passed in the English Parliament and was probably part of Wentworth's general reform agenda with regards to the modernisation of the law. Curiously, this English reforming act is listed as a retained statute in the Statute Law Revision Act, 2007, § 2(2)(a), and Part 2 of Schedule 1 to the act, although, to the best of this author's understanding, it never had legal force in Ireland. This act is not mentioned in Hunneyball's recent article on early Stuart parliamentary privilege, or in many other studies for that matter. P. Hunneyball, 'The development of parliamentary privilege' in C.R. Kyle (ed.), *Managing Tudor and Stuart parliaments: essays in memory of Michael Graves* (Chichester, 2015).

16 11 &12 Edward IV, c. LXXX. An act for the freedom of lords coming to parliament, and their servants. 'Also, at the request of the commons. That whereas by the laudable custom usage and privilege used beyond a time to which any memory runs, that all the lords of the parliament of our sovereign lord the king in this his land of Ireland, and their ministers and servants, coming with them to the said parliament, ought to have free coming and free going to the said parliament, without any vexation to them or any of them done, or being arrested by writ or bill or plaint in any manner of court.'
17 *CJ*, 25 November 1614.
18 *LJ*, 27 February 1635. Indeed, although it is beyond the period examined by this book, by the rule of the Lords as set down early in the 1692 parliament and enhanced in the early eighteenth century, the Lords restricted privilege to forty days after each prorogation and before each resumption of parliament. Rule 26, *LJ*, 2 November 1692; NLI MS 2091. In addition to numerous biblical references, such as Jesus's time of temptation in the desert (Matthew 4:2, Mark 1:13, Luke 4:20), the period between resurrection and ascension (Acts 1:3), and the length of consistent rain at the time of the flood (Genesis 7:4), the use of forty days is probably traceable to the length of time of safe medieval sanctuary. See W.C. Jordan, 'A fresh look at medieval sanctuary' in R.M. Karras, J. Kaye, and E.A. Matter (eds), *Law and the illicit in medieval Europe* (Philadelphia, 2008), p. 23; W.A. Logan, 'Criminal law sanctuaries', *Harvard civil rights – civil liberties law review*, 38 (2003), p. 327.
19 *Modus tenendi parliamentum*, NLI MS 999, f. 343.
20 *CJ*, 23 October 1640, 5 March 1641 (although the entry is a report of a committee meeting that took place on 18 February 1641).
21 *CJ*, 11 May 1647.
22 *CJ*, 19 March 1645.
23 L.J. Arnold, 'The Irish Court of Claims of 1663', *IHS*, 24 (1985), p. 417–30; *The restoration land settlement in County Dublin*; K.S. Bottigheimer, 'The restoration land settlement in Ireland: a structural view', *IHS*, 18 (1972), pp. 1–21; *English money and Irish land: the 'adventurers' in the Cromwellian settlement of Ireland* (Oxford, 1971); Dennehy, 'Sir Winston Churchill and restoration Ireland'.
24 *CJ*, 19 February, 9 April 1666.
25 *CJ*, 3, 17, 19 March 1645, 30 November 1646, 27 January 1647, 30 March 1647.
26 *CJ*, 24 February 1646.
27 For example, at the end of this chapter see disputes relating to Carlingford's rescue of his arrested servant from the Commons in 1662 and also Kingsland's dispute with the lower house in 1666.
28 It is a little difficult to ascertain what general aristocratic privilege might have been as there has not been an in-depth study. However, in this instance, it is probably safe to look to the example of England where aristocratic privilege outside of parliament extended to the right to testify on honour rather than oath, trial by their peers, freedom from arrest on actions from debt, and an entitlement to claim benefit of clergy without the necessity of proof of being able to read on a first offence. See Foster, *The House of Lords*, pp. 138–41.

29 LJ, 2 November 1692; NLI MS 2091.
30 CJ, 22 October 1614.
31 CJ, 20, 21 October, 4, 10 November 1614.
32 In his recent book on honour in Britain and Ireland in the early modern period, Brendan Kane mistakenly refers to the lord chancellor as Dudley Loftus. Although he makes many valid points regarding the nature of the grievance, the problem is more complex, in that in this instance, as well as being lord chancellor and as such a servant of the upper house, the archbishop was also a lord of parliament in his own right, albeit not necessarily a peer. Jones was preceded by Adam Loftus as archbishop of Dublin and lord chancellor, and followed in the post by Adam Loftus, who sat as lord chancellor and speaker in 1634–5 and was also a peer in his own right as Viscount Ely. B. Kane, *The politics and culture of honour honour in Britain and Ireland, 1541–1641* (Cambridge, 2010), pp. 204–5.
33 A gold coin worth roughly 11 shillings English.
34 CJ, 18 April 1614.
35 CJ, 27 April 1615. The work of this committee is, unusually, recorded in great detail.
36 CJ, 28 April 1615.
37 CJ, 6 May 1615.
38 CJ, 18 April 1615.
39 CJ, 29 April 1615.
40 CJ, 2 May 1615. The members were Sir Edward Fisher, Sir Richard Morrison, and Sir William Usher. Full detail on the hearing is a little scant, but it is curious that Howth did not (or perhaps was not allowed) to call in other witnesses that must surely have been at the initial hearing.
41 CJ, 16 May 1615. In many respects the accusations were very accurate. For the colourful life of Miler Magrath, see J. Barry, 'Magrath, Miler (Meiler)', DIB.
42 CJ, 16 May 1615.
43 Interestingly, the Commons tried to use the example of the *lord chancellor v Sherlock* as a precedent later in the century to convince the Lords of their sole right to judicature over their privilege in 1645. CJ, 19 March 1645.
44 LJ, 2 November 1692; NLI MS 2091. In March 1641, Mary Caulfield, the dowager baroness of Charlemont, petitioned the Commons, but it is questionable whether she was entitled to privilege in the Lords and, if so, whether she was bound by the aforementioned rule. CJ, 3 March 1641.
45 LJ, 17, 31 May, 18 June 1661, 6 March 1662.
46 CJ, 6 May 1661.
47 LJ, 21 May 1661.
48 LJ, 4 November 1634.
49 NLI MS 9607, pp. 126–27.
50 P. Marshall, *Mother Leakey and the bishop: a ghost story* (Cambridge, 2007).
51 N. Bernard, *The penitent death of a woefull sinner* (London, 1642), p. 30.
52 CJ, 17 June 1640.
53 A. Clarke, 'A woeful sinner: John Atherton' in V. Carey and U. Lotz-Heumann

(eds), *Taking sides: colonial and confessional* mentalités *in early modern Ireland* (Dublin, 2003), p. 146.
54 Clarke, 'A woeful sinner', p. 146. It is questionable whether this case could have been heard in any of the ecclesiastical courts. The punishment of sodomy (and many of the other things Atherton was accused and found guilty of) was originally tried in ecclesiastical courts, but the reformation secularisation is generally seen as the reason for the passing of the original sodomy bill in England in 1534 (25 Henry VIII, c. VI [Eng.]), as those accused could not avail of benefit of clergy. The law was only passed in Ireland in 1635 as a reaction to the trial of Castlehaven in England some four years earlier. S.E. Lehmberg, *The reformation parliament, 1529–1536* (Cambridge, 1970), p. 185.
55 C. Herrup, *A house in gross disorder: sex, law, and the 2nd earl of Castlehaven* (Oxford, 1999), pp. 63–98. The right to defence counsel in felony trials was not formally legislated for in the United Kingdom until the trials for felony act 1836 (6 & 7 William 4 c 114 [UK]), although it was not uncommon in the eighteenth century. It was available by right for treason trials from 1696 onwards due to the 1696 treason act (The treason act 1695 [7 & 8 William 3 c 3]). J.H. Langbein, *The origins of adversary criminal trial* (Oxford, 2005); 'The prosecutorial origins of defence counsel: the appearance of solicitors', *Cambridge law journal*, 58 (1999), pp. 314–65.
56 Marshall, *Mother Leakey and the bishop*, p. 99.
57 Appointed bishop by letters patent on 4 May 1636, this was almost seventeen months after the bill had received the royal assent in mid-December 1634. See C.E. Neumann, 'Atherton, John (1598–1640)', GLBTQ Enclyopedia, www.glbtqarchive.com/ssh/atherton_j_S.pdf (downloaded 24 June 2017).
58 Rule 75, NLI MS 2091: Resolved upon the question, nem. con. [*nemine contradicente*] that no Lord of Parliament having once obtained the Leave of this House to waive his privilege in any cause, shall at any time after be admitted to resume his privilege in the same Cause, without the Leave of the House.
59 3 Edward IV, c. I; 11 & 12 Edward IV, c. LXXX.
60 *CJ*, 8 November 1614. Star Chamber was the term occasionally used in Ireland, but the official name of the prerogative court was the Court of Castle Chamber.
61 *CJ*, 17 November 1614.
62 *CJ*, 18 November 1614.
63 *CJ*, 23 November 1614.
64 *CJ*, 23 July 1661.
65 *CJ*, 30 July 1661.
66 *LJ*, 17 April 1635.
67 *LJ*, 18 April 1635.
68 *LJ*, 14 December 1665.
69 *LJ*, 14 December 1665.
70 NLI MS 9607, p. 85. *LJ*, 19 February 1641. Replevin was, in the seventeenth century, a counter-action against distress. P. Brand, 'The use and adaption of the action of replevin in Ireland during the reign of Edward I' in P. Brand, K. Costello, and W.N. Osborough (eds), *Adventures of the law: proceedings of the sixteenth British legal history conference, Dublin, 2003* (Dublin, 2005).

71 11 &12 Edward IV, c. LXXX.
72 *CJ*, 29 October 1614.
73 *CJ*, 2 November 1614.
74 *CJ*, 25 November 1634.
75 *CJ*, 2 December 1614. In the following session, Higgins had been incarcerated by the serjeant at arms, and also had a case heard where he was defendant answering a case by Redmond MacJennings, but was ordered to be released with Teige O'Connor (knight of the shire of Sligo) paying all of his fees, although it is not apparent whether these actions were involved with the original arrest of a servant of an MP. *CJ*, 16, 21 February, 5 March 1635.
76 *CJ*, 24 March 1635.
77 *LJ*, 19 February 1635.
78 *LJ*, 20 February 1635.
79 *LJ*, 23, 25 February 1635.
80 *LJ*, 3 June 1662.
81 Foster, *The House of Lords*, pp. 142–43.
82 *CJ*, 6 August 1642.
83 *CJ*, 6, 9 August 1642.
84 Ball, *The judges in Ireland, 1221–1921*, vol. 1, pp. 274–75.
85 *LJ*, 20 May 1645.
86 *LJ*, 31 July 1662.
87 *CJ*, 14 May 1662.
88 The speaker's warrant to the sheriff is printed in full in the journals, something not usually done, and is surely an indication of Ferneley's influence in drawing up the journals.
89 10 & 11 Charles I, c. XII.
    Forasmuch as doubt hath been made heretofore, if any person being arrested in execution, and by priviledge of either of the houses of parliament set at liberty, whether the partie at whose suit such execution was pursued, be for ever after barred and disabled to sue forth a new writ of execution in that case......from henceforth the partie at or by whose suit such writ of execution was pursued, his executors or administrators, after such time as the priviledge shall be so granted shall cease, may sue forth and execute a new writ or writs of execution, in such manner and forme as by the lawes of this realme he might have done if no such former execution had been taken forth or served.
90 See Richardson and Sayles, *The Irish Parliament in the middle ages*, pp. 332–65; Ellis, *Ireland in the age of the Tudors*, pp. 372–75.
91 *CJ*, 9 August 1642.
92 1 James I, c. 13 [Eng.]; Foster, *The House of Lords*, p. 143.
93 This bill raises a rather important issue of judicature of privilege cases after parliament had concluded. As has been discussed above at length, both houses had established a clear and unimpeachable right to sole judicature of their own privileges during the seventeenth century. However, parliamentary privilege lasted forty days longer than parliament did, and so it is questionable as to which court a member or a protected person should approach in complaint of a breach

of privilege after parliament had been determined. No examples of any of the other courts taking on privilege cases after parliament had ended are known and clearly there would be a question over their competency. Interestingly, there are two cases of privilege being retrospectively applied in the 1640s to breaches that occurred in the previous parliament. Sir Piers Crosby complained that his privilege as a member of the 1634–35 parliament had been breached when he was 'violently seized', interrogated and held in Dublin Castle for several days 'upon a bare suspicion of libel only'. Daniel O'Brien complained a month later that during the previous parliament his privileges and 'just liberties ... [were] violently infringed' when a bill was exhibited in the Court of Castle Chamber in July 1634, while parliament was sitting. The fact that both of these complaints were aired some sixteen months after the first sitting of the 1640–48 parliament should make us suspicious that the complaints were at least partially politically motivated. In both cases, the Commons found in favour of the MPs. A. Clarke, 'Sir Piers Crosby, 1590–1646: Wentworth's "tawney ribbon"', *IHS*, 26 (1988), pp. 142–60; *CJ*, 15 July, 7 August 1641.

94 *CJ*, 24, 26 March, 6 April 1635; *LJ*, 6, 18 April 1635. The Lords in particular have the appearance of simply going through the motions, passing another seven bills the same day without division or committals. The Commons passed another six the same day, committing just one.
95 *LJ*, 20 April 1643; *CJ*, 20 April 1643.
96 Catholic members involved in the initial rebellion and the confederacy were obviously excluded from parliament, and therefore any protections they may have made in advance of their absence were void. In England, however, peers who had joined the royalists outside of London were still afforded privilege of parliament for themselves and their attendants and servants until 1644. Foster, *The House of Lords, 1603–1649*, p. 141.
97 *CJ*, 17 February 1644.
98 *CJ*, 31 October 1644.
99 *LJ*, 24 February 1646.
100 James, *Lords of the ascendancy*, p. 85.
101 *CJ*, 6 November 1661.
102 *LJ*, 6 November 1661.
103 *LJ*, 6 December 1661; *CJ*, 6 December 1661.
104 *LJ*, 3 September 1662. The House of Commons assented to this move later in the month. *CJ*, 27 September 1662.
105 *LJ*, 26 February 1663; *CJ*, 5 March 1663. The Commons suggested the idea of an alphabetical parliamentary register of all protected persons, although it is not clear if this was ever assented to by the Lords.
106 *CJ*, 31 January 1666.
107 *CJ*, 12 April 1666; *LJ*, 12 April 1666.
108 *CJ*, 6, 7 July 1666; *LJ*, 11 July 1666.
109 Foster, *The House of Lords*, p. 142.
110 *LJ*, 28 July 1666.
111 *LJ*, 28 June 1666.

112 *LJ*, 24 July 1666.
113 *LJ*, 2 November 1692; NLI MS 2091.
114 *CJ*, 31 October, 3 November 1614.
115 Committal warrants, 9, 16 May 1614, *Acts of the Privy Council of England, 1613–4*.
116 *LJ*, 18 December 1643.
117 Greaves, *Deliver us from evil*, pp. 135–58; Dennehy, 'The restoration Irish parliament', pp. 53–68.
118 Foster, *The House of Lords*, ch. 8; M.A.R. Graves, 'Freedom of peers from arrest: the case of Henry Second Lord Cromwell, 1571–72', *American journal of legal history*, 21 (1977), pp. 1–14; Hunneyball, 'The development of parliamentary privilege'; K.A.T. Stapylton, 'The parliamentary privilege of freedom from arrest, 1603–1629', Unpublished Ph.D. thesis, University College London (2016).
119 *CJ*, 9 August 1642.
120 *CJ*, 20 April 1643.
121 *CJ*, 17 January 1666.
122 Although most interestingly, the complaint of Abdy against Howse heard strong evidence against Abdy insinuating he was in fact the aggressive and violent party. The following day, the Commons divided on the case, thirty-seven finding him guilty with twenty finding in Howse's favour. *CJ*, 21, 22 February 1666.
123 J.C. Beckett, *The cavalier duke: a life of James Butler, 1st duke of Ormond, 1610–1688* (Belfast, 1990), p. 15.
124 McCavitt, *Sir Arthur Chichester*, p. 184; Lye to Williamson, 16 December 1665, *CSPI*; Churchill to Bennet, 27 December 1665, *CSPI*.
125 *LJ*, 18 November 1642.
126 For example, Lord Fitzwilliam of Merrion, who attended regularly until 1646, and the earl of Westmeath in 1645.
127 The phrase '*de scandalo magnatum*' was used by Sir John Everard, knight of the shire for Tipperary, when discussing the case *lord chancellor v Sherlock* (1615). *CJ*, 27 April 1615.
128 J.H. Baker, *An introduction to English legal history* (3rd edn, London, 1990), pp. 496–97.
129 *LJ*, 29 July 1661, 26 June 1662.
130 *CJ*, 19 June 1661.
131 *CJ*, 24 September 1662.
132 *CJ*, 4 February 1663.
133 *CJ*, 12 February 1662.
134 *CJ*, 4 November 1634.
135 In England in the first half of the century, it was not uncommon for members to be brought before the council after parliament had ended and possibly put under house arrest, but Wentworth's move went several steps further. J.P. Kenyon, *The Stuart constitution: documents and commentary* (Cambridge, 1986), p. 24; Hunneyball, 'The development of parliamentary privilege'; Stapylton, 'The parliamentary privilege of freedom from arrest, 1603–1629'.
136 P. Hunneyball, 'The House of Commons, 1603–29' in C. Jones (ed.), *A short*

history of parliament: England, Great Britain, The United Kingdom, Ireland and Scotland (Woodbridge, 2009), p. 104; Smith, *The Stuart parliaments, 1603-1689*, p. 65; BL, Lansdowne MS 1208; NLI, MS 836.

137 *CJ*, 12, 13 December 1665. 17 & 18 Charles II, c. I, an act for the grant of four entire subsidies by the temporalty. This act is recorded in the journals of the Commons and the Lords as being eight subsidies rather than four. Eight would seem to be the more correct figure as we have two printed sources reporting eight, and just one printed source (*The statutes at large*) reporting four. *CJ*, 13, 14, 15, 23 December 1665; *LJ*, 18, 21, 23 December 1665. *The statutes at large*, vol. 3, pp. 1-2.

138 P. Seaward, *The cavalier parliament and the reconstruction of the old regime, 1661-1667* (Cambridge, 1989); C. Russell *The crisis of parliaments: English history, 1509-1660* (Oxford, 1971).

139 *CJ*, 18 December 1665.

140 Dennehy, 'Parliament in Ireland, 1661-6', pp. 113-28. Johnston, 'State formation in seventeenth-century Ireland'. It is noteworthy that after the catastrophe of the early 1640s concurrent parliaments, the government felt confident to convene all three kingdoms' parliaments simultaneously on 8 May 1661.

141 McCavitt, *Sir Arthur Chichester*, pp. 169-89.

142 Clarke, *The Old English in Ireland*, p. 136.

143 For example, see the details of the Norfolk election in 1586. G.R. Elton, *The Tudor constitution - documents and commentary* (Cambridge, 1960), pp. 275-7; *The parliament of England, 1559-1581*, pp. 338-41; D. Hirst, 'Elections and the privileges of the House of Commons in the early seventeenth century: confrontation or compromise?', *Historical journal*, 18 (1975), pp. 852-61; R.C. Munden, 'The defeat of Sir John Fortescue: court versus country at the hustings?', *EHR*, 93 (1978), pp. 811-16.

144 The study of elections, how they were conducted, and strategies of the various competing interests, although clearly of huge importance to a political study of parliament, is not in any meaningful sense a part of this book. It really falls into the remit of interaction between central and local government. For excellent work on electoral practice in Ireland in the seventeenth century, see McGrath, 'The Irish elections of 1640-1'; 'The membership of the Irish House of Commons, 1613-5', pp. 6-25; 'Electoral law in Ireland before 1641' in Dennehy (ed.), *Law and revolution in seventeenth-century Ireland*.

145 The committee 'appointed to examine privileges and returns, etc.' in the 1613-15 parliament was not composed until October 1614 due to the difficulties in the first abortive session in May 1613.

146 *CJ*, 16 March 1640.

147 A double return was made for the borough of Tuam in County Galway, but the former confederate lawyer, Geoffrey Browne, and Thomas Bramhall, described by Orrery as 'an Anabaptist', were deemed not to have been elected. No pronouncement made in this dispute is recorded in the Commons' journals, but the two others returned (Robert Ormsby and Humphrey Abdy) sat, and Browne and Bramhall were not mentioned again. It is perhaps surprising that two figures so obviously outside of the established church should be returned for a borough that

was the seat of the archbishop of Tuam. Orrery to Clarendon, 8 May 1661, Bodl., Clarendon MS 74, ff.383–86. This is not to say that all seats in the vicinity of episcopal seats were controlled by their bishops. Clogher, Leighlin Bridge (Ferns), Irishtown (Ossory), and Armagh were, in addition to Blessington as the personal property of Michael Boyle, archbishop of Dublin, and later Armagh. However, all others were not, including Ardfert, Waterford, Limerick, Cork, Dublin, Tuam. See Dennehy, 'Representation in later medieval and early modern Ireland'.

148 *CJ*, 15 May 1661.
149 *CJ*, 8 July 1661.
150 *CJ*, 11 July 1661.
151 For the best account of the campaign, see McCavitt, *Sir Arthur Chichester*, cc. 10, 11.
152 *CJ*, 15 October 1614.
153 *CJ*, 4 February, 27 May 1641.
154 Carew's remembrances to be thought of touching the parliament. Lambeth Palace Library, Carew MS 629, p. 53.
155 Wentworth to Coke, 24 June 1634, *The earl of Strafforde's letters*, vol. 1, pp. 269–70, 276–92. 'It is therefore ordered, that the awarding of the said writ and the placing of the said lord in the room of his father shall be with a *Salvo Jure* of the said Thomas, in case the said Thomas be living and return; And with this further saving, that in case the said Thomas be living, and that he or his heirs shall at any time hereafter return into this kingdom, and reassume the title of Lord of Slane, that then and in such case the said William, or his heirs, shall take no advantage or benefit by the said writ or any consequent thereof, but shall be altogether secluded from any such title, place or privilege, as he may claim by pretext of that writ, as if the honour and favour, now granted unto him, hand not been; or that no such writ had ever been awarded unto him; under which conditions and *Salvos* the said William did accept of the said favour, and fully consented it might be entered accordingly.' *LJ*, 14 July 1634.
156 *LJ*, 14 July 1634.
157 *CSPI*, 22 December 1660, 15 January 1661, 3 April 1661, 6 May 1661, 18 May 1661, 3 June 1661.
158 *LJ*, 9 May 1661.
159 *LJ*, 20 May, 5 July 1661.
160 Bergin and Lyall (eds), *The acts of James II's Irish parliament of 1689*, pp. xlii–l, 88–167.
161 Rule VII, VIII. *LJ*, 23 July 1634.
162 Rule 8, 9, 29. *LJ*, 2 November 1692; NLI MS 2091.
163 *LJ*, 28 July 1634.
164 *LJ*, 2 August 1634, 24 July 1661.
165 *CJ*, 22 July 1634.
166 *CJ*, 20 October 1614. His nephew, Hugh, MP for Newtownards in County Down, was also permitted to depart due to illness permanently and the House ordered another to be elected in his place. *CJ*, 4 February 1641.
167 *CJ*, 8 May 1615.

168 *CJ*, 7 April 1635. Interestingly, in 1661, the fines were charged at only £5, and the following year, only 2 shillings and 6 pence. *CJ*, 17 June 1661, 21 July 1662.
169 *CJ*, 17 May 1662.
170 Dennehy, 'Privilege, organisation and aristocratic identity', pp. 117–30; Ohlmeyer, *Making Ireland English*, pp. 34–47.
171 Kearney, *Strafford in Ireland*, pp. 50–51; Wentworth to the king, 22 January 1634, *The earl of Strafforde's letters*, vol. 1, pp. 182–87; List of noblemen with a licence to be absent from parliament, June 1634, *CSPI*.
172 *LJ*, 26 July 1634.
173 *LJ*, 13 February 1641.
174 18 May, 16 July 1641, *CSPI*. Grievance – An act should pass to prevent peers who have titles of honour in Ireland, but no lands there, from voting in the Irish house of lords, either by proxy or otherwise. Blank proxies, which allow two or three peers to sway the whole house must be stopped.
   Answer – No nobleman in future shall be capable of more proxies than two. Blank proxies stopped. If those peers who have no estates in Ireland purchase not, within five years, a Baron £200, a Viscount £400, and an Earl £600 per annum, they shall lose their votes until they gain such estates.
175 *LJ*, 10 May 1661.
176 *LJ*, 14 May 1661, LJ Eng., 25 February 1626. J.E. Powell, 'Proxy voting in the house of lords', *Parliamentary affairs*, 9 (1955), p. 203. The same day, the English peers voted that proxies of spiritual lords should be given only to other spirituals, and so too temporals proxies must stay with temporal lords.
177 *LJ*, 11 June 1661.
178 *LJ*, 2 November 1692; NLI MS 2091. This same set of orders ruled that proxies could not be used in judicial causes, which might indicate that they were permitted before this point.
179 *LJ*, 30 July 1634.
180 *LJ*, 1, 2 September 1662. Interestingly, on the same day as the protest by Massareene was entered, there is an order of the Lords for the lord chancellor to send a writ of summons to the marquis of Antrim, which could be indicative of an attempt by a Catholic and a Presbyterian lord from the same corner of the kingdom attempting to work together. What is more, the following day two bishops submitted their proxies to the benefit of the John Bramhall, the archbishop of Armagh, which may further indicate a vindictive action by a reactionary episcopal bench in particular against the two counties with the strongest Presbyterian population.
181 *LJ*, 11 September 1662.
182 *LJ*, 23 December 1665, 15 January 1666. The parishes were Aghad, Corkebegg, Ballinatory, Inishinebarky, Clonmolt, and Dangindonovane.
183 *CJ*, 16 May 1615.
184 Rule 42, *LJ*, 2 November 1692; NLI MS 2091. No Act of Restitution in Blood shall be proceeded upon in Parliament, until the same be first allowed and signed by the King's Majesty, and that then it is first to being in the House of Peers.
185 *CJ*, 17 November 1614.
186 *CJ*, 18 May 1613 – 24 October 1615; Treadwell, 'The House of Lords in the Irish

Parliament of 1613-1615', pp. 92-107. Bills in question included the bill for the attainder of the earl of Tyrone, the bill for the attainder of the earl of 'Sowgan' (Desmond), and the bill for restitution in blood of Maurice FitzGerald.
187 *CJ*, 22 August 1662. This topic is discussed at much greater length in the chapter on legislation.
188 Kelly, 'Monitoring the constitution'; *Poynings' Law*; C.I. McGrath, *The making of the eighteenth-century Irish constitution: government, parliament and the revenue, 1692-1714* (Dublin, 2000).
189 For the full details of the Commons' interpretation of the case, written up to be presented to the king by the commissioners of parliament then in England, see *CJ*, 5 March 1641.
190 The full background to this salacious case is found in McGrath, 'Sex, lies, and rigged elections'.
191 McGrath, 'A bibliographical dictionary of the membership of the Irish House of Commons', pp. 155-56.
192 *CJ*, 26 January 1641.
193 NLI MS 9607, p. 85.
194 *LJ*, 26 February 1641.
195 *LJ*, 25 May 1666.
196 Crawford, *A star chamber court in Ireland*, p. 401.
197 *CJ*, 18 February 1641.
198 *CJ*, 5 March 1641; *LJ*, 4, 5 March 1641; Lords justices and council to Vane, 2 April 1641, *CSPI*; NLI 9607, pp. 117-30; D. Edwards, 'The poisoned chalice: the Ormond inheritance, sectarian division and the emergence of James Butler, 1614-1642' in T.C. Barnard and J. Fenlon (eds), *The dukes of Ormond, 1610-1745* (Woodbridge, 2000), p. 79.
199 *LJ*, 27 November 1662.
200 *CJ*, 10, 20, 27 February 1663; *LJ*, 9, 20 February, 12 March 1663.
201 *LJ*, 17, 24 July 1666.
202 *LJ*, 30 July 1666.
203 Ormond to Bennet, 18 April 1663, Bodl., Carte MS 46, f. 45.

6

Conclusion

One of the most dangerous and more persistent assumptions about the early modern Irish Parliament, especially in the seventeenth century, is that due to its dependence upon the English model for direction in precedence and procedure it was simply a carbon copy of the English assembly. For example, questions of procedure are often treated entirely with reference to the example of England as if the answer can invariably be found by looking to the studies of the English parliament. This book has demonstrated that whereas there were aspects of procedures of the Irish Parliament that were thoroughly and consciously modelled on the English example, there were also significant differences. Examples have been given of cases where contemporary members of the Irish Parliament and contemporary commentators explicitly mentioned the Westminster example as a guide. Yet we have also seen many instances where parliament in Dublin followed its own footprint and developed its own practices.

Parliamentarians and commentators were influential in attempting to ensure explicit adherence to English parliamentary norms. However, it should also be acknowledged that the development of the Irish Parliament along English lines also happened for more organic reasons. Ireland had a political society and, more importantly, a kingdom based closely on that of England. The role of the viceroy in Dublin Castle along with that of his royal officers and the judicial system were also based on the English model, and so it naturally followed that in a political culture and system that bore many resemblances to the English state, the Irish assembly was always likely to develop in a manner that was not too dissimilar to the neighbouring parliament. Thus, just as in Westminster in the seventeenth century, the Irish Parliament consisted of an upper house containing the higher echelons of civil and ecclesiastical society, and a lower house made up of representatives of the country gentry and the towns. It was overseen by a royal representative, assisted by the Privy Council (many of whom sat in parliament), and made use of many state officers, such as the judiciary and other members of the administration. The two houses of parliament worked together to make bills into acts, dispensed justice when it was required, and occasionally undertook to represent grievances of the localities or of the kingdom in general to the viceroy, and sometimes to the king.

However, for all of these similarities, it must also be emphasised that once we delve a little deeper, we find a political culture and state that was uniquely Irish and, despite the hopes of many English politicians and newcomers to Ireland since the reign of Henry II, Ireland was never made English nor British.[1] Like England in the seventeenth century (particularly in the middle third), Irish political society was deeply divided. Perhaps in ways not too dissimilar to those described by Professor Stone and his colleagues, Irish society had been changed in a large way by the transfer of land in the early modern period. In England, the market was based on confiscations of monastic lands, in Ireland it was a more volatile mix of monastic lands with those made forfeit by rebellion.[2] In both kingdoms the reformation may be blamed in part for religious divisions of the seventeenth century, but in a very different fashion. The political classes in England largely made the change to the new religion but soon found that it began to fragment in various ways which were to take their toll on parliamentary politics in the seventeenth century. In Ireland, Protestant divisions were vastly overshadowed by the fact that a substantial majority of the population was Catholic. This majority was being systematically excluded from most positions of influence. Finally, Ireland had an ethnic division that England did not have. A substantial part of the island at the beginning of the seventeenth century held no affinity whatsoever for the outgoing Tudor monarchy or its Stuart successor. Militarily defeated, the Gaelic Irish were subsumed into the new triple monarchy. In theory, exposure to English law, language, and civility should have made them into 'little Englanders' within a few generations at most, but a colonial elite needed to emphasise the differences that made them civil and the natives barbarous, and so the process of cultural and political assimilation was always going to be tricky.

Ireland's unique constitutional status added to the overall complexity. In 1541, Ireland had been transformed by act of parliament that stipulated that Ireland was 'united and knit to the imperial crown of the realm of England'.[3] However, there was no definition of the specific relationship between the English and Irish parliaments. English common law had largely been the common law of Ireland since the early days of the Irish lordship, and so naturally precedents in the English Parliament, as a court of record, were in many instances appropriate for the Irish Parliament. However, political and practical realities since the establishment of English law in the lordship caused the

Irish Parliament to develop in a different manner. Sometimes this was simply a reflection of the fact that the colony in Ireland was never given the full attention of its lord or his resources in England and occasionally had to make its own way. When it became isolated, the transfer of ideas and regulations for the holding of parliament could and did take a different form to England. There were also occasions both in the medieval and early modern periods when the Irish Parliament deliberately managed to ensure that it had a complexion very different from that in Westminster. A legal and administrative history of the passage of legislation can illustrate this fact. Irish legislation, in a very basic analysis, bore a striking resemblance to English legislation in the way that it was formulated and processed. As in England, it had to pass through each house and then receive the royal assent. During its passage through each house, it was generally read three times. However, there were significant differences in the way legislation proceeded before it arrived in each house. Irish legislation was given advance royal assent, and although over time an arrangement was effectively worked out whereby either house could effect changes to legislation or indeed plan new legislation themselves, a detailed examination of overall legislative procedure shows the Irish Parliament processed its business in a drastically different manner to that of England.

So too the manner of access to parliament for the members of the public for either justice or grace, or indeed for members of parliament themselves. Again, we see that there was a similar procedure in the Irish Parliament to that of the Westminster assembly. Ireland also had a marked increase in the use of petitions and parliamentary judicial action during the middle third of the seventeenth century. The fact that parliament in England could and did act as an alternative court and a superior court to the Irish one means that a more detailed study of the judicial role is a necessity. Naturally, this increase in business affected the way that parliament functioned in terms of how the day's business was set out, the role of the legal and clerical officers, and also the necessity to have MPs and peers spend an increasing amount of time on matters pertaining to justice. This kind of justice could become politicised, and indeed the role of parliamentary justice became a key part of the political breakdown in Ireland in the early 1640s.

The role of the speaker and the rest of the officers and servants of parliament can be understood (and indeed, misunderstood) in a similar manner. In an institutional history of parliament, knowing the technical details of the role of these officers is of more importance than the biographical details of members of both houses. As we have seen at various stages, the work of parliament could continue without the vast majority of members, but not without the speaker. Many of the tumultuous events of seventeenth-century parliamentary politics were played out by the speakers and judges in particular, so it is essential to have as thorough as possible a knowledge of their work.

Occasionally, their function mirrored that of their English counterparts, but there were critical times when this was not so, such as those frequent occasions when the lord chancellor undertook the role of lord justice and an alternative had to be found. The fact that many archbishops held the role of speaker of the lords in Ireland mark it out as position quite different from that in England.

Studying the liberties and privileges of parliaments is perhaps the most interesting way to study the institution of parliament. The way in which an institution regulated its own individual members yields great insight on how it worked, how people felt it should have worked, and importantly, how it interacted with the 'outside' world. While a study of privilege will frequently highlight a vain and selfish collection of individuals that use their elected or inherited positions of power to protect and indeed increase their wealth and status, Chapter 5 showed that parliament could sometimes be sensitive to the needs of the population at large and organise their privileges accordingly. It also showed that privilege in Ireland did differ from England in the way that it was legislated for and regulated.

Parliamentary history in Ireland has had mixed fortunes and a complete and thorough understanding of the institution has not yet been fully developed. While this book in no way attempts or claims to have achieved a complete understanding, it does open up the workings of the seventeenth-century Irish assembly. A similar and even more thorough approach across the centuries would provide a more complete picture, but the restrictions of time and space have demanded that it should be curtailed to the seventeenth century and just to events within parliament itself. This study has sought to put parliament into its context as part of the judicial and administrative establishment of the kingdom, rather than following it as a forum for political reaction, opposition, and drama. The Irish Parliament at this time was not democratic in any sense and the ethnic and religious chasms within Irish society make it questionable whether parliament in Ireland in this period could be described as representative. Studying the Irish assembly in a similar fashion to the way in which the English assembly has been studied in the past is a dangerous move. The social and political climate in Ireland was profoundly different. However, what is true for both realms is that the notion of a parliamentary opposition using procedures and procedural innovations to fight a political war as a *sine qua non* does not, for the most part, stand up to scrutiny.[4]

However, there are ways to invert the traditional approach and instead to use a thorough knowledge of the procedural development of parliament during the period in question (and the constitution in general) to come to a greater understanding of political history. With so many procedural issues involved at moments of high political drama (such as the role of petitions in the attack on the Strafford administration in the early 1640s), a well-informed knowledge of how petitions worked and why the use of them developed is essential to a good investigation of how events unfolded. The same can be said in the understanding of the development of the heads of bills process in the seventeenth century, in that in order to understand the events of the sole right dispute and the general use of heads of bills in the long eighteenth century, a working knowledge of the process in the century before is instructive. The role of government placemen within the membership, and later into the eighteenth century the growth of the undertaker movement, can best be grasped if we have a better understanding of the traditional role of various crown officials in parliament, both as members and as servants of that body.

Despite the irregularity of parliament in Ireland, it was still an organic body that developed over time. This can be seen in all aspects of its procedures and processes. Sometimes the catalyst for change came from politics, but more often it came from the contact between parliament and the executive or the judiciary. Most of the time, members of both houses were aware of the institution and how it worked, and they continually used and looked for precedent as a guide to how to organise themselves; both to the English Parliament but also to the Irish assembly as it sat in the centuries before 1613. Despite the traditional assertion that the Irish Parliament was relatively weak and dependent (which to a certain degree it was), we should keep in mind that at the same time as the Irish Catholic party was contesting the speakership and successfully wrecking plans for anti-Catholic legislation, the French *états généraux* were dismissed and to be done without for the following 175 years. In 1661, as the Commons asserted their pre-eminence in money-raising acts, and the Lords their superiority as a court of judicature, the Danish *rigsdag* was entirely abolished. In truth, after centuries of intermittent meetings, the 1650s parliamentary union, and the later seventeenth-century English constitutional (r)evolution and a growing colonial influence in all areas of the state, it is noteworthy in itself that the Irish Parliament survived at all.

NOTES

1 N. Canny, *Making Ireland British, 1580–1650* (Oxford, 2001).
2 L. Stone, *The causes of the English revolution* (London, 1972); C. Hill, *Puritanism and revolution: studies in interpretation of the English revolution of the 17th century* (London, 1958), ch. 2.
3 33 Henry VIII, c. I.
4 Graves, *The House of Lords in the parliaments of Edward VI and Mary I*, p. 141.

Bibliography

MANUSCRIPTS

Armagh Public Library (APL), Armagh
Mss. P00149836X, P001497053, P001497118, P001498149.

Public Record Office of Northern Ireland (PRONI), Belfast
Mss. T. 954, T. 971, T. 765/1.

Cambridge University Library, Cambridge
Mss. Fr. III. 17, Mm. I.46.

Harvard University Library, Houghton, Cambridge (MA)
Mss. Eng. 218. 22–23.

Dublin City Library and Archives, Dublin
Gilbert Coll. Mss. 88–9, 145, 158, 173, 198, 219, 249.

Genealogical Office, Dublin
Mss. 1, 2, 4, 8, 14, 17, 50, 56, 95, 96, 150, 200, 552–3.

King's Inns Library, Dublin
John P. Prendergast Papers.

Marsh's Library, Dublin
Mss. Z.1.1.18, Z3.1.1, Z3.2.5, Z4. 3. 28.

National Archives of Ireland (NAI), Dublin
Mss. M239, M610, M612, M865, M939, M2448–9, M2452, M 2458–60, M2532, M2541, M2829, M3070, M3237, M3571–2, M3575, M4839–40, M5939, M5941, M7004, Ms. C86.

Ms. N16267.
Ms. Lodge.
Ms. R.C. 14/1–3, 5–11.
Ms. Wyche 126.

National Library of Ireland (NLI), Dublin
Mss. 14, 18, 31–6, 40, 88, 184, 195–195B, 692, 802, 816, 836, 999, 1450, 2091, 2189, 2323–62, 2511–3, 2698, 2700–1, 7724, 7733–4, 8008, 8099, 8172, 8389, 8546, 8642, 8646, 8818, 9218, 9607, 11,056, 11.959, 11,973–4, 12,813.
Mss. D. 1871, D. 3941, D. 3958, D. 3978, D. 6914–5, D. 7094, D. 16,430.
Ms. Ainsworth (JF).
Annesley Mss. Misc books no. 5, Lib. G.
Joly Ms. 6.

Oireachtas Library, Dublin
Ms. 8. H. 12.

Royal Irish Academy (RIA), Dublin
Ms. 3. A. 54.
Ms. D. V. 3.
Ms. 24. D. 20.
Upton Papers, No. 6, 13.

Trinity College Library, Dublin
Ms. 578, 587, 613–6, 622, 647, 650–1, 659, 808, 843–4, 1178, 1180, 1444, 1749, 1746.
Ms. V. 4. 4.

British Library (BL), London
Add Mss. 4223, 4771, 4781, 4792, 4819, 5754, 6297, 9715, 11312, 19526–7, 21132, 22548, 29854, 30383, 33505, 33745, 34253, 34773, 35838, 35850–1, 37206–8, 37823.
Cotton Ms. Faustina D.V.
Cotton Ms. Julius F. VI.
Cotton Mss. Titus B.X., B.X.37, B.X.39, B. XIII.
Egerton Mss. 205, 212, 1048, 2537–8, 2541, 2543, 2618.
Hargrave Mss. 216, 278.
Harleian Mss. 1042, 2048, 2120, 2138, 4261, 4892, 4931, 5108.
Lansdowne Mss. 156, 159, 194, 253, 255, 692, 1208.
Sloane Mss. 203, 1008, 1015, 1742.
Stowe Mss. 153, 185, 744.

Lambeth Palace Library, London
Mss. 600, 608, 610, 621, 629.

National Archives (TNA), London
P.C. 1.

PRO 30/5.
PRO 31/8.
SP 63.

Victoria and Albert Museum (National Art Library), London
Forster Mss. 426-7 (47.A.39-46)

Bodleian Library (Bodl), Oxford
Add. Ms. A. 116 (30, 166)
Carte Mss. 31-35, 40, 42-44, 47-49, 51, 60-61, 64-72, 118, 142-47, 158-59, 213-15, 219-21, 232.
Clarendon Mss. 70-89, 121
Laud Misc. Ms. 612.
Rawlinson Mss. A. 237, C. 389, D.922, D.1079.
Tanner Mss. 58, 67, 70, 458.
Willis Ms. 57 (16,351).

PRINTED MATERIAL

Primary sources
An account of the whole proceedings of the parliament in Ireland, beginning March 25 1689, and ending the 29th of June following; with the establishment of their forces there (London, 1689)
Mercurius Hibernicus
Modus tenendi parliamenta in Hibernia, ed. by A. Dopping (Dublin, 1692)
The earl of Strafforde's letters and dispatches with an essay towards his life by Sir George Radcliffe, ed. by W. Knowler (2 vols, London, 1739)
The journal of the proceedings of the parliament in Ireland, with the establishment of their forces there (London, 1689)
Tracts relating to Ireland, ed. by J. Hardiman (Dublin, 1843)
Wentworth papers, 1597-1628, ed. by J.P. Cooper (London, 1973)

Bernard, N., *The penitent death of a woefull sinner* (London, 1642)
Davies, J., Le primer report des cases in les courts del roy (Dublin, 1615), translated as *A report of cases and matters in law resolved and abridged in the king's courts in Ireland* (Dublin, 1762)
Elsynge, H., *The manner of holding parliaments in England* (London, 1768)
___ *Judicature in parlement by Henry Elsyng*, ed. by E.R. Foster (London, 1991)
Locke, J., *Locke: Two treatises of government*, ed. by P. Laslett (Cambridge, 1960)
May, E., *Treatise on the law, privileges, proceedings and usage of parliament*, ed. by D. Lidderdale (19th edn, London, 1976)
Mountmorres, H.R. *History of the principle transactions of the Irish Parliament, from the year 1634 to 1666* (London, 1792)
Molyneux, W., *The case of Ireland stated ...*, ed. by J.G. Simms (Dublin, 1977)
Parliament in Elizabethan England, John Hooker's order and usage ed. by V.F. Snow (Yale, 1977)

Spencer, E., *A view of the State of Ireland* (1633) ed. by A. Hadfield and W. Maley (Oxford, 1997)

Records publications

Acts of the Privy Council of England (London, 1921–40)
Calendar of the Carew manuscripts preserved in Lambeth Palace Library (London, 1867)
Calendar of the Clarendon state papers in the Bodleian Library (Oxford, 1970)
Calendar of the state papers domestic series of the reign of Charles II (London, 1862)
Calendar of the state papers relating to Ireland during the reign of Charles II (London, 1905)

Records of parliament

The journals of the House of Commons (London, 1742–)
The journals of the House of Commons of the Kingdom of Ireland (Dublin, 1752–1800)
The journals of the House of Lords (London, 1767–)
The journals of the House of Lords of the Kingdom of Ireland (Dublin, 1779–1800)
The statutes at large, passed in parliaments held in Ireland (Dublin, 1786–1800)
The statutes of the realm (London, 1810–28)
Viceregal speeches and episcopal votes (London, 1869)

Statutes

Chronological table and index of the statutes affecting Northern Ireland, and dealing with matters with respect to which the parliament of Northern Ireland has power to make laws, covering the legislation to December 31st, 1946 (7th edn, 2 vols, Belfast, 1948)
In this volume are contained all the statutes from the tenthe yere of King Henry the sixth, to the xiii yere of ... Queene Elyzabeth made and established in ... Irelande, ed. by R. Tottell (London, 1572)
Statute rolls of the parliament of Ireland, Edward IV (Dublin, 1914) ed. by H.F. Berry
Statute rolls of the parliament of Ireland, Edward IV (Dublin, 1939) ed. by J.F. Morrissey
Statute rolls of the parliament of Ireland, Henry VI (Dublin, 1910) ed. by H.F. Berry
Statute rolls of the parliament of Ireland, John to Henry V (Dublin, 1907) ed. by H.F. Berry
Statute rolls of the Irish Parliament, Richard III – Henry VIII (Dublin, 2002) ed. by P. Connolly
The Irish statutes: 3 Edward II to the union, A.D. 1310–1800 ed. by W.F. Callinan (London, 1885)
The statutes of Ireland beginning the third yere of K. Edward the second and continuing untill the end of the parliament, begunn in the eleventh yeare of.. King James, and ended in the thirteenth yere ... ed. by R. Bolton (Dublin, 1621)

Irish manuscripts commission

Court of claims: submissions and evidence, 1663, ed. by G. Tallon and intro. J.G. Simms (Dublin: Irish Manuscripts Commission, 2006)

Irish Exchequer payments, 1270–1446: volume II, 1326–1446, ed. by P. Connolly (Dublin, 1998)
Parliaments and councils of mediaeval Ireland, ed. by H.G. Richardson and G.O. Sayles (Dublin, 1947)
Patentee officers in Ireland, 1173–1826, including high sheriffs, 1661–1684 and 1761–1816, ed. by James L.J. Hughes (Dublin, 1960)

SECONDARY MATERIAL

Armstrong, O., 'Manuscripts of the *Modus tenendi parliamentum* in the library of Trinity College, Dublin', *PRIA* 36, C (1921–24)
Armstrong, R., 'Eustace, Sir Maurice (1590x95–1665)', *ODNB*
__ *Protestant War: the 'British' of Ireland and the wars of the three kingdoms* (Manchester, 2005)
Armstrong, R. and Ó hAnnracháin, T. (eds), *Community in early modern Ireland* (Dublin, 2006)
Arnold, L.J., 'The Irish Court of Claims of 1663', *IHS*, 24 (1985)
__ *The restoration land settlement in County Dublin, 1660–1688: a history of the administration of the acts of settlement and explanation* (Dublin, 1993)
Arthurson, I., *The Perkin Warbeck conspiracy, 1491–1499* (Stroud, 1994)
Aylmer, G.E., *The crown's servants: government and civil service under Charles II, 1660–1685* (Oxford, 2002)
__ *The king's servants: the civil service of Charles I, 1625–1642* (London, 1961)
__ *The state's servants: the civil service of the English republic, 1649–1660* (London, 1973)
Bagwell, R., *Ireland under the Stuarts and during the interregnum* (3 vols, London, 1916)
Baker, J.H., *An introduction to English legal history* (3rd edn, London, 1990)
__ '"United and knit to the imperial crown": an English view of the Anglo-Hibernian constitution in 1670' in D. Greer, D. and N. Dawson (eds) *Mysteries and solutions in Irish legal history* (Dublin, 2001)
Ball, F.E., *The judges in Ireland, 1221–1921* (2 vols, Dublin, 1993)
__ 'Some notes on the Irish judiciary in the reign of Charles II, 1660–85, conclusion', *Journal of the Cork Historical and Archaeological Society*, 9 (1903)
__ 'Some notes on the Irish judiciary in the reign of Charles II, 1660–85, continued', *Journal of the Cork Historical and Archaeological Society*, 8 (1902)
Barbour, V., *Henry Bennet, earl of Arlington, secretary of state to Charles II* (Washington, 1914)
Barnard, T.C., 'Boyle, Michael (1609/10–1702)', *ODNB*
__ 'Considering the inconsiderable: electors, Patrons and Irish Elections 1659–1761' in D. W. Hayton (ed.), *The Irish Parliament in the eighteenth century: the long apprenticeship* (Edinburgh, 2001)
__ *Cromwellian Ireland: English government and reform in Ireland, 1649–1660* (2nd edn, Oxford, 2000)
Barnard, T.C. and Fenlon, J. (eds), *The dukes of Ormond, 1610–1745* (Woodbridge, 2000)

Barnwell, P.S. and Mostert, M. (eds), *Political assemblies in the earlier middle ages* (Turnhout, 2003)
Barry, J., 'Magrath, Miler (Meiler)', *DIB*
Bartlett, T. and Jeffery, K. (eds), *A military history of Ireland* (Cambridge, 1997)
Battles, M., *Library: an unquiet history* (London, 2003)
Beckett, J.C., *The cavalier duke: a life of James Butler, 1st duke of Ormond, 1610-1688* (Belfast, 1990)
__ *The making of modern Ireland* (2nd edn, London, 1981)
Bellamy, J.G., *The law of treason in England in the later middle ages* (Cambridge, 1970)
__ *The Tudor law of treason: an introduction* (London, 1979)
Bennett, M., *Lambert Simnel and the battle of Stoke* (Gloucester, 1987)
Benson, C. and Pollard, M., '"The rags of Ireland are by no means the same": Irish paper used in the *Statutes at Large*', *Long Room*, 2 (1970)
Bergin, J., 'Vesey, John', *ODNB*
Bergin, J. and Lyall, A. (eds), *The acts of James II's Irish Parliament of 1689* (Dublin, 2016)
Bond, M.F., *Guide to the records of parliament* (London, 1971)
Bottigheimer, K.S., *English money and Irish land: the 'adventurers' in the Cromwellian settlement of Ireland* (Oxford, 1971)
__ 'The restoration land settlement in Ireland: a structural view', *IHS*, 18 (1972)
Bradshaw, B., *The Irish constitutional revolution of the sixteenth century* (Cambridge, 1979)
__ 'The opposition to the ecclesiastical legislation in the Irish reformation parliament', *IHS*, 16 (1969)
Brady, C. and Ohlmeyer, J.H. (eds), *British interventions in early modern Ireland* (Cambridge, 2005)
Brand, P., 'The birth and early development of a colonial judiciary: the judges of the lordship of Ireland, 1210-1377' in W.N. Osborough (ed.), *Explorations in law and history* (Dublin, 1995)
__ 'The use and adaption of the action of replevin in Ireland during the reign of Edward I' in P. Brand, K. Costello, and W.N. Osborough (eds), *Adventures of the law: proceedings of the sixteenth British legal history conference, Dublin, 2003* (Dublin, 2005)
Brand, P., Costello, K., and Osborough, W.N. (eds), *Adventures of the law: proceedings of the sixteenth British legal history conference, Dublin, 2003* (Dublin, 2005)
Brown, K. and Mann, A.J. (eds) *The history of the Scottish Parliament* (3 vols, Edinburgh, 2005)
Burghclere, W., *Strafford* (2 vols, London, 1931)
__ *The life of James, first duke of Ormonde, 1610-1688* (2 vols, London, 1912)
Butler, T.B., 'The officers of arms in Ireland', *The Irish genealogist*, 2 (1943)
Caldicott, C.E.J., Gough, H., and Pittion, J.P. (eds), *The Huguenots and Ireland: anatomy of an emigration* (Dublin, 1987)
Canny, N., *Making Ireland British, 1580-1650* (Oxford, 2001)

___ *The upstart earl: a study of the social and mental world of Richard Boyle, first earl of cork, 1566-1643* (Cambridge, 1982)
Carey, V. and Lotz-Heumann, U. (eds), *Taking sides: colonial and confessional* mentalités *in early modern Ireland* (Dublin, 2003)
Carroll, S., 'The Dublin parliamentary elections, 1613' in W. Sheehan and M. Cronin (eds), *Riotous assemblies: rebels, riots and revolts in Ireland* (Cork, 2011)
Clarke, A., '28 November 1634: a detail of Strafford's administration', *JRSAI*, 93 (1963)
___ 'A woeful sinner: John Atherton' in V. Carey and U. Lotz-Heumann (eds), *Taking sides: colonial and confessional* mentalités *in early modern Ireland* (Dublin, 2003)
___ 'Colonial constitutional attitudes in Ireland, 1640-60', *PRIA*, 90 C (1990)
___ 'Historical revision XVIII: the history of Poynings' Law, 1615-41', *IHS*, 18 (1972-73)
___ 'Ireland and the general crisis', *Past and present*, 48 (1970)
___ 'Patrick Darcy and the constitutional relationship between Ireland and Britain' in J. Ohlmeyer (ed.), *Political thought in seventeenth-century Ireland: kingdom or colony* (Cambridge, 2000)
___ *Prelude to restoration in Ireland: the end of the commonwealth, 1659-1660* (Cambridge, 1999)
___ 'Sir Piers Crosby, 1590-1646: Wentworth's "tawney ribbon"', *IHS*, 26 (1988)
___ *The graces, 1625-41* (Dundalk, 1968)
___ *The Old English in Ireland, 1625-42* (2nd edn, Dublin, 2000)
Clarke, A. and Fenlon, D., 'Two notes on the parliament of 1634', *JRSAI*, 97 (1967)
Clarke, M.V., *Medieval representation and consent: a study of early parliaments in England and Ireland, with special reference to the* Modus tenendi parliamentum (London, 1936)
Coburn Walshe, H., 'Jones, Thomas (c.1550-1619)', *ODNB*
Collinson, P., 'Elton, Sir Geoffrey Rudolph (1921-1994)', *ODNB*
___ 'Puritans, men of business and Elizabethan parliaments', *Parliamentary history*, 7 (1988)
Conway, A., *Henry VII's relations with Scotland and Ireland, 1485-98* (Cambridge, 1932)
Connolly, S.J., *Contested island: Ireland 1460-1630* (Oxford, 2007)
___ *Divided kingdom: Ireland, 1630-1800* (Oxford, 2008)
___ *Religion, law and power: the making of Protestant Ireland, 1660-1730* (Oxford, 1992)
Cosgrove, A., *Late medieval Ireland, 1370-1541* (Dublin, 1981)
___ 'Parliament and the Anglo-Irish community: the declaration of 1460' in A. Cosgrove and J.I. McGuire (eds), *Parliament and community: historical studies XIV* (Belfast, 1983)
Cosgrove, A. and McGuire, J.I. (eds), *Parliament and community: historical studies XIV* (Belfast, 1983)
Craig, M., *Irish book bindings* (Dublin, 1976)
Crawford, J.G., *Anglicizing the government of Ireland: the Irish Privy Council and the expansion of Tudor rule, 1556-1578* (Dublin, 1993)
___ *A star chamber court in Ireland: the Court of Castle Chamber, 1571-1641* (Dublin, 2005)
Cronin, J. and Clavin, T., 'Lane, George', *DIB*

Cruickshanks, E. (ed.), *The Stuart courts* (Stroud, 2000)
Curry, A., 'Speakers at war in the late 14th and 15th centuries' in P. Seaward (ed.), *Speakers and the speakership: presiding officers and the management of business from the middle ages to the 21st century* (Oxford, 2010)
Curtis, E., *A history of medieval Ireland* (Dublin, 1938)
__ 'Richard duke of York as viceroy of Ireland, 1447–1460', *JRSAI*, 62 (1932)
__ 'The acts of the Drogheda parliament, 1494-5, or "Poynings' Law"' in A. Conway, (ed.), *Henry VII's relations with Scotland and Ireland, 1485-98* (Cambridge, 1932)
Davis, R.W. (ed.), *The origins of modern freedom in the West* (Stanford, 1995)
Davis, T.O., *The patriot parliament* (3rd edn, Dublin, 1863)
Dawson, N.M. (ed.), *Reflections on law and history: Irish legal history society discourses and other papers, 2000–2005* (Dublin, 2006)
Dennehy, C.A., 'An administrative and legal history of the Irish Parliament, 1613–89', Unpublished Ph.D. thesis, University College Dublin, 2011
__ 'Appointments to the restoration Irish bench' in C.A. Dennehy (ed.), *Law and revolution in seventeenth-century Ireland* (Dublin, 2019)
__ 'Dependency and subservience: the Irish Parliament as a "small-state parliament"', *Czasopismo prawno-historyczne*, 61 (2009)
__ 'Institutional history and the early modern Irish state' in V. Carey, S. Covington, and V. McGowan-Doyle (eds), *Early modern Ireland: sources, methods, perspectives* (New York, 2018)
__ (ed.), *Law and revolution in seventeenth-century Ireland* (Dublin, 2019)
__ '*Nisi per legale judicium parium suorum*: trial by peer in the criminal trial in early modern Ireland' in P. Crooks and T. Mohr (eds), *Law and the idea of liberty* (Dublin, 2019)
__ 'Parliament in Ireland, 1661-6', Unpublished M.Litt. thesis, University College Dublin, 2002
__ 'Privilege, organisation, and aristocratic identity in the seventeenth-century Irish House of Lords' in F. Soddu and A. Nieddu (eds), *Assemblee rappresentative, autonomie territoriali, culture politiche. Atti del 59°Congresso dell'International Commission for the History of Representative and Parliamentary Institutions. Alghero 9–12 luglio 2008* (Sassari, 2011)
__ 'Representation in later medieval and early modern Ireland' in M. Damon, J. Haemers, and A.J. Mann (eds), *Political representation: communities, ideas and institutions in Europe, c. 1200 – c. 1650* (Brill, 2018)
__ (ed.), *Restoration Ireland: always settling and never settled* (Aldershot, 2008)
__ 'Sir Winston Churchill and restoration Ireland' in R. McNamara (ed.), *The Churchills and Ireland: connections and controversies from the 1660s to the 1960s* (Dublin, 2012)
__ 'Speakers in the 17th century Irish Parliament' in P. Seaward (ed.), *Speakers and the speakership: presiding officers and the management of business from the middle ages to the 21st century* (Oxford, 2010)
__ 'Surviving sources for Irish parliamentary history in the seventeenth century' *Parliaments, estates and representation*, 3 (2010)

___ 'The Irish Parliament after the rebellion, 1642-8' in P. Little (ed.), *Ireland in crisis: politics and religion during the confederate wars, 1641-1650* (Manchester, 2019)

___ 'The restoration Irish Parliament, 1661-6' in C.A. Dennehy (ed.), *Restoration Ireland: always settling and never settled* (Aldershot, 2008)

Dodd, G., *Justice and grace: private petitioning and the English parliament in the late middle ages* (Oxford, 2007)

Donaldson, A.G., *Some comparative aspects of Irish law* (Durham NC, 1957)

___ 'The application in Ireland of English and British legislation made before 1801', Unpublished Ph.D. thesis, Queen's University, Belfast (1952)

Duxbury, N., *The nature and authority of precedent* (Cambridge, 2008)

Edwards, D., 'Scottish officials and secular government in early Stuart Ireland' in D. Edwards, with S. Egan (eds) *The Scots in early Stuart Ireland: union and separation in two kingdoms* (Manchester, 2016)

___ 'The poisoned chalice: the Ormond inheritance, sectarian division and the emergence of James Butler, 1614-1642' in T.C. Barnard and J. Fenlon (eds), *The dukes of Ormond, 1610-1745* (Woodbridge, 2000)

Edwards, D. with Egan, S. (eds), *The Scots in early Stuart Ireland: union and separation in two kingdoms* (Manchester, 2016)

Edwards, R.D. and Moody, T.W., 'The history of Poynings' Law: part I, 1494-1615', *IHS*, 2 (1940-1)

Egan, S., 'Finance and the government of Ireland, 1660-85', Unpublished Ph.D. thesis, Trinity College Dublin, 1983

Ellis, S.G., *Ireland in the age of the Tudors: English expansion and the end of Gaelic rule* (Harlow, 1998)

___ 'Parliament and community in Yorkist and Tudor Ireland' in A. Cosgrove and J.I. McGuire (eds), *Parliament and community: historical studies XIV* (Belfast, 1983)

___ *Reform and revival: English government in Ireland, 1470-1534* (London, 1986)

Elton, G.R., *Political history: principles and practice* (London, 1970)

___ 'The early journals of the House of Lords', *EHR*, 84 (1974)

___ *The parliament of England, 1559-1581* (Cambridge, 1986)

___ *The Tudor constitution - documents and commentary* (Cambridge, 1960)

Englefield, D.J.T., *The printed records of the parliament of Ireland, 1613-1800: a survey and bibliographical guide* (London, 1978)

___ 'Printing the journal of the Irish house of commons, 1735-1802' in H.S. Cobb, (ed.), *Parliamentary history, libraries and records: essays presented to Maurice Bond* (London, 1981)

Everard, R.H.A.J., 'The family of Everard: part I', *The Irish genealogist*, 7 (1988)

Flaherty, M.S., 'The empire strikes back: *Annesley v. Sherlock* and the triumph of imperial parliamentary supremacy', *Columbia law review*, 87 (1987)

Foster, E.R., *The House of Lords, 1603-1649* (Chapel Hill, NC, 1983)

Fritze, R.H. and Robinson, W.B., *Historical dictionary of late medieval England, 1272-1485* (Westport, 2002)

Gadd, R.P., *Peerage law* (Bristol, 1985)

Gilbert, J.T., *An account of the parliament house, Dublin, with notices of parliaments held there* (Dublin, 1896)
Gillespie, R., 'Arthur Chichester', *DIB*
___ *Reading Ireland: print, reading and social change in early modern Ireland* (Manchester, 2005)
___ 'Richard Head's *The Miss Display'd* and Irish restoration society', *Irish university review*, 34 (2004)
___ *Seventeenth-century Ireland: making Ireland modern* (Dublin, 2006)
Graves, M.A.R., *Elizabethan parliaments, 1559–1601* (Harlow, 1996)
___ 'Freedom of peers from arrest: the case of Henry Second Lord Cromwell, 1571–72', *American journal of legal history* 21 (1977)
___ *The House of Lords in the parliaments of Edward VI and Mary I* (Cambridge, 1981)
___ 'The management of the Elizabethan House of Commons: the council's men of business', *Parliamentary history* 2 (1983)
___ *The parliaments of early modern Europe* (Harlow, 2001)
Greaves, R.L., *Deliver us from evil: the radical underground in Britain, 1660–1663* (Oxford, 1986)
Gribbon, H.D., *Journals of the Irish House of Commons: a list of the printings/editions* (unpublished memorandum: Belfast, c. 1984)
Hand, G.J., *English law in Ireland, 1290–1324* (Cambridge, 1967)
Handley, S., 'Temple, Sir John (1632–1705)', *ODNB*
Hanrahan, D.C., *Colonel Blood: the man who stole the crown jewels* (Stroud, 2003)
Harris, T., *Politics under the later Stuarts: party conflict in a divided society, 1660–1715* (Harlow, 1993)
Hart, A.R., 'Audley Mervyn: lawyer or politician?' in W.N. Osborough (ed.), *Explorations in law and history* (Dublin, 1995)
___ *A history of the king's serjeants at law in Ireland* (Dublin, 2000)
___ 'The king's serjeants at law in Ireland: a short history' in W.N. Osborough (ed.), *Explorations in law and history* (Dublin, 1995)
___ 'The king's serjeant at law in Tudor Ireland, 1485–1603' in D. Hogan and W.N. Osborough (eds), *Brehons, serjeants and attorneys: studies in the Irish legal profession* (Dublin, 1990)
Hart, J., *Justice upon petition: the House of Lords and the reformation of justice, 1621–1675* (London, 1991)
Hawkyard, A., *The House of Commons, 1509–1558: personnel, procedure, precedent and change* (Chichester, 2016)
___ 'The Tudor speakers, 1485–1601: choosing, status, work' in P. Seaward (ed.), *Speakers and the speakership: presiding officers and the management of business from the middle ages to the 21st century* (Oxford, 2010)
Hayton, D.W., 'Introduction: the long apprenticeship' in D.W. Hayton (ed.) *The Irish Parliament in the eighteenth century: the long apprenticeship* (Edinburgh, 2001)
___ *Ruling Ireland, 1685–1742: politics, politicians and parties* (Woodbridge, 2004)
___ (ed.), *The Irish Parliament in the eighteenth century: the long apprenticeship* (Edinburgh, 2001)

___ 'The Stanhope-Sunderland ministry and the repudiation of Irish parliamentary independence', *EHR*, 113 (1998)

Hébert, M., *Parlementer: assemblées representatives et échange politique en Europe occidentale à la fin du Moyen Âge* (Paris, 2014)

Herlihy, K., *The religion of Irish dissent* (Dublin, 1996)

Herrup, C.B., *A house in gross disorder: sex, law, and the 2nd earl of Castlehaven* (Oxford, 1999)

Hibbert, C., *The road to Tyburn* (London, 1957)

Hill, C., *Puritanism and revolution: studies in interpretation of the English revolution of the 17th century* (London, 1958)

Hirst, D., 'Elections and the privileges of the House of Commons in the early seventeenth century: confrontation or compromise?', *Historical journal*, 18 (1975)

Hogan, D. and Osborough, W.N. (eds), *Brehons, serjeants and attorneys* (Dublin, 1990)

Hood, S., *Royal roots, republican inheritance: the survival of the office of arms* (Dublin, 2002)

Hunneyball, P.M., 'Note on the conjectural plan of the palace of Westminster' in C.R. Kyle and J. Peacey (eds), *Parliament at work: parliamentary committees, political power and public access in early modern England* (Woodbridge, 2002)

___ 'The development of parliamentary privilege' in C.R. Kyle (ed.), *Managing Tudor and Stuart parliaments: essays in memory of Michael Graves* (Chichester, 2015)

___ 'The house of commons, 1603–29' in C. Jones (ed.), *A short history of parliament: England, Great Britain, The United Kingdom, Ireland and Scotland* (Woodbridge, 2009)

Hylton, R.P., 'The less favoured refuge: Ireland's nonconformist Huguenots at the turn of the eighteenth century' in K. Herlihy (ed.), *The religion of Irish dissent* (Dublin, 1996)

Jackson, B. (ed.), 'A Document on the parliament of 1613 from St Isidore's College, Rome', *AH*, 33 (1986)

James, F.G., *Lords of the ascendancy: the Irish House of Lords and its members, 1660–1800* (Dublin, 1995)

Johnston, N., 'State formation in seventeenth-century Ireland: the restoration financial settlement, 1660–62', *Parliaments, estates and representation*, 36 (2016)

Johnston-Liik, E.M., *History of the Irish Parliament, 1692–1800* (6 vols, Belfast, 2002)

___ *MPs in Dublin: companion to the history of the Irish Parliament, 1692–1800* (Belfast, 2006)

Jones, C., *A short history of parliament: England, Great Britain, The United Kingdom, Ireland and Scotland* (Woodbridge, 2009)

Jordan, W.C., 'A fresh look at medieval sanctuary' in R.M. Karras, J. Kaye, and E.A. Matter (eds), *Law and the illicit in medieval Europe* (Philadelphia, 2008)

Judge, D., 'Public petitions and the House of Commons', *Parliamentary affairs*, 31 (1978)

Kane, B., *The politics and culture of honour in Britain and Ireland, 1541–1641* (Cambridge, 2010)

Karras, R.M., Kaye, J., and Matter, E.A. (eds), *Law and the illicit in medieval Europe* (Philadelphia, 2008)
Kearney, H.F., *Strafford in Ireland, 1633-41: a study in absolutism* (Manchester, 1959)
Kelly, J., 'Monitoring the constitution: the operation of Poynings' Law in the 1760s' in D.W. Hayton (ed.), *The Irish Parliament in the eighteenth century: the long apprenticeship* (Edinburgh, 2001)
__ *Poynings' Law and the making of the of law for Ireland, 1660-1800* (Dublin, 2008)
__ 'The making of law in eighteenth-century Ireland: the significance and import of Poynings' Law' in N.M. Dawson (ed.), *Reflections on law and history: Irish Legal History Society discourses and other papers, 2000-2005* (Dublin, 2006)
Kenny, C., *King's inns and the Kingdom of Ireland: the Irish 'inns of court': 1541-1800* (Dublin, 1992)
__ '"Nothing could be more pernicious": King James II and parliament at King's Inns, Dublin, 1689', *Parliaments, estates and representation*, 37 (2017)
Kenyon, J.P., *The history men: the classic work on historians and their history* (London, 1983).
__ *The Stuart constitution: documents and commentary* (Cambridge, 1986)
Key, N.E. '"High feeding and smart drinking": associating Hedge-Lane lords in exclusion crisis London' in J. McElligott, (ed.), *Fear, exclusion and revolution: Roger Morrice and Britain in the 1680s* (Aldershot, 2007)
Kinsella, E., 'A "new interest" politician in the service of the house of Stuart, 1689-1691' in *History matters II: selected papers from the School of History and Archives postgraduate conference, 2004-5* (Dublin, 2006)
__ *Catholic survival in Protestant Ireland, 1660-1711: Colonel John Browne, landownership and the Articles of Limerick* (Woodbridge, 2018)
__ '"Dividing the bear's skin before she is taken": Irish Catholics and land in the late Stuart Monarchy, 1683-91' in C.A. Dennehy (ed.), *Restoration Ireland: always settling and never settled* (Aldershot, 2008)
Koenigsberger, H.G., *Medieval Europe, 400-1500* (London, 1987)
Kyle, C.R., *Theater of state: parliament and political culture in early Stuart England* (Stanford, 2012)
Kyle, C.R. and Peacey, J. (eds), *Parliament at work: parliamentary committees, political power and public access in early modern England* (Woodbridge, 2002)
Langbein, J., *The origins of adversary criminal trial* (Oxford, 2005)
__ 'The prosecutorial origins of defence counsel in the eighteenth century: the appearance of solicitors', *Cambridge law journal*, 58 (1999)
Lambert, S., *Bill and acts: legislative procedure in eighteenth century England* (Cambridge, 1971)
__ 'Committees, religion, and parliamentary encroachment on royal authority in early Stuart England', *English historical review*, 105 (1990)
Lawless Lee, G., *The Huguenot settlements in Ireland* (London, 1936)
Lehmberg, S.E., *The reformation parliament, 1529-1536* (Cambridge, 1970)
Lennon, C., *Dublin, part II: 1610-1756* (Dublin, 2008)
__ *Sixteenth-century Ireland: the incomplete conquest* (Dublin, 1994)

Little, P., *Lord Broghill and the Cromwellian union with Ireland and Scotland* (Woodbridge, 2004)
__ (ed.), *Ireland in crisis: war, politics and religion, 1641-1651* (Manchester, 2019)
__ 'The first unionists?: Irish Protestant attitudes to union with England, 1653-9', *IHS*, 32 (2000)
__ 'The Geraldine ambitions of the first earl of Cork', *IHS*, 32 (2002)
Logan, W.A., 'Criminal law sanctuaries', *Harvard civil rights – civil liberties law review*, 38 (2003)
Lyall, A., *The Irish House of Lords: a court of law in the eighteenth century* (Dublin, 2013)
Lydon, J.F. (ed.), '"Ireland corporate of itself": the parliament of 1460', *History Ireland*, 3 (1995)
__ *The lordship of Ireland in the middle ages* (Dublin, 1972)
MacCurtain, M., *Tudor and Stuart Ireland* (Dublin, 1972)
MacDonald, A.R., 'Uncovering the legislative process in the parliaments of James VI', *Historical research*, 84 (2011)
MacLysaght, E., *Irish life in the seventeenth century* (3rd edn, Dublin, 1979)
Madicott, J., *The origins of the English Parliament, 924-1327* (Oxford, 2010)
Marongiu, A., *Medieval parliaments: a comparative study* (London, 1968)
Marshall, A., *Intelligence and espionage in the reign of Charles II* (Cambridge, 1994)
Marshall, P., *Mother Leakey and the bishop: a ghost story* (Cambridge, 2007)
McCafferty, J., 'Bramhall, John (bap. 1594, d. 1663)', *ODNB*
__ 'John Bramhall's second Irish career, 1660-1663' in J. Kelly, J. McCafferty, and I. McGrath (eds), *People, politics and power: essays on Irish history, 1660-1850* (Dublin, 2009)
__ *The reconstruction of the Church of Ireland: Bishop Bramhall and the Laudian reforms 1633-1641* (Cambridge, 2007)
__ '"To follow the late precedents in England": the first Irish impeachment proceedings in 1641' in D. Greer and N. Dawson (eds), *Mysteries and solutions in Irish legal history* (Dublin, 2001)
McCarthy, P., *'A favourite study': building the king's inns* (Dublin, 2006)
McCavitt, J., 'An unspeakable parliamentary fracas: the Irish House of Commons, 1613', *AH*, 37 (1995-96)
__ *Sir Arthur Chichester, lord deputy of Ireland, 1605-16* (Belfast, 1998)
McElligott, J. (ed.), *Fear, exclusion and revolution: Roger Morrice and Britain in the 1680s* (Aldershot, 2007)
McGrath, B., 'A bibliographical dictionary of the membership of the Irish House of Commons, 1640-1.' Unpublished Ph.D. thesis, Trinity College, Dublin, 1997
__ 'Electoral law in Ireland before 1641' in C.A. Dennehy (ed.), *Law and revolution in seventeenth-century Ireland* (Dublin, 2019)
__ 'Parliament men and the confederate association' in M. Ó Siochrú (ed.), *Kingdoms in crisis: Ireland in the 1640s* (Dublin, 2001)
__ 'Sex, lies and rigged returns – the Kerry county parliamentary election of 11 June 1634 and its consequences', *Parliaments, estates and representation*, 37 (2017)

___ 'The Irish elections of 1640-1' in C. Brady and J.H. Ohlmeyer (eds), *British interventions in early modern Ireland* (Cambridge, 2005)
___ 'The membership of the Irish house of commons, 1613-5.' Unpublished M.Litt. thesis, Trinity College, Dublin, 1985.
McGrath, C.I., *The making of the eighteenth-century Irish constitution: government, parliament and the revenue, 1692-1714* (Dublin, 2000)
___ 'English ministers, Irish politicians and the making of a parliamentary settlement in Ireland, 1692-5', *EHR*, 119 (2004)
___ 'Securing the Protestant interest: the origins and purpose of the penal laws of 1695', *IHS*, 30 (1996)
McGuire, J.I., 'A lawyer in politics: the career of Sir Richard Nagle, c. 1636-1699' in H.B. Clarke and J. Devlin (eds), *European encounters: essays in honour of Albert Lovett* (Dublin, 2003); also published in N.M. Dawson (ed.) *Reflections on law and history: Irish legal history society discourses and other papers, 2000-2005* (Dublin, 2006)
___ 'Policy and patronage: the appointment of bishops, 1660-61' in A. Ford, J. McGuire, and K. Milne (eds), *As by law established. The Church of Ireland since the reformation* (Dublin, 1995) '
___ The Irish parliament of 1692' in T. Bartlett and D.W. Hayton (eds), *Penal era and golden age: essays in Irish history, 1690-1800* (Belfast, 1979)
Monahan, A.P., *Consent, coercion, and limit: the medieval origins of parliamentary democracy* (Montreal, 1987)
Moody, T.W., 'The Irish Parliament under Elizabeth and James I: a general survey', *PRIA*, 45 C (1939-40)
Moody, T.W., Martin, F.X., and Byrne, F.J. (eds), *NHI*
Munden, R.C., 'The defeat of Sir John Fortescue: court versus country at the hustings?', *EHR*, 93 (1978)
Neale, J.E., *Elizabeth I and her parliaments, 1584-1601* (Oxford, 1957)
___ *The Elizabethan House of Commons* (Oxford, 1963)
Neumann, C.E., 'Atherton, John (1598-1640)', *GLBTQ Encyclopedia*, www.glbtqarchive.com/ssh/atherton_j_S.pdf (downloaded 24 June 2017)
Noble, M., *A history of the college of arms and the lives of all the kings, heralds, and pursuivants* (London, 1804)
Notestein, W., 'The winning of the initiative by the House of Commons', *Proceedings of the British Academy*, 11 (1924-25)
Notestein, W. and Relf, F.H. (eds), *Commons debates for 1629* (Minneapolis, 1929)
Ó hAnnracháin, T., 'Imagining political representation in seventeenth-century Ireland' in R. Armstrong and T. Ó hAnnracháin (eds), *Community in early modern Ireland* (Dublin, 2006)
O'Brien, G. (ed.), *Parliament, politics and people: essays in eighteenth-century Irish history* (Dublin, 1989)
O'Callaghan, J.F., *The cortes of Castile-Leon, 1188-1350* (Philadelphia, 1989)
O'Donoghue, F.M., 'Parliament in Ireland under Charles II', Unpublished M.A. thesis, University College, Dublin (1970)
Oldham, J.B., 'Hobson, Geoffrey Dudley (1882-1949)', rev. Marc Brodie, *ODNB*

O'Flanagan, J.R., *The lives of the lords chancellors and keepers of the great seal of Ireland: from the earliest times to the reign of Queen Victoria* (London, 1870)
Ollard, R., *Clarendon and his friends* (New York, 1987)
O'Malley, E., *The singing flame* (Dublin, 1978)
O'Riordan, T., 'Lodge, John', *DIB*
Ó Siochrú, M., 'Catholic confederates and the constitutional relationship between Irelan and England, 1641–1649' in C. Brady and J.H. Ohlmeyer (eds), *British interventions in early modern Ireland* (Cambridge, 2005)
__ *Confederate Ireland, 1642–1649: a constitutional and political analysis* (Dublin, 1999)
__ (ed.), *Kingdoms in crisis: Ireland in the 1640s* (Dublin, 2001)
Ohlmeyer, J.H. (ed.), *Ireland from independence to occupation, 1641–1660* (Cambridge, 1995)
__ *Making Ireland English: the Irish aristocracy in the seventeenth century* (New Haven, 2012)
__ (ed.), *Political thought in seventeenth-century Ireland: kingdom or colony* (Cambridge, 2000)
__ 'Power, politics and parliament in seventeenth-century Ireland' in M. Jansson (ed.), *Realities of representation: state building in early modern Europe and European America* (London, 2007)
__ 'The Irish peers, political power and parliament, 1640-1' in C. Brady and J.H. Ohlmeyer (eds), *British interventions in early modern Ireland* (Cambridge, 2005)
__ 'The wars of religion, 1603–1660' in T. Bartlett and K. Jeffery (eds), *A military history of Ireland* (Cambridge, 1997)
Ormrod, W.M., Killick, H., and Bradford, P. (eds), *Early common petitions in the English Parliament, c.1290–1420* (London, 2017).
Osborough, W.N. (ed.), *Explorations in law and history* (Dublin, 1995)
__ 'In search of Irish legal history: a map for explorers', *Long room*, 35 (1990)
__ 'Puzzles from Irish law reporting history' in P. Birks (ed.), *The life of the law: proceedings of the tenth British legal history conference, Oxford 1991* (Rio Grande, 1993)
__ *Studies in Irish legal history* (Dublin, 1999)
__ 'The legislation of the pre-union Irish parliament' in *The Irish statutes revised edition: Edward II to the union, AD 1310–1800* (Dublin, 1995)
Otway-Ruthven, A.J., *A history of medieval Ireland* (London, 1980)
Paley, R. (ed.), *The House of Lords* (5 vols, Cambridge, 2016)
Paley, R. and Seaward, P. (eds), *Honour, interest and power: an illustrated history of the House of Lords, 1660–1715* (Woodbridge, 2010)
Pawlisch, H.S., *Sir John Davies and the conquest of Ireland: a study in legal imperialism* (Cambridge, 1985)
Peacey, J. (ed.), 'The House of Lords and the "other house", 1640–1660' in C. Jones, *A short history of parliament: England, Great Britain, The United Kingdom, Ireland and Scotland* (Woodbridge, 2009)
__ *The print culture of parliament, 1600–1800* (Edinburgh, 2007)
Perceval-Maxwell, M., *The outbreak of the Irish rebellion of 1641* (Dublin, 1994)

Pollard, A.F., 'The clerk of the crown', *EHR*, 57 (1942)
___ *The evolution of parliament* (London, 1920)
Pollard, M., *Dictionary of members of the Dublin book trade, 1550–1800* (Dublin, 2000)
Post, G., '*Plena potestas* and consent in medieval assemblies: a study in Romano-canonical procedure and the rise of representation, 1150–1325', *Traditio*, 1 (1943)
___ 'Roman law and early representation in Spain and Italy, 1150–1250', *Speculum*, 18 (1943)
Potterton, M. and Herron, T., *Ireland in the renaissance, c.1540–1660* (Dublin, 2007)
Powell, J.E., 'Proxy voting in the House of Lords', *Parliamentary affairs*, 9 (1955)
Power, T.P. and Whelan, K. (eds), *Endurance and emergence: Catholics in Ireland in the eighteenth century* (Dublin, 1990)
Quinn, D.B., 'Government printing and the publication of the Irish statutes in the sixteenth century', *PRIA*, 44 C (1943)
___ 'Parliaments and great councils in Ireland, 1461–1586', *IHS*, 3 (1942–3)
___ 'The bills and statutes of the Irish parliaments of Henry VII and Henry VIII', *AH*, 10 (1941)
___ 'The early interpretation of Poynings' Law, 1494–1534', *IHS*, 2 (1940–41)
Rait, R.S., *The parliaments of Scotland* (Glasgow, 1924)
Ranger, T.O., 'Richard Boyle and the making of an Irish fortune, 1588–1614', *IHS*, 10 (1957)
Richardson, H.G., 'The Irish parliament rolls of the fifteenth century', *EHR*, 58 (1943)
Richardson, H.G. and Sayles, G.O., *The administration of Ireland, 1172–1377* (Dublin, 1963)
___ *The Irish Parliament in the middle ages* (Philadelphia, 1952)
Routledge, F.J., 'Journal of the Irish House of Lords in Sir John Perrot's parliament (3 May 1585–13 May 1586)', *EHR* 29 (1914)
Russell, C., 'The British background to the Irish rebellion of 1641', *Bulletin of the Institute of Historical Research*, 61 (1988)
___ *The crisis of parliaments: English history, 1509–1660* (Oxford, 1971)
Sayles, G.O., *The king's parliament of England* (London, 1975)
Schweizer, K.W. (ed.), *Parliament and the press, 1689–c. 1939* (Edinburgh, 2006)
Seaward, P., *The cavalier parliament and the reconstruction of the old regime, 1661–1667* (Cambridge, 1989)
Shaw, D., 'Restoration through ritual in Ireland: the celebrations of 1661' in M. Potterton and T. Herron (eds), *Ireland in the renaissance, c.1540–1660* (Dublin, 2007)
___ 'Thomas Wentworth and monarchial ritual in early modern Ireland', *History journal*, 49 (2006)
Silke, J., 'Primate Lombard and James I', *Irish theological quarterly*, 22 (1955)
Simms, J.G., *Jacobite Ireland* (London, 1969)
___ *The Jacobite parliament of 1689* (Dundalk, 1966)
Smith, D.L., *The Stuart parliaments, 1603–1689* (London, 1999)
Smyth, C.J., *Chronicle of the law officers of Ireland* (London, 1839)

Stapylton, K.A.T., 'The parliamentary privilege of freedom from arrest, 1603–1629.' Unpublished Ph.D. thesis, University College London (2016)

Stater, V., 'Fitton, Alexander, Jacobite Baron Fitton (d. 1699)', *ODNB*

Stone, L., *The causes of the English revolution, 1529–1642* (London, 1972)

Stubbs, W., *The constitutional history of England* (3 vols, 5th edn, Oxford, 1891–98)

Terry, C.S., *The Scottish Parliament: its constitution and procedure, 1603–1707* (Glasgow, 1905)

Tierney, B., 'Freedom and the medieval church' in R.W. Davis (ed.), *The origins of modern freedom in the West* (Stanford, 1995)

Tite, C.C.G., *Impeachment and parliamentary judicature in early Stuart England* (London, 1974)

Townshend, C., *Easter 1916: the Irish rebellion* (London, 2006)

Treadwell, V., *Buckingham and Ireland, 1616–1628: a study in Anglo-Irish politics* (Dublin, 1998)

__ 'Sir John Perrot and the Irish Parliament of 1585–6', *PRIA*, 85 (1985)

__ 'The House of Lords in the Irish Parliament of 1613–1615', *EHR*, 80 (1965)

__ 'The Irish Parliament of 1569–71', *PRIA*, 65 (1966/7)

Twomey, M., 'The financial and commercial policy of the English administration in Ireland, 1660–70.' Unpublished M.A. thesis, University College Dublin, 1954

Velona, J., 'The speech of Sir Audley Mervyn, speaker of the Irish House of Commons, demanding reforms in the Court of Claims: a reinterpretation through the lens of legal history' in C.A. Dennehy (ed.), *Law and revolution in seventeenth-century Ireland* (Dublin, 2019)

Victory, I., 'The making of the 1720 declaratory act' in G. O'Brien (ed.), *Parliament, politics, and people* (Dublin, 1989)

Wagner, A., *Heralds of England: a history of the college of arms* (London, 1967)

Wedgewood, C.V., *Thomas Wentworth, first earl of Strafford, 1593–1641: a revaluation* (London, 1961)

Wells, J., *The House of Lords: from Saxon wargods to a modern senate* (London, 1997)

Weiser, B., 'Access and petitioning during the reign of Charles II' in E. Cruickshanks (ed.), *The Stuart courts* (Stroud, 2000)

Williams, O.C., *The clerical organisation of the House of Commons, 1661–1850* (Oxford, 1954)

Wolfe, E.L., '"Into the custody of the serjeant at arms": inducing parliamentary attendance in Dublin and Westminster, 1690–1859', *Parliaments, estates and representation*, 38 (2018)

Wood, H., *Guide to the records deposited in the Public Record Office of Ireland* (Dublin, 1919)

__ 'The destruction of the public records: the loss to Irish history', *Studies: an Irish quarterly review*, 43 (1922)

__ 'The public records of Ireland before and after 1922', *Transactions of the Royal Historical Society*, 13 (1930)

Woolyrch, H.W., *Lives of eminent serjeants at law of the English bar* (2 vols, London, 1869)

Young, J., 'Charles I and the 1633 parliament' in K. Brown and A.J. Mann (eds), *The history of the Scottish Parliament* (3 vols, Edinburgh, 2005), vol. 2

__ *The Scottish Parliament, 1639-1661: a political and constitutional analysis* (Edinburgh, 1996)

Index

1649 officers 37
1782, constitution of 63

Abdy, Humphry 184, 203 (n. 147)
absence 29–30, 34, 117, 128, 191
   fines for 34, 192
acts
   £23,500 136, 140, 144
   adventurers' 61, 68
   attainder 190
   declaratory 1689 70
   declaratory 1720 3, 52 (n. 42), 61
   explanatory 60
   kingly title 62, 208
   Ormond 89, 193
   penal 96
   printing 148
   private 16 (n. 47), 144
   privilege (1463) 171–72, 176
   privilege (1634) 171, 176, 181, 200 (n. 89)
   protection (1471) 176, 178, 197 (n. 16)
   public 16 (n. 47), 117
   remittal of rents 59
   settlement 60, 120
   statute law revision (2007) 196 (n. 15)
   treason 199 (n. 55)
   trial for felony act 199 (n. 55)
acts of state 61, 98
Adair, Archibald *see* Killala
adjournment 13 (n. 14), 132, 171–72
agenda 74, 117, 122
agents 124–26, 187–88
Alexander, Jerome 128

Antrim, Randall MacDonnell, 1st marquis of 41, 191, 193, 205 (n. 180)
   Rose MacDonnell, marchioness of 41
appellate 30, 61, 70
archbishops *see* spiritual lords
Arlington, Henry Bennet, 1st earl of 77, 155 (n. 77), 187
Armagh, James Ussher, archbishop of 32, 148, 178
Armagh, John Bramhall, archbishop of 40, 107 (n. 154), 111–13, 115, 126, 146, 151 (n. 2), 180, 205 (n. 180)
Armagh, Michael Boyle, archbishop of *see* Dublin
assault 184–85
assent *see* royal assent
Aston, William 128
Athlone pursuivant at arms 149–50
attachment *see* custody
attendance 8–9, 79, 125, 128, 191
attorney *see* counsel
attorney general *see* law officers

Bagnall, George 183
bail *see* bond
Baltimore, County Cork 24
bar 16 (n. 34), 23, 39, 74, 85–86, 88, 112, 115–16, 123, 138
Barnewall, Robert and William 119, 146, 195
battle of Aughrim 69
battle of Stoke 63
battle of the Boyne 69
Bellew, John 188

Bellingham, Daniel 150, 166 (n. 326)
Bible 197 (n. 18)
bills 66, 122, 131
  advance consultation on 67–68
  amendment 64–65, 80, 83, 85, 91, 106 (n. 141), 127
  buggery 72, 83, 176
  drafting 90
  engrossment 83–85
  explanation 37, 76–77, 84, 126
  gunpowder 60, 98 (n. 18)
  heads of 11, 92–93, 194
  indemnity 84, 127
  initiation 91
  Jesuits 60
  money 11, 60, 88–89, 194
  movement of 62–63
  private 71, 120, 138, 143, 154 (n. 63)
  pro forma 76
  readings 71, 73–78
  rejected 75, 85, 127, 183
  relating to alcohol
  settlement 37, 76, 84, 126
  time to pass 72, 104 (n. 116)
  transmiss(ion) 64–68, 70–73, 102
biography 2
black rod, gentleman usher of the 115, 122, 128, 130, 145–47, 173, 195
  yeoman usher 145–47
Blennerhasset, John 32, 141, 189
Blennerhasset, Robert 177
Blood's Plot 26, 123, 184
Blood, Neptune 27
Blood, Thomas 26–27
blood, restitution in 36–37, 56 (n. 199), 193, 205 (n. 184)
  bishops *see* spiritual lords
bond 56 (n. 117), 136, 141
Borlase, Edmund 178
boroughs, 3, 42
  controlled by ecclesiastical hierarchy 204 (n. 147)
  creation, 3, 58–59
Bourke, Theobald
Boyle, County Roscommon 8
Boyle family 8
Boyle, Michael *see* Dublin
Bradley, William 15 (n. 28), 103 (n. 88), 133–35
Bramhall, John *see* Armagh
Bramhall, Thomas 203 (n. 147)
bribery 15 (n. 29), 22, 173

Browne, Geoffrey, 123, 203 (n. 147)
Butler, Walter, of Kilcash 29
butter 37
Buttevant, David de Barry, 5th viscount 190

Canterbury, William Laud, archbishop of 40
Cantwell, sheriff of Waterford 9
capital trials 175–76
Carlingford, Theobald Taaffe, 1st earl of 136, 195
Carlow 8
Carney, Richard 150
Carpenter, Joshua 41
Carpenter, Philip 142
Cashel, Miler Magrath, archbishop of 38–40, 174–75, 185
  James, his son 38–39
Cashel, Oliver 188
Castle Chamber 30–31, 126, 172, 177, 194, 201 (n. 93)
Castlehaven, Mervyn Tuchet, 2nd earl of 176
Catelin, Nathaniel 9, 121, 126
Catherine of Braganza 187
Catholic
  confederacy *see* confederacy
  'party' 32, 38, 96, 125, 188
  walk-out 110, 188–90
Cavan County 190
censorship 147–48
  see also John Sterne
censure 116, 124, 138, 177–79, 185
chamber 127
Chancery (administrative side)
  seal 68, 102 (n. 75), 118, 160 (n. 180), 190
Chancery (court) 30, 112, 118–19, 137
  examiners in 34
  masters of 113, 128, 158 (n. 149)
chaplain 125, 147, 179
Chappell, William 24, 40
charity 125, 136, 191
Charlemont, Mary Caulfield, dowager baroness of 198 (n. 44)
Chichester, Arthur 65, 91
Chichester House 134, 150
Chief Place *see* King's Bench
Child, John 176
Christ-Church, Dublin 136
Churchill, Winston 77
Church of Ireland 40, 131, 156 (n. 106), 191

Chute, Richard 32, 189
civil war 2, 179
Clancarty, Donagh MacCarthy, 1st earl of 35
Clarendon, Edward Hyde, 1st earl of 108 (n. 175)
Clanrickard, Richard Burke, 6th earl of 28, 41, 42, 179, 185
Clarke, Marcus 179
Clayton, Randolph 36
clerical proctors 3, 65, 99 (n. 31), 101 (n. 51) 171
clerk 9, 15 (n. 29), 133–40, 160 (n. 179)
   accounts 136
   administrative 133–35
   appointment 133–34
   bills 7, 72, 74, 86, 89, 105 (n. 116), 134
   committees 134
   fees 16 (n. 47), 21, 137–40
   housekeeping 135, 150
   petitions 23, 138
   registration of protections 182
clerk of the crown and hanaper 118, 124, 151, 189
committees 6, 78–83, 92, 95, 117
   acts 131
   ad hoc 6, 23
   benefits of 80
   chairmen 79–80
   evidence before 120, 174
   grand (committee of the whole house) 6, 23, 32, 80, 126
   grievances 23, 142
   privileges 23, 32, 180, 185, 189
   privileges and grievances 23
   quorum 79, 157 (n. 120)
   rate 80–83
   re-committal 80
   report 83, 95
   second 83
   standing 6
common law 30–31, 61, 94, 127, 132, 171, 208
commons, split from lords 114
confederacy (Kilkenny) 68, 201 (n. 93)
conference 11, 15 (n. 11), 40, 85, 107 (n. 155), 169, 172, 182, 193, 195
Convocation 106 (n. 145), 130, 159 (n. 158)
constitution 1
contempt 119, 156 (n. 102), 185
Conway and Kilulltagh, Edward Conway, 3rd viscount 27

copy 23
Cork 8
Cork, bishopric 8, 193
Cork, Richard Boyle, 1st earl of 37, 176
Cork, Richard Boyle, 2nd earl of 8
corporal punishment 38, 157 (n. 119), 176, 183, 185
Council Board *see* Privy Council
counsel 35–36, 55 (n. 85), 71, 79, 91, 123, 143, 177
courts 25, 125, 127, 176, 199 (n. 54)
Court of Claims 30, 123, 126–27, 166 (n. 326), 172, 185
   Common Pleas 103 (n. 88)
court of record 10, 55 (n. 81), 112, 170, 183, 208
covenant 112, 124, 156 (n. 106)
covered 116, 158 (n. 136)
Craig, William 150
Crawford, Lawrence 9
Cressy, Hugh 128, 159 (n. 159)
Cromwell, Oliver 68
Crosby, Piers 201 (n. 93)
Crosby, Thomas 189
custody 32–33, 36, 123, 138, 140–43, 146, 150, 183, 186
   breaking 195
   jail 136, 141, 157 (n. 119), 174, 183–84

Darcy, Nicholas 27–28
Darcy, Patrick 61
Davies, John 92, 133–34
Davys, Paul 124, 177
de la Mare, Peter 121
debate 74–83, 117
debt 31–32, 171, 178, 182, 184
delinquent 138, 140, 146
Desborow, John 185
Desmond, daughters of 36, 193
diaries 7
Dillon, Carey 26, 150, 185
dissolution 11, 18, 71, 88, 195, 201 (n. 93)
distrainment 35–36, 42, 178, 182, 199 (n. 70)
distress *see* distrainment
divisions 7, 85, 121
Dixon, Richard and Sir William 20
Dolphin, Robert 195
Domville, William 110–111, 129
Donegal 24
doorkeeper 130, 142, 150
Drogheda, Henry Moore, 1st earl of 37

Dublin, Adam Loftus, archbishop of 198 (n. 32)
Dublin Castle 34, 70, 91, 94, 117, 121–22, 174, 180, 187
   Bermingham's Tower 136
Dublin City 37
Dublin, Michael Boyle, archbishop of 112, 193
Dublin, Thomas Jones, archbishop of, 15 (n. 29), 33, 112, 173–74, 185
Dungan, John 186
Dungannon, Marcus Trevor, 1st viscount 145
Dunsany, Patrick Plunkett, 9th baron 31, 33–34, 184

elections 6, 32, 66–67, 124, 128, 151, 185, 188, 203 (n. 144)
   double return 153 (n. 42), 203 (n. 147), 189
   new 9, 151
   writs 112, 151, 172
electoral fraud 188–90
Elphin, Henry Tilson, bishop of 9
Elsynge, Henry 6, 169
Ely, Adam Loftus, 1st viscount 151 (n. 1), 180, 197 (n. 32)
English parliament 61–62, 132–33, 188
English parliamentary model 7, 20, 22, 30, 62–63, 70, 71, 83, 94, 110, 115, 128, 145, 149, 151, 169–170, 179, 181, 207
   appointment 146
   enlargement 32–33
Ennis, County Clare 42
equity 30
equity jurisdiction *see* appellate, exchequer, chancery
états généraux 208
Eustace, Maurice 111, 124–27
Evans, Thomas 186
Everard, John 110–11
exceptionalism of Irish parliament 3, 88, 170–71, 207–08
   see also English parliamentary model
Exchequer (administrative side) 90, 103 (n. 88), 127, 160 (n. 186)
Exchequer (court) 30
executive *see* Dublin Castle, privy council, lord deputy

Falkland, Henry Cary, 1st viscount 66–67
fees 21, 33–34, 143–44, 146, 148–49

Ferneley, Philip 9, 16 (n. 47), 103 (n. 88), 139, 160 (n. 179), 180
fines 10, 30, 34, 124, 125, 128, 136, 142, 174, 191–92, 194–95, 205 (n. 168)
Fishe, John, 130
Fisher, Edward 198 (n. 40)
Fitzharris, Edward 28
Folliot et al v Castle-Stewart 149
forgery 38, 118, 183
forty-day rule 31, 37, 171–72, 177, 197 (n. 18), 200 (n. 93)
freedom of speech 187

Geashill, Robert Digby, 1st baron 74
Gibbes, Thomas 178
Goldsborow, Henry 20
Gookin, Vincent 67, 170
graces 4, 59, 66–67, 117
Grainer, Isaac 42

Hamilton, Hans 36
Harrison, John 32
Harrison, Matthew 10
hats *see* covered
Head, Richard 31
Henry VII 63
High Commission 30–31, 123–24, 137, 176
Hill, Peter 29, 56 (n. 106), 136
historiography
   English 1–3, 58
   international 211
   Irish 3–5, 58, 208
History of Parliament Trust 2
Hooker, John *alias* Vowell *see* Orders and usage 6, 12 (n. 13)
Howth, Christopher St Lawrence, 10th baron of 170, 174–75
Huguenot 142
Hutchinson, Daniel 185

illegality of Jacobite parliament 5, 69–70
in forma Pauperis 26, 120
Ingoldsby, Henry 195
Inistiogue, Kilkenny 194
impeachment 29, 34, 56 (n. 105) 67, 113, 132, 152 (n. 21), 176, 188
imprisonment *see* custody
Inchiquin, Murrough O'Brien, 1st earl of 193

jail *see* custody
James I 65

James II 68–69
Johnson, John 172
Johnson, Thomas 181, 184
Jones, Michael *see* Dublin
journals 5, 7–12, 60
  compilation 8
  editing 10
  errors 8
  fair / rough 9
  petitions in 19, 28
  scribe 22
judges 24, 72, 79, 93, 95, 113–14, 127–33, 194
  legal advice 130–33
  as messengers 130–31
  as MPs 128–29
judicial functions 112, 170
  see also court of record

keeper of the parliament house 150
Kennedy, Richard 128
Kerry 24
Kerry v Fitzgerald 133, 172, 194
Kildare County 190
Kildare, Gerald Fitzgerald (Gearóid Mór), 8th earl of 63
Kildare, Thomas Price, bishop of 28
Killala, Archibald Adair, bishop of 153 (n. 42)
Kilrush, County Clare 27
King, Ralph 25, 175
King's Bench 30, 118–21, 125, 147, 178, 180, 190
King's County 118
Kingsland, Henry Barnewall, 2nd viscount 119, 146, 186, 195
knights of the shire, 8, 9, 26, 32, 124, 144, 155 (n. 76), 174, 188–89
Kirwin, Patrick 195

Lake, Edward 123
Lambert, Laurence 181, 184
Lambert v Hatfield, et al 119
Lane, George 103 (n. 88), 133, 187
law officers 72, 93, 95, 113–14, 127, 195
law reporting 61
lawyers *see* counsel
Laud, William *see* Canterbury
Lecale, Thomas Cromwell, 1st viscount 37
legislation 36
Leslie, John *see* Raphoe
Leverett, Albion 149–50
libel 185

liberties of parliament 186–95
Lisle, Philip Sidney, viscount 9
Little, Thomas 41
location of parliament 69, 107 (n. 156)
Loftus, Adam *see* Dublin
Loftus, Arthur 28, 126
Loftus, Dudley 198 (n. 32)
Loftus, Robert 194
Lone, Highgate 150
lord chancellor 15 (n. 29), 23, 72, 78–79, 86, 112, 118–20, 152 (n. 32), 164 (n. 279)
lord deputy 3, 60, 69, 85–90, 179, 187, 207
lord lieutenant *see* lord deputy
lords justices *see* lord deputy
lord high steward of Ireland 35
Lowther, Gerard 128, 146, 171, 194
Lutterell, Thomas 174

mace 115, 122, 140, 145, 177
Magrath, Miler *see* Cashel
Magrath, Terence 184
Martin, Richard 195
Massareene, John Clothworthy, 1st viscount 131, 193, 205 (n. 180)
master of the rolls 90, 114, 126, 137
Mayart, Samuel 31, 159 (n. 156)
Meath, William Brabazon, 1st earl of 179–80
Medhop, Edmond 77, 103 (n. 88), 133–34, 160 (n. 179)
'men of business' *see* privy councillors, members in parliament
Mervin, Audley 111, 121–27, 129, 151 (n. 7), 155 (n. 77), 157 (n. 120)
messages 114, 130–31, 137, 146
Modus tenendi parliamentum 6, 169
Molyneux, William 61
monarch 58, 60, 85–90
  access to 187
monopolies 40–41, 132
Montgomery, Hugh 204 (n. 166)
Montgomery, James 191
Morrison, Richard 198 (n. 40)
Morton, Francis 178
Morton, John 32, 35, 178
motion 75–76, 78–79, 83–84, 148
Mountrath, Charles Coote, 1st earl of 179

naturalization 71, 143
Netterville, Nicholas Netterville, 1st viscount 78
newspapers 7, 13 (n. 27)

nisi prius 124
Nugent, Gerald 38–39, 174

oath 23, 62, 112, 120, 136–37, 170, 197 (n. 28)
O'Brien, Daniel 201 (n. 93)
O'Connor, Teige 200 (n. 75)
O'Higgins, Teige 179, 200 (n. 75)
opposition 12 (n. 6), 101
opprobrious words
   scandalum magnatum 116, 130, 174–75, 185
   see also scandalous
Orders and usage 6, 13 (n. 13), 135, 169–70
order, keep 116, 140
Ormond, James Butler, 1st duke of 89–90, 131, 151 (n. 3), 184, 193
Ormsby, Robert 203 (n. 147)
Orrery, Roger Boyle, 1st earl of 90, 111, 179
Osborne, Richard 123
Ossory, Thomas Butler, 6th earl of 151

Pattershall, Robert 27
paper / parchment 21–22, 52 (n. 17), 83–85, 116
peerage 114, 116, 131, 175–76, 192
   fees 137, 147
   introduction 149, 190
   in the commons 173–74
   outlawed 190
Perrot, Letitia 133
petitions
   detail 19
   fees 21
   medieval 20
   notification 24
   paper / parchment 21–22, 52 (n. 17)
   printed 19–20
   procedure 22, 135
   rejected 27–28
   scandalous 23, 27, 174
   time 24–25
   theory 18
   withdrawn 27
Petty, William 142, 185
Philpot, John 159 (n. 159)
Piggott, Alexander 36
Plunkett, Christopher 75
Plunkett, William 172
Porter, Charles 152 (n. 21)
Poynings, Edward 64

Poynings' Law 3, 58, 60, 88–89, 102 (n. 75), 183, 193
   amendment 65–66
   origins 63–65
   repeal, attempted 70
   reform 92
   suspension 65–66, 92
prayers 125, 147, 191
precedence 149, 169
precedent 55 (n. 81), 73, 170
Presbyterian 40, 147, 205 (n. 180)
Preston, Thomas 56 (n. 106), 149
Price, Charles 186
Price, Thomas *see* Kildare
print 8, 89–90, 148
privilege 38, 137, 141, 168–206, 197 (n. 28)
   abuse 181–84
   breach by counsel 177
   legal action in contravention of 177–79
   legislation *see* acts, privilege
   no distinction between lords 175
   restricting 171–72, 181–84
   retrospective application 201 (n. 93)
   servants of members 178, 181, 185
      menial servants rule 182
   sole competence 169, 171–73, 188, 192, 200 (n. 93)
   theory 168–69
   treatises 169–70
   waive 199 (n. 58)
Privy Council
   English 3, 36, 60, 66–67, 92, 174, 188
   Irish 3, 30, 60, 71, 78, 91–93, 111, 113, 115, 187
   members in parliament 79, 85, 91
productivity 2
   legislative 4, 93–95
   petitions 28–42
prorogation 36, 56 (n. 117), 88, 151, 171
prerogative jurisdiction *see* Castle Chamber, High Commission
protection 138, 180, 182,
   sale of 183
   forgery 38, 118, 183
protest 7, 193
Protestant
   'party' 96, 123, 125
   refugees 136
   representation 3
proxy 9, 137–38, 147, 149, 180, 191–92, 205 (n. 174)
purge the house 186, 189

queries 15 (n. 27), 132–33

Radcliffe, George 198
Ranelagh & Keating v Molloy 118
Ranelagh, Arthur Jones, 2nd viscount 129, 131
Raphoe, John Leslie, bishop of 40
Raymont, Samuel 177
replevin 35, 178, 199 (n. 70)
representation, principles of 61–62
residency rules 13 (n. 13), 52 (n. 69), 192, 205 (n. 174)
Roman law 62
restoration settlement 4, 60, 62, 68, 94
revenue 16 (n. 47), 34–35, 62, 72, 74, 98 (n. 27), 108 (n. 158), 192–93
Ridgeway, Thomas 74
rigsdag 208
Robertson, Thomas 20
robes 8, 115
 keeper of the king's 146, 164 (n. 281)
Robinson, William 150
rolls 52 (n. 3), 89–92, 99 (n. 41), 113, 135
Roscommon, Robert Dillon, 7th earl of 182
royal assent 68, 86–90, 107 (n. 158), 151
 refused 88
royal interest 40, 179
royal mandate 61
Ruish, Francis 140, 178
rules 76, 111, 171, 182, 191
 see also residency
Ryves, Dorothy 34, 121, 127
Ryves, William 110–113, 121

sanctuary 197 (n. 18)
Sanderson, Thomas 195
Sandys, William 134
Santry, James Barry, 1st baron vi, 111, 119, 147, 152 (n. 8), 153 (n. 48)
Savage, Valentine 119, 178
scandalum magnatum 33, 130, 174–75, 185
 see also opprobrious words
Scotland 6, 67, 139
seal *see* Chancery (administration)
seating 8, 11, 16 (n. 30) 26, 79, 87, 114, 126, 147, 149, 153 (n. 34), 160 (n. 179), 165 (n. 292), 174–75, 179
secrecy 114, 141–42, 150
Selden, John 6, 170, 196 (n. 9)

serjeant at arms 24, 35, 115, 122, 130, 136, 140–45
 fees 143–44
serjeant at law *see* law officers
Shapcote, Robert 26
sheriffs 34–35, 140–41, 172, 179, 185, 189
Sherlock, Paul 15 (n. 29), 33, 173–74
Shrewsbury, Francis Talbot, 11th earl of 35
Simnel, Lambert 63
slander 38, 123, 185
Slane, Thomas Fleming, 13th baron of 190, 204 (n. 155)
Slane, William Fleming, 14th baron of 190, 204 (n. 155)
sodomy *see* buggery
sole competence 169, 194
 see also privileges
solicitor general *see* law officers
Southerby, Roger
speaker 34, 76, 110–27
 commission of 113–14
 communication 114–15, 122, 124, 125
 election / selection 110, 121, 129, 188
 function 114
 income 120, 127
 presentation 121, 186
 qualifications 111, 126, 155 (n. 73)
 rejection 110
 replacement 56 (n. 105), 113
 speech 121
speaker's chamber, keeper of 150
spiritual lords 36, 149, 156 (n. 106), 173, 175, 192
St George, Henry 149
St George, Oliver 141
St George, Richard 149–50
Stafford, Maurice 121
Stanhope, Michael 123
Stanihurst, James 130
stare decisis 10
 see also precedent
Sterne, John 148
Stewart, Archibald 25, 149, 175
Strafford, Thomas Wentworth, 1st earl of 4, 40–41, 59, 67, 88, 90, 92, 94, 151 (n. 1), 181, 188, 192, 196 (n. 15)
Stratford, Bernard 179
Subpoena ad testificandum 119, 179
supply, financial 67, 88, 112, 117
 see also revenue
supremacy, ecclesiastical 63
 oath of *see* oath

summoning of parliament 66
　writ of summons 112, 118, 128, 153 (n. 48), 172, 184, 190, 204 (n. 155)
summons 139, 141
suspension 26

Temple, John (solicitor general) 8, 129
Temple, John (master of the rolls, author) 8
temporal lords *see* peerage
Thimbleby, William 179
Thorpe, Richard 179
tobacco 27, 41
tonnage and poundage 37
Thomond, Barnabas O'Brien, 6th earl of 30, 35, 178
throne 153 (n. 34)
translation to the upper house 151
Trinity College, Dublin, 40, 148
Tuam 189
Tuam, archiepiscopal see of 204 (n. 147)
Tuam, Richard Boyle, archbishop of 40, 175
Tyrconnell, Oliver Fitzwilliam, 1st earl of (second creation) 185
Tyrconnell, Richard Talbot, 1st earl of (third creation) 69

Ulster king of arms 148–50
umbrage between houses 27, 58, 91, 126, 173
Ussher, James *see* Armagh
Ussher, William 198 (n. 40)

Vesey, John 147

wages, MPs' 124, 145, 189
Walsh, Nicholas 130
Wandesford, Christopher 132, 194
war-time 124, 132, 134, 172, 180
Warbeck, Perkin 63
Warburton, Richard 56 (n. 106), 156 (n. 83)
wardrobe, yeoman of the 127
warrant 24, 26, 36, 102, 118–19, 124–25, 135, 139, 141, 153 (n. 42), 200 (n. 88)
Warren, George 195
wars of the roses 63
Waterford and Lismore, John Atherton, bishop of 176
Westmeath, Richard Nugent, 1st earl of 191
White, Arthur 32
Wicklow County 34
William III 190
Willoughby, Francis 119
'winning the initiative' 1–2, 18, 31, 78
Wiseman, William 34, 191
witness 23,
women 41–42
work rate *see* productivity
writ, application by 61
writ of *Certiorari* 119
writ of error 35, 70
writ of *Habeas corpus* 36, 119, 195
writ of *Habere facias possessionem* 124
writ of summons *see* summoning
writ of *Supersedeas* 118, 194
writ of *Quo Warranto* 42, 132

EU authorised representative for GPSR:
Easy Access System Europe, Mustamäe tee 50,
10621 Tallinn, Estonia
gpsr.requests@easproject.com

www.ingramcontent.com/pod-product-compliance
Lightning Source LLC
Chambersburg PA
CBHW070340240426
43671CB00013BA/2386